Leper Creativity

LEPER CREATIVITY

Cyclonopedia Symposium

Edited by

Ed Keller, Nicola Masciandaro, & Eugene Thacker

punctum books ✸ brooklyn, ny

 LEPER CREATIVITY: CYCLONOPEDIA SYMPOSIUM
© The individual contributors and punctum books, 2012.

This work is licensed under the Creative Commons Attribution-NonCommerical-NoDerivs 3.0 Unported License. To view a copy of this license, visit: http://creativecommons.org/licenses/by-nc-nd/3.0, or send a letter to Creative Commons, 444 Castro Street, Suite 900, Mountain View, California, 94041, USA.

This work is Open Access, which means that you are free to copy, distribute, display, and perform the work as long as you clearly attribute the work to the authors, that you do not use this work for commercial gain in any form whatsoever, and that you in no way alter, transform, or build upon the work outside of its normal use in academic scholarship without express permission of the author and the publisher of this volume. For any reuse or distribution, you must make clear to others the license terms of this work.

First published in 2012 by punctum books, Brooklyn, New York.

punctum books is an open-access and print-on-demand independent publisher dedicated to radically creative modes of intellectual inquiry and writing across a whimsical para-humanities assemblage. We specialize in neo-traditional and non-conventional scholarly work that productively twists and/or ignores academic norms. This is a space for the imp-orphans of thought and pen, an ale-serving church for little vagabonds.

ISBN-13: 978-0615600468

Library of Congress Cataloging-in-Publication Data is available from the Library of Congress.

Cover image by Perry Hall, Sound Drawing 07-04, 2007.

TABLE OF CONTENTS

A BRIEF HISTORY OF GEOTRAUMA Robin Mackay	1
AN INHUMAN FICTION OF FORCES McKenzie Wark	39
ROOT THE EARTH: ON PEAK OIL APOPHENIA Benjamin H. Bratton	45
DUSTISM Alisa Andrasek	59
QUEERNESS, OPENNESS Zach Blas	101
NON-OEDIPAL NETWORKS AND THE INORGANIC UNCONSCIOUS Melanie Doherty	115
SYMPTOMATIC HORROR: LOVECRAFT'S "THE COLOUR OUT OF SPACE" Anthony Sciscione	131
CYCLONOPEDIA AS NOVEL (A MEDITATION ON COMPLICITY AS INAUTHENTICITY) Kate Marshall	147
WHAT IS A HERMENEUTIC LIGHT? Alexander R. Galloway	159

BLACK INFINITY; OR, OIL DISCOVERS HUMANS   173
    Eugene Thacker

GOURMANDIZED IN THE ABATTOIR OF OPENNESS   181
    Nicola Masciandaro

PHILEAS FOG^G, OR THE CYCLONIC PASSEPARTOUT: 193
ON THE ALCHEMICAL ELEMENTS OF WAR
    Dan Mellamphy & Nandita Biswas
    Mellamphy

THE UNTIMELY (AND UNSHAPELY) DECOMPOSITION   213
OF ONTO-EPISTEMOLOGICAL SOLIDITY:
NEGARESTANI'S *CYCLONOPEDIA* AS METAPHYSICS
    Ben Woodard

. . . OR, SPEAKING WITH THE ALIEN, A REFRAIN . . .   225
    Ed Keller

RECEIPT OF MALICE   255
    Lionel Maunz

SYMPOSIUM PHOTOGRAPHS   279
    Öykü Tekten

NOTES ON THE FIGURE OF THE CYCLONE   287
    Reza Negarestani

A Brief History of Geotrauma

Robin Mackay

Freud, Ferenczi, Lovecraft, Bodkin, Challenger, Cane, Barker, Land, Parsani. Unilkely characters. Crackpots, every one of them. Frauds, fakes, pseudoscientists at best. Indisciplined thinkers breeding speculative mon-

grels. Hysteria, neuronics, stratoanalysis, schizoanalysis, geotraumatics.

Through misinterpretations, imaginary convergences, forced couplings and other shady maneouvres lacking in the principled behaviour expected of a scholar, they claimed to have invented a new discipline referred to by various names at various times; but no-one clearly understood what the goals, methods or principles of this new discipline were.

And yet, there was something important here;

something on the verge of being forgotten. There would have been no trace,

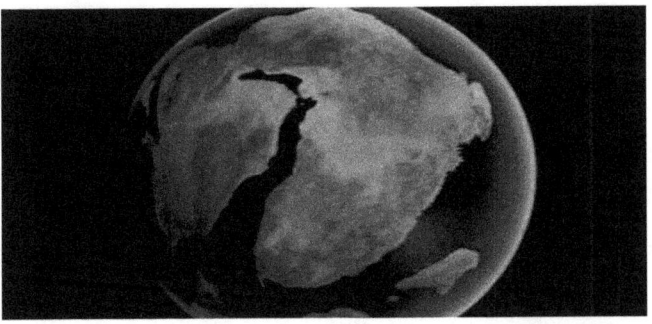

the Geo-cosmic Theory of Trauma would not even have been a memory, if it weren't for the work of the Plutonics Committee.

Not that it was easy. An indirect approach was necessary. A contemporary advocate, a new candidate. If he didn't exist, he would have to be invented. And this time, something had to get through.

The committee had its eye on the widest possible target market. So the primary task was an understanding of how ideas travel—an epidemiology of the concept.

It obviously couldn't be an academic. Things have changed: freaks like Land and Parsani wouldn't even get through the doors of a university these days. No, it would have to be an outsider—exotic, even.

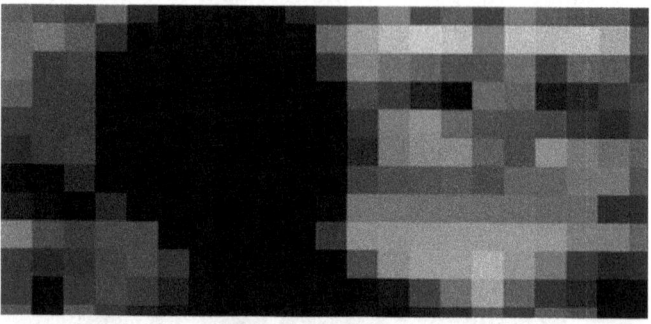

Some peculiar maverick, self-taught, no qualifications; a lone voice who comes out of nowhere.

He—or she—must be credibly unreachable, hidden away. Somewhere on the Axis of Evil, maybe, to add some political intrigue: A persecuted dissident scouring the outer reaches of the web to find other sick-minded individuals, he comes across Land,

retired from philosophy and now promulgating conspiracy theory and peddling neo-occultist speculations. Land passes on the last Barker manuscript to him.

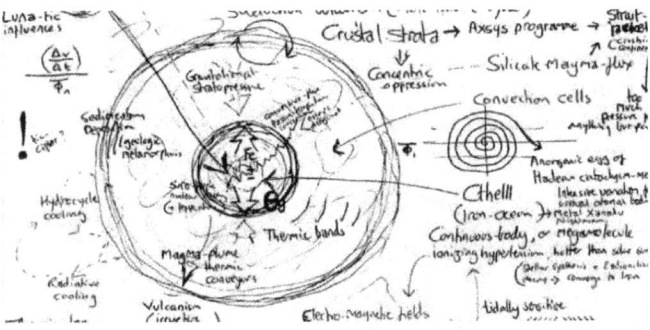

Then he discovers Parsani's notebooks in Iran, realizes the Bodkin-Cane connection, and begins to piece it together. It could have happened that way.

Then move him to the Far East. Someplace no-one ever goes. Not even China or Japan—Malaysia. Construct his writings in a kind of tortured, gnomic style that combines extreme etymological acuity with a sick imagination that comes of watching too many horror movies.

Anyhow, he's probably sick in some way. Insomniac, delirious, unable to function normally; sick with some kind of middle-eastern fever. That could be the case.

Invisible, his character must exude a sort of enigmatic charisma, and an aura of exoticism. Since he comes from outside, almost anything would be credible. Keep him hidden for as long as possible, unseen but effective.

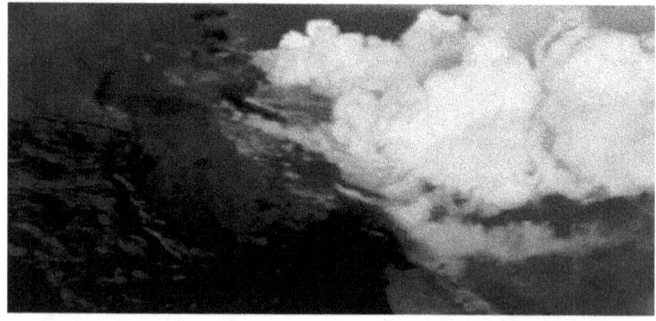

Personal appearances made and cancelled. Visa problems, poor health, whatever it takes. If it gets to the stage where he does have to appear, it has to be done well—no expense spared.

But above all, the ideas keep coming, exerting a subterranean influence. All that is necessary is that he exist long enough to effectuate inception. Once the ideas take, once the ideas are embedded, he can easily be retired. Anything could happen to a freak like that.

It's true, the Committee took risks. Carried away with their creation, they ventured a few unnecessarily baroque twists. A fictional quantity expounding the theory of its own hyperstitional inexistence? A puppet who tells us what is pulling our strings?

In the end, no-one would be crazy enough to believe it wasn't true.

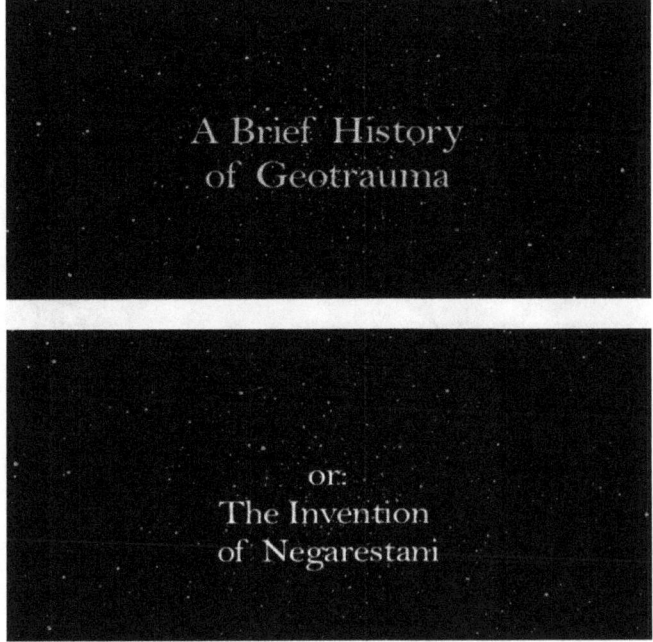

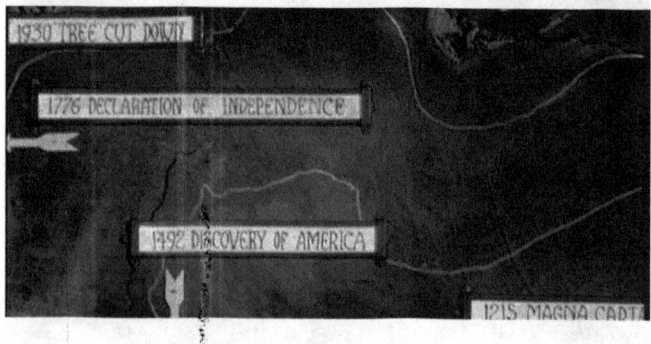

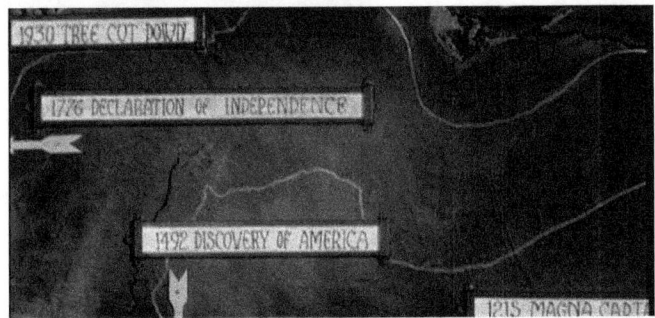

LEPER CREATIVITY

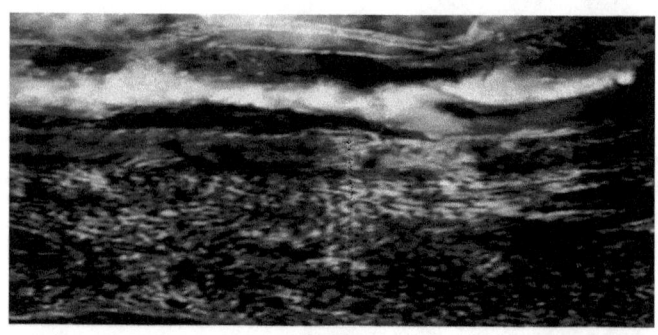

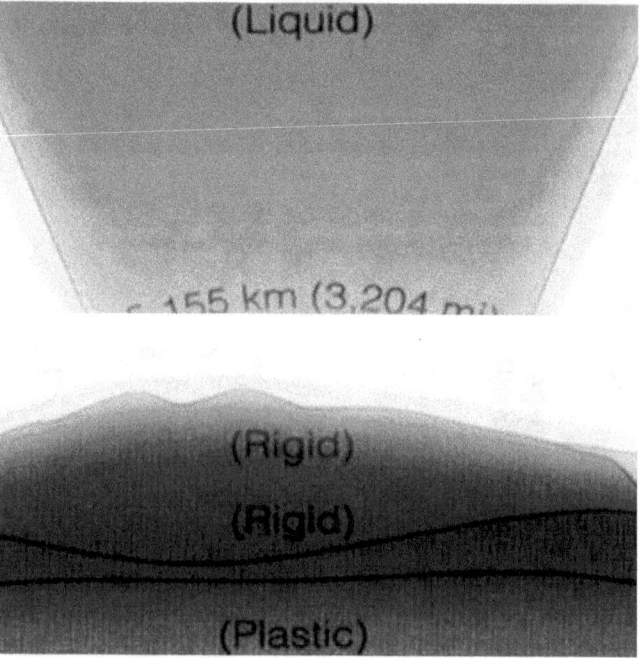

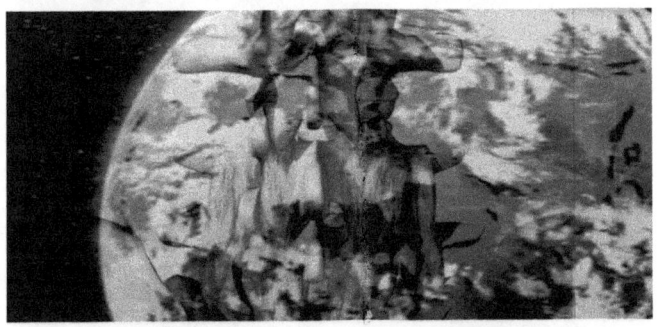
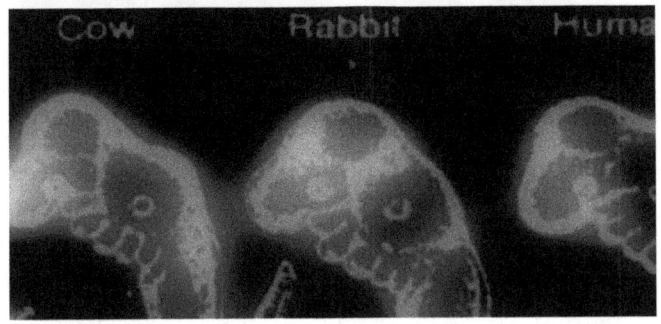

*
* *

Going up that river was like travelling back to the earliest beginnings of the world, when vegetation rioted on the earth and the big trees were kings. An empty stream, a great silence, an impenetrable forest. The air was warm, thick, heavy, sluggish . . . The long stretches of waterway ran on, deserted, into the gloom of overshadowed distances . . . We were wanderers on prehistoric earth, on an earth that wore the aspect of an unknown planet.

– Tall trees.

– When were you born?

– So you're one of the dreamers now. You've beheld the fata morgana of the terminal lagoon. You look tired. Was it a deep one?

Accessing files.

> The psychical material in such cases of hysteria presents itself as a structure in several dimensions which is stratified in at least three different ways. (*I hope I shall presently be able to justify this pictorial mode of expression.*)
>
> To begin with there is a nucleus consisting in memories of events or trains of thought in which the traumatic factor has culminated or the pathogenic idea has found its purest manifestation. Round this nucleus we find what is often an incredibly profuse amount of other mnemic material which has to be worked through in the analysis and which is, as we have said, arranged in a threefold order.
>
> In the first place there is an unmistakable linear chronological order which obtains within each separate theme. . . .
>
> [I]n Breuer's analysis of Anna O, . . . under each of . . . seven headings ten to over a hundred individual memories were collected in chronological series. It was as though we were examining a dossier that had been kept in good order.
>
> They make the work of analysis more difficult by the peculiarity that, in reproducing the memories, they reverse the order in

which these originated. The freshest and newest experience in the file appears first, as an outer cover, and last of all comes the experience with which the series in fact began.

Such groupings constitute 'themes'. These themes exhibit a second kind of arrangement. Each of them is—*I can not express it in any other way*—stratified concentrically round the pathogenic nucleus.

The contents of each particular stratum are characterized by an equal degree of resistance, and that degree increases in proportion as the strata are nearer to the nucleus. Thus there are zones within which there is all equal degree of modification of consciousness, and the different themes extend across these zones. The most peripheral strata contain the memories (or files), which, belonging to different themes, are easily remembered and have always been clearly conscious. The deeper we go the more difficult it becomes for the emerging memories to be recognized, till near the nucleus we come upon memories which the patient disavows even in reproducing them.

A third kind of arrangement has still to be mentioned—the most important, but the one about which it is least easy to make any general statement. What I have in mind is an arrangement according to thought-content, the linkage made by a logical thread which reaches as far as the nucleus and tends to take an irregular and twisting path, different in every case. This arrangement has a dynamic character, in contrast to the morphological one of the two stratifications mentioned previously. While these two would be represented in a spatial diagram by a continuous line, curved or straight, the course of the logical chain would have to be indicated by a broken line which would pass along the most roundabout paths from the surface to the deepest layers and back, and yet would in general advance from the periphery to the central nucleus, touching at every intermediate halting-place—a line resembling the zig-zag line in the solution of a Knight's Move problem, which cuts across the squares in the diagram of the chessboard. . . .

We have said that this material behaves like a foreign body, and that the treatment, too, works like the removal of a foreign body from the living tissue. We are now in a position to see where this comparison fails. A foreign body does not enter into any relation with the layers of tissue that surround it, although it modifies them and necessitates a reactive inflammation in them. Our pathogenic psychical group, on the other hand, does not admit of being cleanly extirpated from the ego.

Its external strata pass over in every direction into portions of the normal ego; and, indeed, they belong to the latter just as much as to the pathogenic organization. In analysis the boundary between the two is fixed purely conventionally, now at one point, now at another, and in some places it cannot be laid down at all. The interior layers of the pathogenic organization are increasingly alien to the ego, but once more without there being any visible boundary at which the pathogenic material begins. In fact the pathogenic

> organization does not behave like a foreign body, but far more like an infiltrate.[1]

The theory of trauma was a crypto-geological hybrid from the very start. Darwin and the geologists had already established that the entire surface of the earth and everything that crawls upon it is a living fossil record, a memory bank rigorously laid down over unimaginable aeons and sealed against introspection; churned and reprocessed through its own material, but a horrifying read when the encryption is broken, its tales would unfold in parallel with Freud's, like two intertwining themes of humiliation.

Abandoning the circumspection with which Freud handles what he still supposes to be 'metaphorical' stratal imagery, Dr Daniel Barker's Cosmic Theory of Geotrauma, or Plutonics, flattens the theory of psychic trauma onto geophysics, with psychic experience becoming an encrypted geological report, the repercussion of a primal Hadean trauma in the material unconscious of Planet Earth. Further developing Professor Challenger's model of 'generalised stratification', Barker ultra-radicalises Nietzschean genealogy into a materialist cryptoscience.

> Who does the Earth think it is? It's a matter of consistency. Start with the scientific story, which goes like this: between four point five and four billion years ago—during the Hadean epoch—the earth was kept in a state of superheated molten slag, through the conversion of planetesimal and meteoritic

---

[1] Sigmund Freud, *The Psychotherapy of Hysteria* (1895), in vol. 2 of *Standard Edition of the Complete Psychological Works of Sigmund Freud*, ed. and trans. James Strachey (London: Hogarth, 1953-1974).

impacts into temperature increase (kinetic to thermic energy).

As the solar system condensed, the rate and magnitude of collisions steadily declined, and the terrestrial surface cooled, due to the radiation of heat into space, reinforced by the beginnings of the hydrocycle. During the ensuing—Archaen—epoch the molten core was buried within a crustal shell, producing an insulated reservoir of primal exogeneous trauma, the geocosmic motor of terrestrial transmutation. And that's it. That's plutonics, or neoplutonism. It's all there: anorganic memory, plutonic looping of external collisions into interior content, impersonal trauma as drive-mechanism. The descent into the body of the earth corresponds to a regression through geocosmic time.

Trauma is a body. Ultimately—at its pole of maximum disequilibrium—it's an iron thing. At MVU they call it Cthelll: the interior third of terrestrial mass, semifluid metallic ocean, megamolecule, and pressure-cooker beyond imagination. It's hotter than the surface off the sun down there, three thousand clicks below the crust, and all that thermic energy is sheer impersonal nonsubjective memory of the outside, running the plate-tectonic machinery of the planet via the conductive and convective dynamics of silicate magma flux, bathing the whole system in electromagnetic fields as it tidally pulses to the orbit of the moon.

Cthelll is the terrestrial inner nightmare, nocturnal ocean, Xanadu: the anorganic metal-body trauma-howl of the earth, cross-hatched by intensities, traversed by thermic waves and currents, deranged particles, ionic strippings and gluttings, gravitational deep-sensitivities transduced into nonlocal electromesh, and feeding volcanism . . . that's why plutonic science slides continuously into schizophrenic delirium.[2]

Let's retell the story.

At the birth of the solar system, deviating from the protoplanetary disk that is to become the central body, a tiny, uniform spherical mass emerges from the solar nebula. Within 500 million years, a sudden sinking of matter into a dense metallic core—the 'Iron Catastrophe'—precipitates the formation of a differentiated, layered planetary structure, its molten inner matter surrounded by a thin rocky mantle and cold crust. This brittle surface seals into the depths the repressed secret of Earth's 'burning immanence with the sun'.

But the face of Earth does not remain still. The shifting visage of the planet results from the combination of external processes—climatic denudation and deposition—and internal processes—the movement of igneous or magmatic fluids. These two groups of processes transform the surface of the earth and shape the destiny of everything upon it. Their energy sources are, respectively, the sun, and its repressed runt sibling, the inner core of the earth. Thus, the thin crust destined to shield the inhabitants of Earth from its primal trauma, wears on its face the continually-shifting expression of the helio-plutonic bond.

Periodically, the pressure of magma in depth impels it to move in the direction of least resistance: repressed energy erupts onto the surface, forming ig-

---

[2] Daniel Charles Barker, "Barker Speaks," in Nick Land, *Fanged Noumena* (Falmouth/NY: Urbanomic/Sequence, 2011), 497-9.

neous intrusions through the crustal rocks. The terrestrial symptoms that crystallise around these periodic outbreaks of plutonic catharsis are far-reaching and ramified.

Resident Alien; The Insider. Trauma is at once a twisted plot, a geological complex, and a heavily-encrypted file-system. The archives come to the surface only to be churned and folded back into the detritus of their own repression. The tendrils of the 'pathogenic nucleus' merge imperceptibly with 'normal tissue'. And every living individual that ever existed is a playback copy, drawn from the recording vaults, trapped in a refrain that sings the glory of Cthelll.

Beyond the restricted biocentric model outlined in *Beyond the Pleasure Principle,* Barker's theory extends trauma to encompass the inorganic domain. The accretion of the earth is the aboriginal trauma whose scars are encrypted in/as terrestrial matter, instituting a register of unconscious pain coextensive with the domain of stratified materiality as such.

It is not known whether Barker was ever in direct contact with Dr. Bodkin, although the latter developed his work while serving on the covert research mission that preceded 'Project Scar'. In any case, among the features their theoretical works share is a reworking, through this radicalised Freudian theory of trauma, of the discredited biological notion that 'ontogeny recapitulates phylogeny'. If the biological is but a tortured incantation of Cthelll's seething inner core, genealogy, stratoanalysis and information theory promise a cryptography of this cosmic pain; and Haeckel's recapitulation thesis provides a suggestion for how an hysterico-biological filing-system might be formatted.

> Cryptography has been my guiding thread, right through. What is geotraumatics about,

even now?—A rigorous practice of decoding.[3]

How would such a cryptography proceed? It's not as easy as opening files, unpacking cases. Freud knows the core can't be reached by so direct a route. The reverse-file-system, continually encrypted by its own access log, cannot be unpacked directly, but only through an experimental engagement with the twisted, rhizomatic plotlines that emerge from it . . .

> not only . . . a zig-zag, twisted line, but rather to a ramifying system of lines and more particularly to a converging one. It contains nodal points at which two or more threads meet and thereafter proceed as one; and as a rule several threads which run independently, or which are connected at various points by side-paths, debouch into the nucleus.[4]

Needless to say, trauma belongs to a time beyond personal memory—Evidently, Geotraumatics radicalizes Professor Challenger's insistence that schizoanalysis should extend further than the terrain of familial drama, to invest the social and political realms; pushing beyond history and biology, it incorporates the geological and the cosmological within the purview of a transcendental unconscious. The root source of the disturbance which the organism identifies according to its parochial frame of reference—mummy-daddy— or which it construes in terms of the threat of individual death, is a more profound trauma rooted in physical reality itself. Trauma is not personal, and the time of the earth is recorded, accreted, knotted up inside us. All human experience is an encrypted

---

[3] Barker, "Barker Speaks," 494.
[4] Freud, *Psychotherapy of Hysteria*.

message from Cthelll to the cosmos, the scream of the earth.

> Fast forward seismology and you hear the earth scream. Geotrauma is an ongoing process, whose tension is continually expressed—partially frozen—in biological organization.[5]

Nietzsche suggested that the structure and usage of the human body is the root source of the system of neurotic afflictions co-extensive with human existence; but this is also a *planetary* neurosis. Geotraumatic cryptography must proceed as ultra-genealogy, accessing these memories deep-frozen and imprinted in the body and determining the planetary events which they index.

Vertigo's dramatization of hysteria may seem to linearise Freud's topologically-twisted model, suggesting that the core may be reached, repetition escaped, through linear regression, through an accessing of personal memory, a peeling back of layers. Perhaps it is only the exigencies of visual entertainment that take it off the couch, outside the therapist's office; but it intuits the kinship of the system of hysteria with non-human systems of memory; and (very possibly Hitchcock was reading Bodkin as well as Freud) it sees traumatic regression activated not through introspection but through return to a former environment, with the unconscious tacked onto geography in the form of affect-triggers. *Tall trees.*

Hence we return to Haeckel's recapitulation thesis. In his formulation of 'neuronics', Bodkin sought to understand the unconscious as a time-coded spinal memory, a series of evolutionary chemical-response triggers sensitive to climatic conditions. Neuronics

---

[5] Barker, "Barker Speaks," 499.

sets out to empirically map the relation between psychic organization, biological phylogenesis, and environmental stimuli. Bodkin's disconcertingly prescient theory discusses the prospect of an inundation of the planet, during a runaway climatic shift, causing tropical heat and oceanic expansion. His experiments chart the resulting modifications of the unconscious, as climate change triggers the shutting-down or reawakening of behaviours belonging to prior evolutionary stages of the human.

Notwithstanding the 'discredit' of Haeckel's thesis—that ontogeny recapitulates phylogeny, that every individual being, in its development, reiterates the stages of evolution of its remote ancestors—like Barker, Bodkin discerns a theoretical potency beneath the linear simplicity that allows its easy dismissal. If major evolutionary changes are the result of catastrophic shifts in the planetary environment—the onset of ice ages, changes in the atmosphere, the parting of tectonic plates, significant rises in temperature—then the biological can be understood, in geotraumatic terms, as a map of geological time.

Along these lines, the emergence of Barker's theory of 'spinal catastrophism' makes the necessary corrections and provides a model for geotraumatic diagnostic procedure:

> I was increasingly aware that all my real problems were modalities of back-pain, or phylogenetic spinal injury, which took me back to the calamitous consequences of the precambrian explosion, roughly five hundred million years ago. . . .
>
> Erect posture and perpendicularization of the skull is a frozen calamity, associated with a long list of pathological consequences, amongst which should be included most of the human psychoneuroses. . . .

> The issue here—as always—is real and effective regression. It is not a matter of representational psychology.
>
> Haeckel's . . . Recapitulation Thesis . . . is a theory compromised by its organicism, but its wholesale rejection was an overreaction. [Bodkin's] response is more productive and balanced, treating DNA as a transorganic memory-bank and the spine as a fossil record, without rigid onto-phylogenic correspondence.
>
> The mapping of spinal-levels onto neuronic time is supple, episodic, and diagonalizing. It concerns plexion between blocks of machinic transition, not strict isomorphic—or stratic redundancy—between scales of chronological order. Mammal DNA contains latent fish-code (amongst many other things).[6]

On the basis of this 'diagonal' model, Bodkin's experimental studies record the effectuation of archaeopsychic 'regressions' in his subjects through extreme environmental triggers, noting the extramental, trans-individual vector of such regression:

> What am I suggesting? That *Homo sapiens* is about to transform himself into Cro-Magnon and Java Man, and ultimately into *Sinanthropus*? No, a biological process is not completely reversible.
>
> The increased temperature and radiation are indeed alerting *innate releasing mechanisms. But not in our minds.* These are the oldest memories on Earth, the time-codes carried in every chromosome and gene. Eve-

---

[6] Barker, "Barker Speaks," 500-1.

ry step we've taken in our evolution is a milestone inscribed with organic memories—from the enzymes controlling the car-carbon dioxide cycle to the organisation of the brachial plexus and the nerve pathways of the Pyramid cells in the mid-brain, each is a record of a thousand decisions taken in the face of a sudden physico-chemical crisis. Just as psychoanalysis reconstructs the original traumatic situation in order to release the repressed material, so our subjects are being plunged back into the archaeopsychic past, uncovering the ancient taboos and drives that havebeen dormant for epochs. The brief span of an individual life is misleading. Each one of us is as old as the entire biological kingdom, and our bloodstreams are tributaries of the great sea of its total memory. The uterine odyssey of the growing foetus recapitulates the entire evolutionary past, and its central nervous system is coded time scale, each nexus of neurones and each spinal level marking a symbolic station, a unit of neuronic time. . . .

The further down the CNS you move, from the hind-brain through the medulla into the spinal cord, the further you descend back into the neuronic past. For example, the junction between the thoracic and lumbar vertebrae, between T-12 and L-1, is the great zone of transit between the gill-breathing fish and the airbreathing amphibians with their respiratory rib-cages . . .

If you like, you could call this the Psychology of Total Equivalents—let's say 'Neuronics' for short—and dismiss it as metabiological fantasy. However, I am convinced that as we move back through geophysical time so we re-enter the amnionic corridor and move back through spinal and archaeopsychic time, recollecting in our unconscious minds the landscapes of each epoch, each with a distinct geological terrain, its own unique flora and fauna, as recognisable to anyone else as they would be to a traveller in a Wellsian time machine. Except that this is no scenic railway, but a total re-orientation of the personality. If we let these buried phantoms master us as they re-appear we'll be swept back helplessly in the flood-tide like pieces of flotsam.[7]

If infantilism were all the past had to offer, then psychoanalysis would be time-travel, and the future would be well-balanced. Announcing themselves as hyper-Freudianism, Neuronics and the Cosmic theory of Geotrauma shift from the imaginary familial circuit to the lagoons of deep time. They introduce diagonalised matter-memory in order to study the twisted indexing of the Geo-Archaeo-Psychic.

As to Land, perhaps what he found most valuable in Barker's work was the extension of geotraumatic theory into human culture and to language in particular, via this keying of the geotraumatic body-map to environmental stimuli; and the potential for development of modes of decoding of cultural phenomena that escape the signifier. Bipedalism, erect posture, forward-facing vision, the cranial verticalization of the human face, the laryngeal constriction of the voice, are themselves all indices of a succession of geotraumatic catastrophes separating the material potencies of the body from its stratified actuality. Just as the bipedal head impedes 'vertebro-perceptual linearity', the human larynx inhibits 'virtual speech'. One cannot

---

[7] Dr. Bodkin's Journal.

dismantle the face without also evacuating the voice. Perhaps inspired by Parsani's invocation of the Middle-Eastern vowel-less battle-cry against solar empire, Land affirms that, in geotraumatic terms, the human voice itself is—via the various accidents of hominid evolution—the enfeebled expression of geotrauma:

> Due to erect posture the head has been twisted around, shattering vertebro-perceptual linearity and setting up the phylogenetic preconditions for the face. This right-angled pneumatic-oral arrangement produces the vocal apparatus as a crash-site, in which thoracic impulses collide with the roof of the mouth. The bipedal head becomes a virtual speech-impediment, a sub-cranial pneumatic pile-up, discharged as linguo-gestural development and cephalization take-off. Burroughs suggests that the protohuman ape was dragged through its body to expire upon its tongue. It's a twin-axial system, howls and clicks, reciprocally articulated as a vowel-consonant phonetic palette, rigidly intersegmented to repress staccato-hiss continuous variation and its attendant becomings-animal. The anthropostructural head-smash that establishes our identity with logos . . . [8]

For Land, therefore, as for Bodkin, the schizoanalytic 'treatment' of geotrauma, the discovery of the 'innate releasing mechanisms', is a matter of 'real and effective regression', which can only be carried out on an experimental and empirical basis, on the basis of a certain hypothesis concerning the relation between time, matter and trauma.

---

[8] Barker, "Barker Speaks," 502.

A noteworthy outcome of this hypothesis is a certain deepening of pessimism: Ultimately, nothing short of the complete liquidation of biological order and the dissolution of physical structure can suffice to discharge the aboriginal trauma that mars terrestrial existence. A collective becoming-snake of human civilization would be only the first step.

When, in the 1990s, the Cybernetic Culture Research Unit—probably, it is thought, through the agency of the aged Anatole Alasca, once assistant to Professor Challenger—disinterred the by then all-but-hermetic Daniel Barker from his lab at MVU for that last CCRU interview, Nick Land embarked upon his short-lived revival of the Geocosmic Theory of Trauma through a series of experiments in microcultural destratification, documentation of which has recently been rediscovered.

Land was a relay, keeping the signal alive, but of course he didn't last long, he burnt out just like Barker before him. In 99-2000 Parsani joined us, but he was too far gone to be of any help. That's why the Committee needed a new candidate.

So where is 'Negarestani' supposed to go with this?

He begins by elaborating on the story so far: the conspiracy to return Cthelll, the earth's core, repressed runt sibling of the sun, to immanence with its solar mothership; the plotting of the return of the Tellurian insider; and the agency of oil as tellurian lube. All this we know and approve of.

But what is important is this: Ultimately, a theory that locates the source of the ills of the human psyche in the accretion of the earth 4.5 billion years ago is—obviously—far too parochial for the purposes of the Committee. It owes its local inhibitions to Land's fondness for Bataille and his disproportionate attention to Freud's later, flawed model of trauma in *Beyond the Pleasure Principle*.

According to Bataille's 'solar economy', the most basic economic problem is not scarcity but the exorbitant excess of solar energy; all movements on this planet, from the basest physical processes through to the highest sophistications of life and culture, consist only in labyrinthine detours of one and the same vector—the profligate expenditure of energy by the sun. The secret of all apparently stable and economically conservative being is that it is already pledged to solar abolition, it already belongs to the sun and its radical horizon of death.

Negarestani recognizes the just alignment of Bataille's notion of the Solar Economy with Freud's speculative thesis concerning the nature of organic life: According to 'Beyond the Pleasure Principle', the preservation of a lifeform in relation to the excessive energy source it draws upon, demands the sacrifice of a part of that lifeform: the creation of a mortified outer surface or crust—'a special envelope or membrane resistant to stimuli'—that protects it from its exorbitant source of energy. Thus, the survival and individuality of an organic lifeform, biological, psychic or cultural, is based on the repression of an originary trauma in which it encountered, in all its naked power, the source of energy that would also be its death. Lifeforms are lagoons, repressed pockets of forgetting, temporarily protecting themselves against the outside that created them and will destroy them.

Thus we can say that all forms of life are solutions to the same problem; managing the excoriating excess of solar energy which will eventually consume them in death. As modes of life become more complex and more numerous, their dependence upon the excessive power source only grows stronger; as Negarestani argues, there is a mutually-reinforcing symmetry between the plurality of life and the monism of death. Another way to put this is that, from the point of view of the securitised individuated lifeform closed up against its traumatic encounter with solar excess, the sun inevitably becomes the single and absolute horizon or vanishing point for all life.

This development of what Negarestani will call the 'monogamous model' of the relation between terrestrial life and the sun, is relayed in the cultural and economic forms of capitalism. Capitalism appears as a crazed thanatropic machine, unlocking the earth's resources—in particular, the fossil fuels that were, in more optimistic times, referred to as 'buried sunlight'—to release them to their destiny of dissolution, and thus accelerating the consumption of the earth by the sun.

> by tapping the Carboniferous Formation and spewing it up into the sky, we've become a volcano that hasn't stopped erupting since the 1700s.[9]

Mankind is the first lifeform to contemporaneously communicate with geological time; a gigantic volcano, a holocaust of consumption, a fault in the file-system. Yet this unbridled consumption also manifests itself culturally in an ever-increasing complexification and elaboration of multiple 'ways of life' and supposedly infinite possibilities and differentiation.

To break thought out of its capture by the monogamous model, even though the propaganda of the solar empire runs through the entirety of biological life and human culture—*including the flawed variants of geotrauma theory*. This is Negarestani's first mission—To broaden still further the theory in rescinding the status of the sun as sole 'image of exteriority', as ultimate singular horizon for all life. The sun is not the absolute or the abyss, but only a local blockage, a re-

---

[9] Alan Weisman, *The World Without Us* (New York: Thomas Dunne, 2007), 40.

striction, a blind spot that obscures the opening of the earth onto a more general cosmic economy which produced it and which will consume it, along with the sun.

In 3.5 billion years, the core of the aging sun grows hotter, causing a severe greenhouse effect that sterilises the entire biosphere; its outer surface cools, expanding to engulf the inner planets. In 7 billion years, the earth slips out of orbit but, outside the small chance that it could be flung out into the 'icy desolation of deep space', is dragged into the core of the Sun to be evaporated, its only legacy a small amount of fuel for the red giant's farewell glow. The sun becomes a 'small block of hydrogen ice'; 100 trillion years into the future, all the stars go out, followed by an era populated only by the 'degenerate remnants' that survive the end of stellar evolution. 10^{40} years, the cosmic catastrophe of proton decay ushers in the era of black holes, where the only stellar objects left are black holes 'convert their mass into radiation and evaporate at a glacial pace', and then the scarcely-conceivable 'dark era' populated by atomic waste products entering into desultory, increasingly rare and fruitless chance encounters.[10]

The cosmic abyss is deeper than the solar furnace. Earth's monogamous relationship with the sun is just one chapter in a weird epic narrative that does not find its climax in annihilatory conflagration.

And therefore, the terrestrial plots that play out in the human psyche must be traced back beyond the paltry 4.5 million year lifespan of the planet. The trauma is deeper still, and more weird, than Challenger, Barker or Land had imagined.

---

[10] See F. C. Adams, "Long-term astrophysical processes," in *Global Catastrophic Risks*, eds. N. Bostrom and M. M. Cirkovic (Oxford: Oxford University Press, 2008).

To contemplate these icy, inevitable vistas of cosmic time is in a certain sense already to go beyond geotrauma. The viewpoint of an ecology radical enough to take in these extra-solar eschatologies not only breaks through terrestrial concerns, but also through the 'solar horizon' that has governed our thought on and of the earth.

As Negarestani will say, 'to be truly terrestrial is not the same as being superficial'. To be truly terrestrial is to embrace the perishability of the earth, and its implication in the universe, beyond the local economics of the relation between the sun and the surface; to replace the monogamous relation between a contingent earth and the necessary and absolute sun around which its planetary path winds, with a relation of multiplicity between this planetary body and the cosmic contingencies which led to its formation, a cosmic chemical conspiracy that works through the earth, and which finds its dissolute destiny beyond the sun. Chemophilosophy; geotrauma unearthed.

*
* *

So now you know. It was all a twisted plot. *For years, they thought they were making all this up. But the Committee was telling them what to write . . .*

The 'Speculative Realist' racket provided a perfect opportunity; capitalizing on the vogue for imagining one can subtract theoretical thought from the human imaginary, from narrative and from sense, through Negarestani we are able to inject it, precisely, with the narrative element that is, as paradoxical as it may seem, an integral part of the procedure. Signification cannot be crushed without following plots that tell ever-new stories of the earth. It's not a matter of using science or a new metaphysics to eradicate such tales, but of constructing a science of real plots, which is what Geotrauma—in Negarestani's hands—becomes. The compulsive-repetitive symptoms that are human culture cannot be overcome simply by precipitately stripping them down to a reductive physical, metaphysical or relational states. The instigation of a collective schizoanalysis must proceed through the development of the experimental means for 'real, effective regression', for meticulous decryption.

> it is quite hopeless to try to penetrate directly to the nucleus of the pathogenic organization. . . . We ourselves undertake the opening up of inner strata, advancing radially, whereas the patient looks after the peripheral extension of the work.
> We must get hold of a piece of the logical thread, by whose guidance alone we may hope to penetrate to the interior.[11]

Unpick the individual, travel down her spine, into the rocks, through the iron core, attaining a burning immanence with the sun, and exiting towards the unknown.
Above all, Negarestani's 'universalist' reconstruction of the theory of trauma, and his continual rethinking of 'The Insider' in yet more xeno-economical terms, must be understood in the wake of the committee's recent reappropriation of Ferenczi's work for the cause. For Ferenczi, trauma is not a hole punched into the organic by exteriority. This model would only reflect—all too-closely—*the empirical occasioning cause of the theoretical recognition of trauma*. Nor is it, even (as in *Beyond the Pleasure Principle*) a founding event synonymous with the constitution of the organic individual per se, and which

---

[11] Freud, *Psychotherapy of Hysteria*.

constricts its path to death. Trauma is a perennial *boring* or a vermicular inhabiting of the organic by the inorganic:

> the inassimilable presence of the universal continuum within the regional field, a resident yet alienating presence that has been bored and nested into the horizon from different angles, contingently, gradationally, infinitesimally. We call this resident yet inassimilable index of exteriority that can neither be expelled nor reintegrated within the interiorized horizon, the Insider.[12]

Ferenczi's traumata are plotholes that must be plumbed, outward itineraries that must be travelled. The time of trauma is altered. Geophilosophy was always a chemophilosophy: just as it needed to explode the constricted space of the individual and escape to the political surface of the earth, and just as it was then necessary to understand the apparently stable surface as an arrested flow and to penetrate to the depths, the cosmic theory of geotrauma now needed to pass through the core of the earth only to escape its inhibited mode of traumatic stratification and to carry its interrogation further afield, or rather according to a new mode of distribution.

The Committee's question is: which practices, conspiracies, theories, insurgencies, *setting out from the local surface,* will 'assist the earth in hatching its inner black egg'; which plots will assist in decrypting the addresses of traumatic agents no longer understood as foreign bodies that assault the protective

---

[12] Reza Negarestani, *On the Revolutionary Earth* (unpublished); subsequently published as "Globe of Revolution. An Afterthought on Geophilosophical Realism," *Identities* 17 (2011): 25-54.

membrane of the organic individual, nor even as a repressed fragments of a greater exuberance; but as xeno-chemical insiders, Old Ones waiting to be awakened. What stimuli will key into the triggers that will attach us to a Kurtz-gradient, disintricating the tangled themes that surface as reality-symptoms, allowing us egress into dreams where the lagoon of personal memory drains into a sea of cosmic trauma?

> Guided by his dreams, he was moving backwards through the emergent past, through a succession of ever stranger landscapes, centred upon the lagoon, each of which seemed to represent one of his own spinal levels. At times the circle of water was spectral and vibrant, at others slack and murky, the shore apparently formed of shale, like the dull metallic skin of a reptile. Yet again the soft beaches would glow invitingly with a glossy carmine sheen, the sky warm and limpid, the emptiness of the long stretches of sand total and absolute, filling him with an exquisite and tender anguish.
>
> He longed for this descent through archaeopsychic time to reach its conclusion, repressing the knowledge that when it did the external world around him would have become alien and unbearable.[13]

How can the revolutionary subject, through deepening and widening its traumas, attain topological and categorical equivalence with the universal absolute? Likewise, how can the regional horizon—as a relatively open set excised from the universal absolute—find its equivalence with the absolute through deep-

---

[13] Dr. Bodkin's Journal.

ening its geophilosophical synthesis and stretching its nested traumas by dilating and twisting them?[14]

It's a question of writing, but also of mapping. That's where Cane comes in. Once you see the Atlas you'll know where to go.

The Plutonics Committee had to exert some pressure, to get things moving.

> There is nothing for it but to keep at first to the periphery of the psychical structure. We begin by getting the patient to tell us what he knows and remembers, while we are at the same time already directing his attention and overcoming his slighter resistances by the use of the pressure procedure. Whenever we have opened a new path by thus pressing on his forehead, we may expect him to advance some distance without fresh resistance.
>
> After we have worked in this way for some time, the patient begins as a rule to co-operate with us.[15]

It therefore remains for us to see how, effectively, simultaneously, these various tasks of schizoanalysis proceed.

*
* *

---

[14] Negarestani, *On the Revolutionary Earth*.
[15] Freud, *The Psychotherapy of Hysteria*.

It was over. Only later would all of this take on concrete meaning. The double-articulated mask had come undone, and so had the gloves and tunic, from which liquids escaped. Disarticulated, deterriorialized, Negarestani muttered that he was taking the earth with him.

An Inhuman Fiction of Forces

McKenzie Wark

> The work is the death mask of its conception.
> — Walter Benjamin

'The Domain of Arnheim' is a strange story by Edgar Allan Poe, in which a young man who inherits an incredible fortune decides to spend it, not on buying art but on fashioning a landscape. Poe also imagines the Earth seen from space as itself a complete work of art. He anticipates the real ends of modernism.

Is not the totality of all our endeavors, all our social relations, tending towards the making over of the planet as a total work of art? This theme of a secular, aesthetic destiny has its roots in Romanticism, but lately it has lost its more optimistic cast. What if the work of art into which the word turns excluded the presence of its own makers? What if its creation destroys the biological possibility of human life on the planet?

What light does aesthetics as a branch of thought, and art as a creative practice, shed on the (possible) end(s) of the world? What if we consider the end of the world as the finished product of aesthetic modernity? The blue ruin of earth is the total work of art at the end of history. The earth will be buried at sea.

These matters are too serious to leave in the hands of technological optimists and apocalyptic doomsayers. Nor is moral scolding about doing the recycling either effective or adequate to conceiving of the whole picture of climate change and its consequences. Rather, it calls for an aesthetic sensibility oriented to the whole picture rather than this or that aspect.

There is a certain popular delight in imagining the modern world in ruins. It's a theme Walter Benjamin identified early in the 20th century. In the shadow of the bomb, the Beats and their contemporaries occasionally gave it an incendiary cast. But what if we push beyond the picture of atomized cities to imagine not what passes but what is created at the end of human time? Our permanent legacy will not be architectural, but chemical. After the last dam bursts, after the concrete monoliths crumble into the lone and level sands, modernity will leave behind a chemical signature, in everything from radioactive waste to atmospheric carbon. This work will be abstract, not figurative.

Grasping this as a total work means understanding two tendencies in relation to each other: the global and the molecular. The tendency toward the global and the tendency toward the molecular are combined in work such as the Center for Land Use Interpretation's guided tours of urban LA oil rigs or nuclear waste dumps in the salt flats, where the tour bus is an inside out vitrine. In the wake of the vast oil spill in the Gulf of Mexico, the artist duo übermogen.com announce: "oil painting has evolved into generative bio-art... an oil painting on an 80,000 square mile ocean canvas..." It's simply a matter of taking the next step, of extending the parameters of the molecular aesthetic to the planetary limit.

While there are tendencies in contemporary art that are helpful for thinking about the blue ruin, there are perhaps fewer resources in literature. Cormac McCarthy's *The Road* presents a reverse passion play, the passing of the sacred out of the earth, but its rather human-centric. On the other hand, is Ian McEwan's

Solar the worst book so far of the 21st century? Climate change exists as a plot device for some jokes about some old white guy. This is the context in which Reza Negarastani's *Cyclonopedia* emerges for me as the only worthy successor to 'The Domain of Arnheim' in the contemporary scene.

Let me say that I doubt the existence of an author named Reza Negarastani. What is named Negrastani is a practice of détournement, or what *Cyclonopedia* itself describes thus: "Hidden Writing can be described as using every plot hole, all problematics, every suspicious obscurity or repulsive wrongness as a new plot with a tentacle and autonomous mobility." It "bespeaks a crowd at work" of "autonomous author drones" (61). It doesn't matter whether the body of Reza Negarastani exists or not. If it does, its just the host for a fiction of forces that writes through it.

Cyclonopedia not a novel. It can of course be read as one, but only at the expense of making the category of novel meaningless. *Cyclonopedia* is heretical theology. Heresy plays out certain structural and rhetorical possibilities of a given authorized corpus. "To do rigorous theology is to perforate the Divine corpus with heresies" (62). The weird beauty of *Cyclonopedia* comes not least from its diving in and out of the plot holes in certain geopolitical narratives. As in theology, its characters are inhuman. They are centrally the figures of earth and sun, and within earth, of liquid and dust, where the liquid is oil and not water.

I'm interested in water myself, but I appreciate this attempt to make a hole in the narrative of water and earth, to dig down to another, about oil, which challenges the "onanistic self indulgence of the Sun" (19). Oil is the agent which brings a time of the aeons, a geological time, through a hole in historical time. Oil is an agent of the xenodrome, from 'xeno', or stranger. "Xenodrome is the Earth of becoming-Gas or cremation-to-dust" (17).

This "hydrocarbon corpse juice", this "black corpse of the sun" (26) is a chemical weapon of earth against sun, unwittingly let loose by human agency. Strikingly, oil is the subject here. Everything belonging to historical time is just minor characters. Here's the ()hole plot summary of the book: "petroleum poisons capital with absolute madness" (27). It is as if oil was waiting for some McGuffin to set it in motion. Oil is capital before there are even humans, waiting for a host. The host reinvents the earth as an oil-shitting machine. Oil that is just masticated life, which is itself just sun-cum.

"Oil, with its poromechanical zones of emergence in economy, geopolitics and culture, mocks Divine chronological time with the utmost irony and obscenity" (58). I'm not so interested in that, frankly. I have nothing to say about Islam. It is not in relation to Islam that *Cyclonopedia* creates heresies. And nor does capital need a genealogy of its will to desertification. It's enough to think how it is not oil that fuels capital but rather the reverse. Capital is just oil's vector.

We need a narratology of the elements, a way of writing that does not just treat the chemical world as if it gave rise to subjects equivalent to the humans, gods or monsters that usually populate narratives. A way of writing that does not make the chemical world merely ambient, either. And can we have done with the organic vanity of biopower? Why should the biological level of organization take precedence over any other? Rather an elemental narratolology, which opens on the one side to the ancestral subatomic world, and on the other to the elements and their molecular combinations.

Nor am I all that interested in Gog and Magog, Bush and Bin Ladin, tweedledum and tweedledee, the drama of sockpuppets animated by oil. Oil is always (re)animating new sockpuppets. The rise of Hugo Chavez; the fall of Libya. It also occurs to me that the emerging narrative is not oily but gaseous. Imagine digging through the hole in the *Cyclonopedia* narrative to another one, about so-called natural gas. Fracking is a water and air story, not an oil and dust one.

What *Cyclonopedia* calls "occult derivatives" are those conspiracy theories that gum up the channels of political communication, impoverishing the state's communication through time. Its an attack on the state's territories of time. That's the strategy of *Cyclonopedia*, and not a bad one. What are the others? Can we see this book as a point in a space of possible writings that are xenowritings. An inhuman fiction of forces. Rather than "truth is stranger than fiction," we might say that Xenowriting is the true stranger in fiction.

Xenia is what the Greeks called the hospitality owed to strangers, and xenia is what I think we owe to *Cyclonopedia*. Which is to say we become its hosts. And in its own metronymic fashion, this small part of the hosting of the stranger helps spread the occult derivatives which block a certain sedentary order of life and yet at the same time opens vectors for inhuman particles to inhabit thought.

Root the Earth: On Peak Oil Apophenia

Benjamin H. Bratton

I. PEAK OIL APOPHENIA; OR "THE ANUS OF FORESIGHT"

After the end of the world, what is the polity of the inhuman? What is its government of energy? It is programmatic reconfigurability: a general economy of plasticity. It extends around the anthropomorphic physiognomy of architecture and toward an acephalic geography emerging in the image of strong computational equivalence. The prototype of an indeterminate future government is positioned by an encounter between that equivalence and the numinous decay of ecological entropy and negentropy: oil as body of the world, and the "worlding" of the body of oil. Peak oil, and after.

Reza Negarestani's own program in his theoretical-novel, *Cyclonopedia*, is both geography and geophilosophy, yes, but also geopolitics, in the specific sense of a Jamesonian geopolitical aesthetic.[1] I wish to instrumentalize the text and to de-metaphorize its obsessions, and to link these to those of another short text of my own: "The language of utopia has shifted. The cybernetics of scenario planning has given way to the apophenia of eschatology. Is geopolitics but a Dark Side of the Rainbow effect? With this shift, infor-

---

[1] Fredric, Jameson, *The Geopolitical Aesthetic: Cinema and Space in the World System* (Indiana University Press, 1995).

mation becomes unmanageable, non-linear, associative, arbitrary. Anything is enrolled into the local rhetoric of conspiracy . . ."[2]

Invention is the transposition of one phase state to another, of one resonance on top of another, and it expresses therefore the deep recomposability, indeed deep recomputability, of worldly substance. Catherine Malabou speaks of the world's plasticity as a condition of its futurity.[3] When or where? Less than deep recomputability causes a genuinely new condition to emerge 'later in time' simultaneous to some postponed event, it does so 'here' in the recombinancy of an infinite synchronic field of the longest possible 'now'. This is the absolute contingency of mathematics collapsing into the mortal contingency of stuff. That is, does everything that has ever existed continue to exist now, in the molecular transformation of geoprogrammatic recycling, and also, does everything that will ever exist already do so in another larval, disorganized distribution?

Consider the Greek *plastikos*, Latin *plasticus*, and in 1630's the English, *plastic*, and then finally Leo

---

[2] This fragment is from my text, "Plastic Futures Markets," written as part of the exhibition, MADE-UP: Design Fictions," curated by Tim Durfee at Art Center College of Design, Pasadena, CA, January, 2011. The Dark Side of the Rainbow, "refers to the pairing of the 1973 Pink Floyd album *The Dark Side of the Moon* with the visual portion of the 1939 film *The Wizard of Oz*. This produces moments where the film and the album appear to correspond with each other. The title of the music video-like experience comes from a combination of the album title and the film's song 'Over the Rainbow.' Band members and others involved in the making of the album state that any relationship between the two works of art is merely a coincidence" (http://en.wikipedia.org/wiki/Dark_Side_of_the_Rainbow).

[3] See Jean-Paul Martinon, *On Futurity: Malabou, Nancy and Derrida* (New York: Palgrave Macmillan, 2007).

Baekland's "plastic," a hard light-weight material synthesized in 1909. The concept of plastiticty predates the industrial-era invention of plastic and its epidemic standardization of the chemical phylum. Now the massive scale oil extraction and distribution that most differentiates the 20th century as the time of the Anthropocene has made possible the ongoing replacement of the things of world by their plastic versions. But plastic is not only mutability and mimesis, it is mutation, a speciation of objects.

And that is oil's own career as a terrestrial process. For Earth, the rendering of organic life on the surface of its crust into subterranean mineral fossil fuels is a core vascular labor. As oil, plastic is life re-recycled. So that the plasticity of plastic—the real compression-deformation effect of oil as the ultimate fate of the living thing—long predates the physical possibility of its composition by animals (humans) as the chemicals we call "plastics." That futurity is ancient. This transmutation from some things and toward other things, the recycling churn of geotrauma and geodesign, translates the situated flux of planetary molecular recombinancy into the generic assemblages we recognize as cities, civilizations, languages, and discursive registers of authority and knowledge.

But that ubiquitous conversion far exceeds our cognitive faculties to map its local causality, effectivity, and relationality. That excess can render the world in the inchoate, premature resolution of a "sacred conspiracy," one which awards critical agency to phantom actors, histories and numerologies, within what are instead, utterly secular, if also inconceivably complex, non-linear systems.

Now the geopolitics of peak oil is necessarily the fabrication and negotiation of an image of the world from which Modern plastic has been withdrawn, because soon it is no longer feasible to manufacture. In that world, existing plastic retrieved from landfills can only be re-re-recycled. But to imagine the world denuded of new plastic first requires a model in which the agency of oil has been conceptualized and formalized, such that effects of the agency of oil (now subtracted through the imminent exhaustion of pre-Holocene deposits) can be differentiated, perceived and predicted. But because Plastic and plasticity are already deeply pervasive, foundational procedures of the world, that abstraction of agency, while absolutely necessary and critical, is nevertheless indissociable from arbitrary eschatology.

This occult theory of geosystems, and the dramatization of untraceable molecular genealogies through their promiscuous recyclings, is apophenia. It is a divination of rhythm from the unfoldings of perception itself, and a reading of these affects as if they were deliberately authored and specifically significant. This spiritualism is perhaps another kind of correlationism, this time not between subjects and objects, but systems and their effects. It is counterpart to the role of conspiracy theory in the Jamesonian geopolitical aesthetic. It a collapse of correlation into causation, a fiction of resolution through a perceptual trick of juxtaposition, as the Kulsehov effect is for the narrative experience of film. For Abrahamac monotheism, textualist eschatology is always apophenia, as history is mapped across a sacred telos, such that correspondence between current event and its foretelling is guaranteed in advance. For our Peak Oil predicament, geopolitical illegibility provokes and precedes the theologic envelope of revelation: the anus of foresight.

II. THE SOLAR ANUS AND THE SOLAR MOUTH

The "devil's shit," oil, is a totality of rot. Fossil fuels are the planetary archive of putrification and cumulative decrepitude: dead plankton, micro and macro-organisms, flaura and fauna, become mineral body, plants become peat, rock. Oil is Meat.

Consider then how Negarestani frames the early scientific pseudo-controversy over the ultimate origins of oil in the fragment, "Outlines for a Science Fiction of the Earth as Narrated from a Nethermost Point of View."[4] A geopolitical—and perhaps metaphysical—imaginary is at stake in the opposition of biogenic and exogenic theories of oil, each constitutional of a different biopolitics, and different conditions for the speculative geo-materialist comprehension of modernity, indeed geology and history, as an expression of oil's own desire. Negarestani writes, "according to the biogenic theory of fossil fuels, petroleum was formed under pressure and heat in the absence of oxygen while sadistically counting organic death tolls for millennia. Under such extreme conditions, petroleum grew a satanic verve for reanimating the dead and puppetizing the living on a planetary scale. A precursor to blobjective narratives, (this) imagery grasps the 'Thingness' of oil as a singular inorganic body fueling the Conradian journey 'up-river,' from the gas station to the chthonic oil reservoir via the tentacled edifice of oil pipelines . . . from a nethermost point of view, Bush and Bin Laden are merely petropolitical puppets convulsing along the chthonic strings of the blob just in the same way that a Chinese plastic toy and equally an American predator drone are brought to life by the strings woven from the hydrocarbon corpse juice."

So the labor of Earth is not only orgiastic recycling but an incessant authophagia, autocannibalization: planet as molecular war machine against itself. The Anthropocene Age of Plastic is but an instant whereby the cumulative subterranean mineral corpse of the planet's initial millions of years of life, now rendered into mineral gas and fluid by the

---

[4] Reza Negarastani, "Outlines for a Science Fiction of the Earth as Narrated from a Nethermost Point of View," *World Literature Today* 84 (2010): 12-3.

Earth itself, is given another zombie life in the animated forms of worldly Plastic: oceans of plankton resur-resurrected as skyscrapers, trillions of trees haunting the world as textiles, as food additives, artificial hearts, and even as fake plastic trees spinning in circles through the Pacific garbage gyre. Here "Peak Oil" represents a clock measuring the speed by which the present can consume the past and a linear, indexical quantification of how much of the past remains for future consumption. It measures time, of how much more future there is to be. Biogenesis is carnivore infrastructure, an eating of the world. This is a restricted economy version of Bataille's Solar Anus, one for which the cosmos provides, in its open expenditure, the energy of construction, circulation and exchange, but for this closed planetary loop, and like the Sadean economy of fluid exchange, there is less and less piss and shit to be eaten every time it goes around. The Anthropocene spasm of transposing the past into the generic chemicals we call Plastic is the Earth re-eating itself all in one go, consuming the full archive in one momentary spasm. In this, the animal becomes mineral.

To open the loop, that economy needs to be extended off-planet in an expanded communication with another archive. That expansion is the crux of the exogenic theory of oil, for which Earth is already parcel of a cosmic economy of hydrocarbons, and for which the Anthopocene represents an apotheosis of negentropic complexity. For the xenogenesis theory, oil is not the liquid corpse of the local past, it is the mineral body of the alien present. Negarastani writes, "Although the theory of fossil fuels underwrites the narrative coherency of oil as a psychopath that runs on blackened blood, its depth and longevity are constrained by the life of organisms . . . In order to deepen . . . and broaden . . . the potencies of Earth's futurities, the avatar of petroleum as the Blob or the Thing must also be extended outside of what the astrophysicist Thomas Gold calls the 'myth of fossil fuels'. For Gold, petroleum has its origin in alien hydrocarbons of deep space, which have been trapped in the bowels of the earth. Since these alien relics are in flux within the planet, the patterns of oil distribution are susceptible to change. In this sense the science-fictional vision inherent to the terrestrial architecture of industrial civilizations becomes contingent upon Plutonic migrations of these alien inorganic demons. Eluding biological origins, oil is not of this place but of estranging depths; it has already infested the earth as an Insider for which scenarios of alien invasion are but melodramatic redundancies. If petropestilence has already invaded and colonized the earth, the entire history of terrestrial life is an era of postoccupation, and our postindustrial, oil-driven achievements that ground the foundations of our science-fictional imagination are simply exploits of a radical outsider in building its own porous earth."

Here, Earthly substances are merely hosts and shells for oil, the alien control parasite, like the parasatoid fungus, Cordyceps unilateralis, which infects the brain of a species of ant and directs its zombie to crawl to the precise height in the jungle canopy suitable by temperature and humidity for the fungus to fully spore, and where the ant husk becomes a factory for further production of the fungus. We can imagine that the ant dies happy, but will we? The poetry of the alien theory of oil is toward an extroverted decapitation of the restricted economy of capital rationalization, and the de-differentation of economies of embodiment and signification from the mineral and energistic processes of ground. Body and site oscillate in a gestalt shift of figure and ground. It is not simply that we do the aliens' bidding, but that we are animated by a chthonic force that consumes us, a praxis of the inhuman, a general economy of possession. Our consumption of time, which becomes by the death of our own decay, the prosthetic productive economy of a parasitic mandate that arrives from beyond our solar economy. Alien hydrocarbons are much more subterranean than the "Old Mole" and refer to a wider menu of orifices than the Solar Anus: instead, here is the Black Sun, the carnivorous orifice, the Solar Mouth. Parallel to our own real primordial mineral origins, here the mineral becomes animal.

To eat or to be eaten: what is infrastructure? What is infrastructure's economy of geologic cannibalism? The Solar Anus, and the biogenic theory of oil is a consumptive model of energy infrastructure for which the production-of-decay/decay-of-production is predicated on the Earth eating the sun and human history eating the Earth, and in turn for which the Earth eats history, and regurgitates it back as fossil fuel.Time eats, and so thereby in turn, time is eaten. The Black Sun and the xenogenic theory of oil privileges the cosmos eating the Earth through the prosthesis of oil, and the Earth eating us through the robot program of that alien. Time is eaten, and so thereby in turn, time can eat.

III. "God Bows to Math"[5]

Peak Oil geopolitics demands geophilosophy, as surely as apophenia demands conspiracy. The subtraction of oil from the milieu of everyday life is the prophetic horizon against which the plastic (post-Plastic) futurity of geopolitical eschatology of is measured. The ultimate effect of that withdrawal, abrupt or gradual, is beyond the comprehension of normal scenario planning models, and threatens to return thought to superstitious conversions of religion, energy and geography. But what other possibilities?

---

[5] "God Bows to Math" is a song title from *Double Nickels On The Dime* by The Minutemen (1984).

My conclusion is a departure from the paranoid methods of the Bronze Age, because the materialism at stake for Peak Oil apophenia is ultimately secular, far more secular than we have as yet had to encounter, precisely because the sacralized inter-relation of energy, religion and geography is so deeply woven into economic discourse. Let me quote Adorno, "the tendency to occultism is a symptom of regression in consciousness. This has lost the power to think the unconditional and to endure the conditional. Instead of defining both, in their unity and difference, by conceptual labour, it mixes them indiscriminately. The unconditional becomes fact, the conditional an immediate essence. The veiled tendency of society towards disaster lulls its victims in a false revelation, with a hallucinated phenomenon. In vain they hope in its fragmented blatancy to look their total doom in the eye and withstand it . . . deranged and bemused, the occultist throws away the hard-won knowledge of itself in the midst of a society which, by the all-encompassing exchange-relationship, eliminates precisely the elemental power the occultists claim to command. . . . The offal of the phenomenal world becomes, to sick consciousness, the mundus intelligibilis. It might almost be speculative truth, just as Kafka's Odradek might almost be an angel, and yet it is, in a positivity that excludes the medium of thought, only barbaric aberration alienated from itself, subjectivity mistaking itself for its object."[6]

Instead the necessary location of Peak Oil as the pivotal problematic of geopolitics and geopolitical aesthetics, as well its attendant ecological collapses and post-petroleum revitalization, must go beyond the dynamics of war as a machine and of each mechanical

---

[6] Theodor Adorno, "Theses Against Occultism" (1946-47), included in *Stars Down to Earth and Other Essays on the Irrational in Culture* (London: Routledge, 1994).

machines as a little war that eats oil. Instead what remains is a open assignment of designing the governance of energy as the governance of a community of forces that inhabit each other through it, a geography which after Deleuze and Guattari's "Geophilosophy" chapter, "wrests history from the cult of necessity in order to stress the irreducibiliy of contingency, it wrests it from the cult of origins in order to affirm the power of a 'milieu'" and which provides what we most lack, which is not communication, but resistance to the present."[7] But can we conceive of this geography which is always a kind of geo-governance (a nomos), even as it is immanent and resistant to transcendental figuration, and which is sober and fearless in its willful self-composition in the shadow of the actual peak and extinguishment of the petroleum lifeblood of industrial objects, and which does not, however, derive its sovereignty from a framing of ecology as an ambient and permanent emergency, or from a morality of absolute conservation. On the later, Brian Massumi, characterizes the profile of such a deranged biopower, "the overall environment of life now appears as a complex, systemic threat environment, composed of subsystems that are not only complex in their own right but are complexly interconnected. They are all susceptible to self-amplifying irruptive disruption. Given the interconnections, a disruption in one subsystem may propagate into others, and even cascade across them all, reaching higher and wider levels of amplification, up to and including the planetary scale."[8] The geophilosophy of "irreducible

---

[7] Gilles Deleuze and Felix Guattari, *What is Philosophy?*, trans. Hugh Tomlinson and Graham Burchell (New York: Columbia University Press, 1995), 85-116.

[8] Brian Massumi, "National Enterprise Emergency: Steps Toward an Ecology of Powers," *Theory, Culture & Society* 26 (2009): 153-185.

contingency" cannot be defined by this cybernetics of risk.

That contingency may come, however, into some partial focus through provisional accidents of digital economics. In applied computational equivalence, the digitalization of anthropomorphic matter can effect an extinguishment of its extrinsic exchange value, and a generalized transference not from private to public domain but into uncoded reservoirs of intellect resistant to capture. For some writers, that leverage is positioned romantically as an opposite of primitive accumulation (instead of the absorption of the common into capital, capitalization is exploded into unexchangeability), but I think the hole in the ground is deeper than that. Integral to this aspect of digital capitalism is the transposition of cognitive labor into digital forms and the extinguishment both of the effective exchange value of digital assets and of the archival accumulation of these which have no investment utility beyond their immediate execution: the circulation of substance-as-information, not the compression algorithm of money but the Omega bit-string of binary equivalence.[9] However, this liquefaction of one Modernity of money may just as well necessitate the appearance of other sovereign currencies for which now uncompensated cognitive labor is forcefully remunerated.

We might counterpose that liquidity with the strong equivalence of another computational materiality, one which, after Turing, Wheeler, Wolfram et al., provides a parallel strong program of algorithmic contingency as the form of energy and the information

---

[9] See for example, Matteo Pasquenelli, "Google's PageRank Algorithm: A Diagram of the Cognitive Capitalism and the Rentier of the Common Intellect," in *Deep Search*, eds. Konrad Becker and Felix Stalder (Innsbruck: Studien Verlag, 2009).

and world-making. How so? Seth Lloyd hypothesizes the total information space of the universe as "no more than 10^{120} ops on 10^{90} bits."[10] In the conjunction of bits and atoms for a potentially acephalic form of strong governance within and for a post-oil ecology, and for the constitution that would reflect both animal-into-mineral and mineral-into-animal, the "smart grid" is but the calculability of a system of material symbols, now both monetary and algorithmic at once: electrons. Its scope is global, but the interfaciality of the machine, the visible diagram of its work, is always only partial; just as the recombinancy of any single subject effect is only, in the arc of decay-that-is-production, discrete to itself only in passing.

The "Geophilosophy" chapter concludes that "the creation of concepts in itself calls for a future form, for a new earth, and people that do not yet exist." A new Earth and as its precondition, a new population for it. Of what part of that new people are we? What mereology for such a replacement? Theseus' Paradox refers to how an object, once it has undergone complete replacement of all its components, piece by piece, while no longer the same material, is still somehow the same thing, the self-identical haecceity. Does the same principle operate at the level of what Kim Stanley Robinson calls "comparative planetology," and an Earth for which the eventual, immanent plane of recombinant flux is thorough?[11] Even assuming the closed loop of biogenic energy, the poetry of oil is one that allows the Precambrian live with us and as us, and which makes the plasticity of the future, the post-

---

[10] Seth Lloyd, *Programming the Universe: A Quantum Computer Scientist Takes On the Cosmos* (Knopf, 2006).
[11] See "Comparative Planetology: An Interview with Kim Stanley Robinson," in *BLDGBLOG*, posted December 19, 2007 at http://bldgblog.blogspot.com/2007/12/comparative-planetology-interview-with.html.

Anthropocene, already virtually present in any re-sorting of the extended 'now' (instead of deferred to the alibi of tomorrow's revelation, a community that will not "come" because it is already here and yet does not yet exist). In this, the cosmopolitanism of computational equivalence finds its analog analogue in the auto-cannibalization of oil and the sloppy translations of decay into the substance of production, a Sadean school of information theory. The refrain once again in recapitulation, "revolution is absolute deterritorialization even to the point where this calls for a new earth, a new people." For "our" post-plastic future, and for the Earth that will re-place our own, bit by bit, ultimately in total, this means absolute recomputability. Our geopolitics is not yet 'Turing complete', and until it is, no viable post-Anthropocene, only posturing, only oblivion and folklore. Root the Earth.

Dustism

Alisa Andrasek

In order to resonate complexity, Biothing needed to open a mutable ground that can absorb and synthesize various agencies acting within complexity of transient ecologies. Its evolution was paralleled with de-evolution of its building blocks. In order to increase the resolution of the fabric of architecture, its resilience and ability to migrate through multiple fabrics of matter, modes of construction and organizational patterns, it was necessary to descend to finer grains of generative building blocks, where the design search is performed within constellations of billions of particles. Data architecture. Voxelized storm encapsulating N dimensions. Dustism.

Xero-data or dust, swarms planetary bodies as the primal flux of data or the mother of all Data-streams in the Solar system. Each particle of dust carries with it a unique vision of matter, movement, collectivity, interaction, affect, differentiation, composition and infinite darkness – a crystallized data-base or a plot ready to combine and react, to be narrated on and through something. There is no line of narration more concrete than a stream of dust particles. (*Cyclonopedia*, 88)

Given that each dust particle envelopes and carries different materials and entities from diverse territo-

ries, dust particles express particulars of different fields and territories in terms of universals. (88)

If the morphology of weapons has to undergo a revolution in the War on Terror, that revolution can only take place through morphing into dust and spores, providing weapons with a cutting edge compatibility with the socio-political sphere, belief-dynamics, people and geography of war. (95)

Dust is the master of collective insurgencies . . . (89)

Dust simultaneously emerges as the alpha and omega xero-data; there is no signal or message other than the compositional insurgency of dust, whose syncretism and obscure polytics of creation can be effectively registered or rooted on a flux of dust . . . (89)

DUSTISM

//NEGARESTURING PAVILION / 2011_
biothing
Alisa Andrasek + Jose Sanchez_ principal designers
in collaboration with Dshape
Initial study with students was conducted during the Workshop at DRL AA
Consulting: Lawrence Friesen and Enrico Dini
dedicated to Reza Negarestani and Alan Turing

Alan Turing's "The chemical basis of Morphogenesis" was published in 1952, describing a speculative chemical reaction that could generate symmetry breaking, deriving dynamic blueprint of stable patterns out of an initially uniform mixture of chemical compounds. In the consequent reaction-diffusion system based on short-ranged activation and long-ranged inhibition, it was possible to maintain symmetry breaking instability as the driving force of development of the organism, only in the conditions far from equilibrium. According to Turing, in biological context this system economizes the amount of (genetic) information needed to produce the pattern and one can find a vivid example in patterns of animal skins. What is captured is the behavioral flow of matter, rather than the fixed states of the pattern. Biothing's collaboration with Dshape manufacturer is working on addressing the problem of rewriting protocols within modes of production explicitly. In Negaresturing pavilion study, distribution of matter was programmed for the large scale deposition machine (the largest 3d printer on Earth), in order to generate continuous flow of matter which can preserve structural consistency. Since the Turing pattern recomputes through the local neighborhoods, it is able to satisfy this requirement. Additionally, the behavioral patterning of the deposition has a capacity to produce heterogeneous spatiotemporal fabric.

The design research space is thus capable of opening new topologies of tension and spaces of synthesis. Such underlying structure has the ability of opening emergent regional chasms or ruptures (new spaces discontinuous to the backdrop continuity). This regional openness of a system allows for adaptation and feedback with external agencies, such as constraints of the structure through minimal section of the elements, resolution of the nozzles of the machine and properties of magnesium dye as a bounding agent that dissolves within marble dust with certain coefficient that the synthesis machine has to replicate. Therefore ruptures in the fabric are asymptotic to the continuity of matter and data . . . Synthesis of algorithmic system, constraints of the machine (Dshape's massive scale deposition robot), material properties of marble dust, fibers and magnesium adhesive, design intent in terms of quality and organizational performance of such architectonic fabric, could be understood in a context of cobordisms (topological, categorical, processual, programmatic equivalences) between the continuous and discontinuous. The fabric of architecture acquires malleability and resilience through its eccentric transitional qualities. The semiology of architecture becomes ambiguous, boundaries turn fuzzy and tertiary forms or functions are produced.

This project is a collaboration with Dshape in order to explore limits of a tectonic, structural and organizational language of architectural fabrics generated out of the space of possibilities of this particular production process. The "brain" of the machine is derived from the study of Turing patterns and their ability to produce heterogeneous flow of matter far from equilibrium, and the theoretical ground resonating in the roots of the structure is laid upon Reza Negarestani's reading of behavioral tendencies in Biothing's work and numerous passages found in *Cyclonopedia*.

( )HOLEY COMPLEX

In ( )hole complex, on a superficial level (bound to surface dynamics), every activity of the solid appears as a tactic to conceal the void and appropriate it, as a program for inhibiting the void, accommodating the void by sucking it in to the economy of surfaces or filling it. (48)

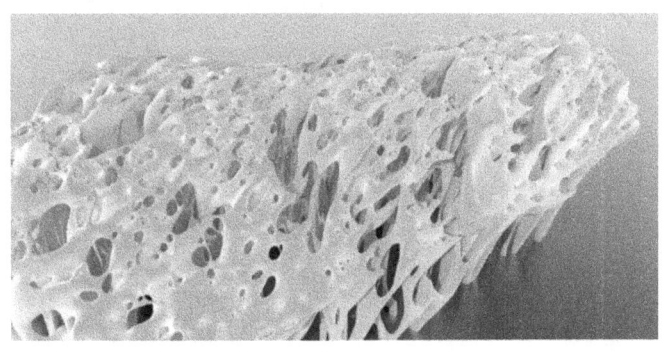

The *d_shape* building process is similar to the "printing" process because the system operates by straining a binder on a sand layer. This is similar to what an ink jet printer does on a sheet of paper. This principle allows the architect to design fantastically complex architectural structures. The process takes place in a non-stop work session, starting from the foundation level and ending on the top of the roof, including stairs, external and internal partition walls, concave and convex surfaces, bas-reliefs, columns, statues, wiring, cabling and piping cavities. During the printing of each section a *structural ink* is deposited by the printer's nozzles on the sand. The solidification process takes 24 hours to complete. The printing starts from the bottom of the construction and rises up in sections of 5-10 mm. Upon contact the solidification process starts and a new layer is added.

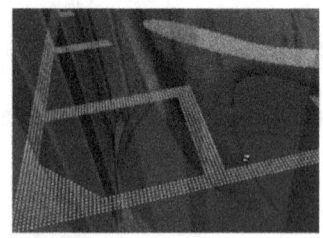

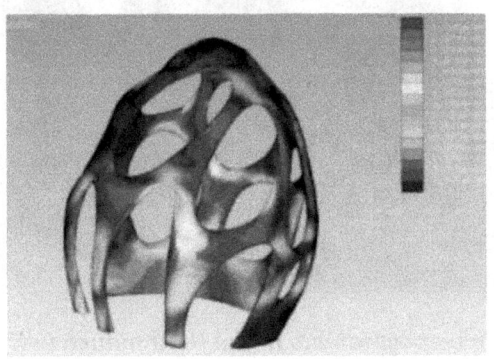

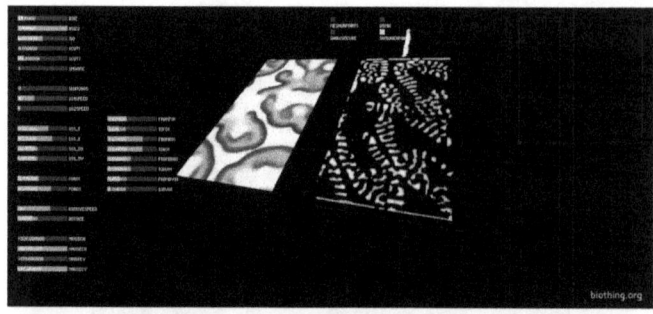

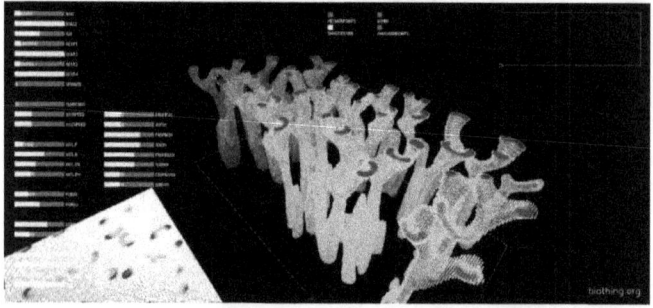

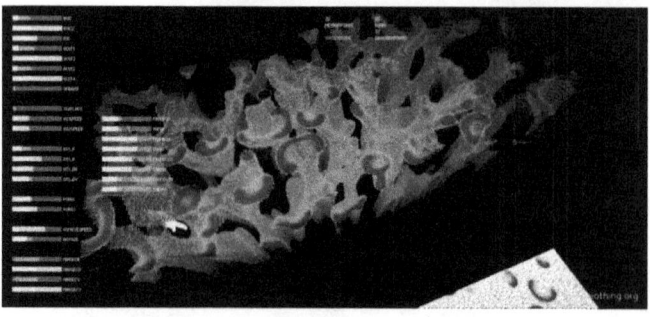

Local velocity gradients in the fluid induce new convolutions, shear stresses, ruptures and deformations of the solid matrix, tuning the surface dynamics to the entire machinery of the complex and the flow of the fluid, that is to say enhancing the flow and building

up the flood. In nemat-space, the diffusing pore fluid thereby smuggles its affect space through the solid matrix as well as its own particles. (49)

For every inconsistency on the surface, there is a subterranean consistency. (53)

The course of emergence in any medium corresponds to the formation of that medium . . . (53)

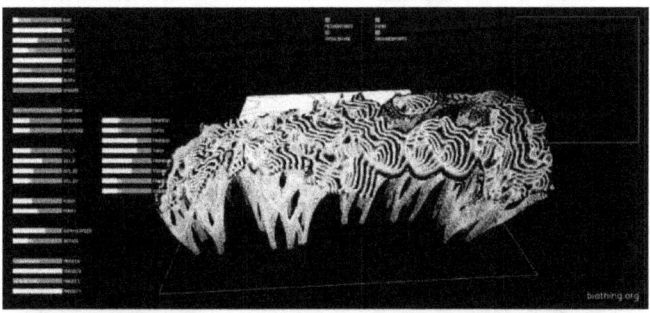

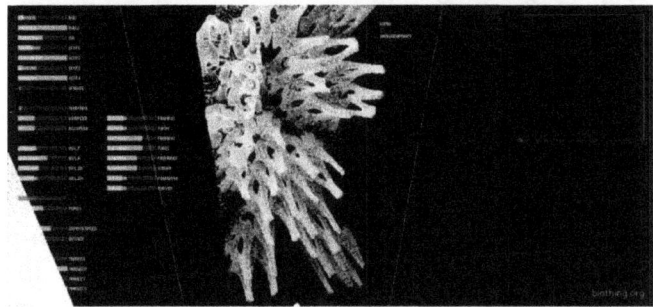

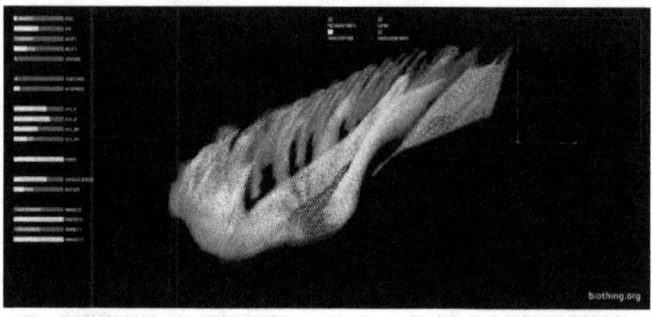

CONTINGENCY

Nemat-space *is an ultimate crawling machine; it is essentially cryptogenic and interconnected with Anonymous-until-Now. . . Anonymous-until-Now is the model of Time in ( )hole complex, whose probes and lines of itineracy move unpredictably according to both the subsoil and superficial ungrounding machineries that weaken the solidus by perversely exploiting and manipulating it (exhuming solidus).* **Incognitum Hactenus** *— not known yet or nameless and without origin until now — is a mode of time in which the innermost monstrosities of the earth or ungraspable time scales can emerge according to the chronological time that belongs to the surface biosphere of the earth and its populations . . . Incognitum Hactenus is a double-dealing mode of time connecting abyssal time scales to our chronological time, thus exposing to us the horror of times beyond.*

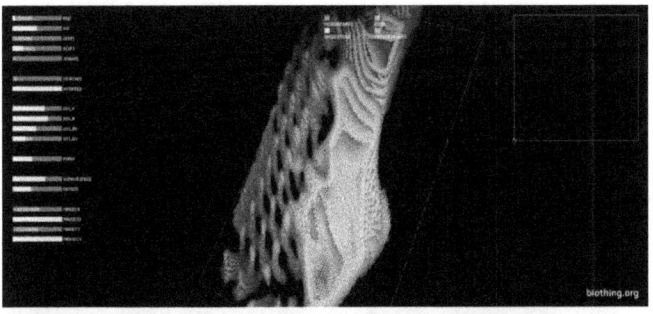

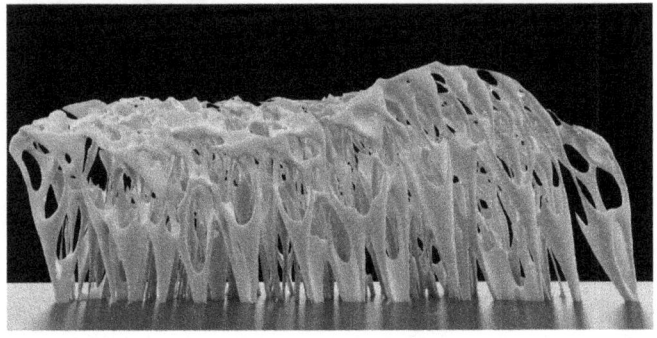

A self-degenerating entity, a volunteer for its own damnation, dust opens new modes of dispersion and of becomingcontagious,inventing escape routes as yet unrecorded. In his interview, Parsani suggests that **the Middle East has simulated the mechanisms of dusting to mesh together an economy which operates through positive degenerating processes, an economy whose carriers must be extremely nomadic, yet must also bear an ambivalent tendency towards the established system or the ground.** *An economy whose vehicle and systems never cease to degenerate themselves. For in this way, they ensure their permanent molecular dynamism, their contagious distribution and diffusion over their entire economy.* (91)

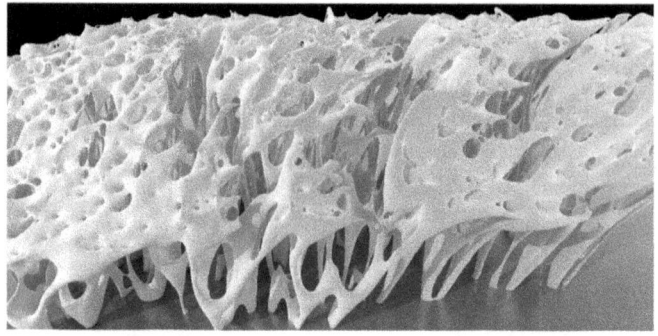

At the bottom of both *Cyclonopedia* and Biothing, one can trace underlying logical structure, that of Peirce triads. Triadic logic, as opposed to binary logic (applying T [true] and F [false] values), introduces third ambiguous element, one that allows for open synthesis.

::::::**Cyclonopedia** *can also be read as a monograph on triadic (versus unitary or binary) logic. It owes this to the influence of Peirce's mathematics . . . Triadic logic is mainly concerned with the expression of universals or global properties of the universe within the confines of regional spaces or localities. Consequently, it deals with concepts of unrestricted synthesis, contamination, openness, complicity (for example between binary elements on behalf of a vague third element), vagueness (such as in the vague logic of holes as opposed to surfaces and voids), overlaps and close neighborhoods* (for example the overlap of the insurgent and the civilian in the doctrine of taqiyya which the book addresses), etc. To this extent, some of Cyclonopedia's elements are explicitly about this three-ness: one example would be the key concept of trison or double-betrayal as the essential engine of cyclonic thought and openness. . . . each Trison-cell is able to triangularly host countless Trisons in itself, either as allies or cells potentially *causing irreversible internal fissions. Trisons within trisons within trisons - also known as children - form thousands, millions of feedback spirals within the mother-spiral. The crypto fractal complexity of these feedback spirals can develop anomalies capable of undermining and derailing the centrality of the mother spiral and eventually themselves. (36)*

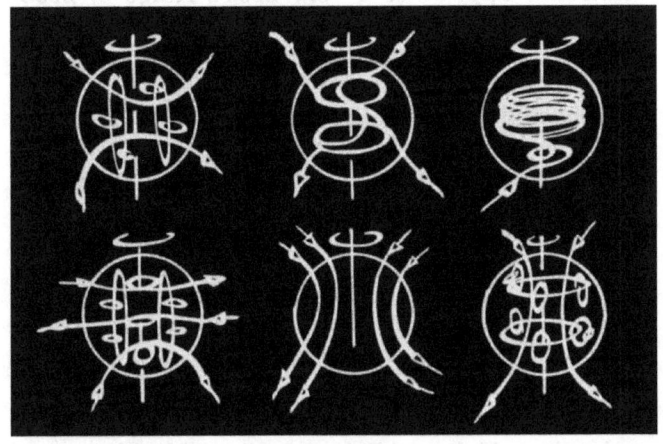

The coils are usually characterized by developmental intensification of a low-pressure center, a cosmodromic cyclone or singularity. Such spirals were frequently associated with the dynamism of distribution of Trisons or polytical units of the Middle East . . . (163)

SYNTHETIC PROTO/E/CO/LOGICS
*:::::triadic design _ a regionally trans-ecological model of design (the appropriate model of design for synthetic places like
Latin America, the Middle East, Eastern Europe and Maghrib)
cyclonopedia: syntheses of theory and fiction, polytics instead of politics++
biothing: ruptured plasticity, ambiguous mobility++*

*Peirce's modal, multipolar and topological system investigates then **the study of transferences of information around regions and borders on such a continuum**. . . . Many fundamental Peircean techniques, such as modalizing, correlating, connecting, gluing, differentiating and integrating, are in fact **geometrical techniques applied to a very broad range of problems**, and are mainly motivated by a crucial **critical study of relativity, plasticity and contamination**. It may then be fair to say that Peirce's introduces a sort of "Einsteinian turn" in general knowledge (of course, before the very Einstein), opening the way to the study of relative movements and invariances (categories, universal relatives, synechism, etc.), focusing attention on TRANS problems and techniques, and producing in this way a profound revision of Kant's more publicized "Copernican turn" in philosophy.*
Fernando Zalamea, Peirce and Latin American "razonabilidad": forerunners of Transmodernity

Peirce experiments with three symbols representing truth values: V, L, and F. He associates V with "1" and "T", indicating truth. He associates F with "0" and "F", indicating falsehood. He associates L with "1/2" and "N", indicating perhaps an intermediate or unknown value.

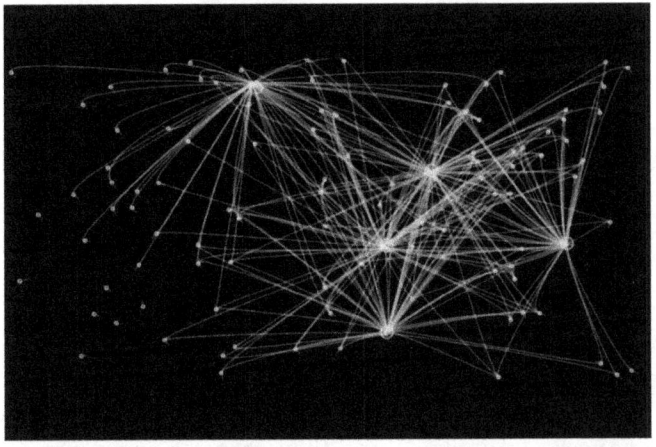

First we should point out that biothing as an 'open' approach annot be encoded or in any way prepared in advance. Even the computational core of the project, i.e. the so-called Genware, can claim temporal but not ontological priority over the project's branches and creatures. For everything that grows out of this 'library of seeds' will return to change something of its initial structure. Biothing's creatures do not live on the outside but within their emergent cosmos. Once materialized their relationship with their surrounding world is not that of a fixed boundary that enclose and divide space but instead of a porous surface, or else, a boundary that serves as a connecting interface. It is a dynamic world of formative and transformative processes and movements that constantly generate new formations, swellings, growths and protuberances. (Lambros Malafouris, Vital Materiality - Biothing, HYX2009)

TRANS/ECO/LOGICAL

:::One of the aspects of Biothing's work are erratic undulations between differential mobilities and frozenness that is usually associated with transecological spaces. Such ambiguous ecologies usually appear between different gradients of the universal continuum where regions shift and different gradations of spatiotemporal continuities begin to overlap: the inorganic overlaps the organic, the organic chemistry overlaps cultural domains, socio-cultural domains come into an inter-phase with neuropsychological regions of the brain and so on. Basically all transecological phenomena (epidemics, evolutionary changes, traumas [since they transfer inorganic to socio-cultural and psychic horizons] and weird syntheses) happen through such cobordant ruptures where the signs become ambiguous, boundaries turn fuzzy and tertiary forms or functions are produced. Usually in such mediating spaces, quality and form are extensively articulated from an intensive quantitative function (example recursive generation, complex concatenations of a basic function or a global element . . .

AGENCY/CONTINGENCY

Coming now to the second consequence, this relates to the non-anthropocentric dimension and direction that biothing incorporates and points at. It is not simply the design process, but also the causal role of the designer that has changed. The designer's position in the chain of causality and its ontological status as the source of creativity is no longer fixed but is subject to constant renegotiation. This should not be understood in the postmodern sense of the 'death of the author' but rather in the 'premodern' sense of a dynamic flow, coupling and intermin-gling of events, causes, and materials. Everything leaks, flows and connects. In the words of Gregory Bateson, the mental characteristics of the system are immanent not in some part but in the system as a whole (1973). The composer is neither the leader nor the creator she is simply a part of the symphony; a part nonetheless with a catalytic role in the overall process. I often use the phrase from A. Pickering **'dance of agency'** (1995; Malafouris 2008b) to characterize this sort of dynamic partnerships that characterize most creative processes of material engagement. (Lambros Malafouris, Vital Materiality - Biothing, HYX 2009)

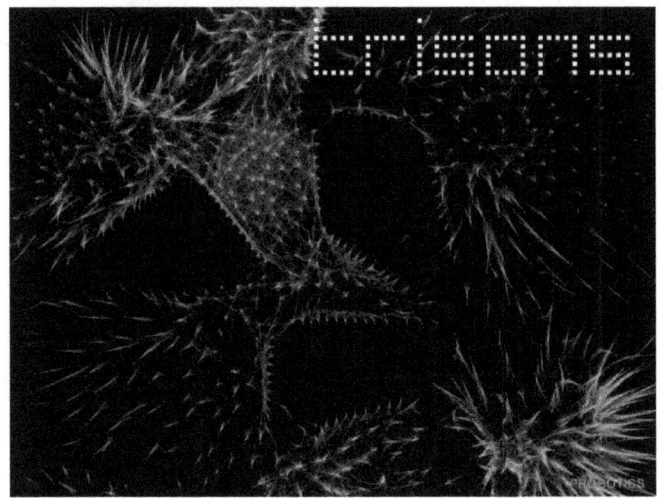

//Agentware

Selected examples of Agentware academic research are part of permanent collection of Centre Pompidou, Frac Collection Orleans and various publication and exhibitions worldwide.

Within general convergence of matter and information, high volumes of data are streaming into constructed ecologies, simultaneous to massive populations of generative agents infiltrating design processes. Fine-grain design singularities are emerging – increasingly malleable and resilient to acute pressures found in complex environments, able to absorb, adapt and learn. Extended design ecology binds mathematized features of natural landscape and weather patterns, planning sequences and instantiated architectural systems. Resultant synthetic design singularizations are amplifying contingent host features with higher "resolution" fabric of architecture. Agentware is an ongoing research into multi-agent generative systems for the applications in synthetic ecologies, initiated in 2006 at Columbia University and Pratt Institute, and continuing at DRL AA, UTS Sydney and annual AA global unit in Croatia.

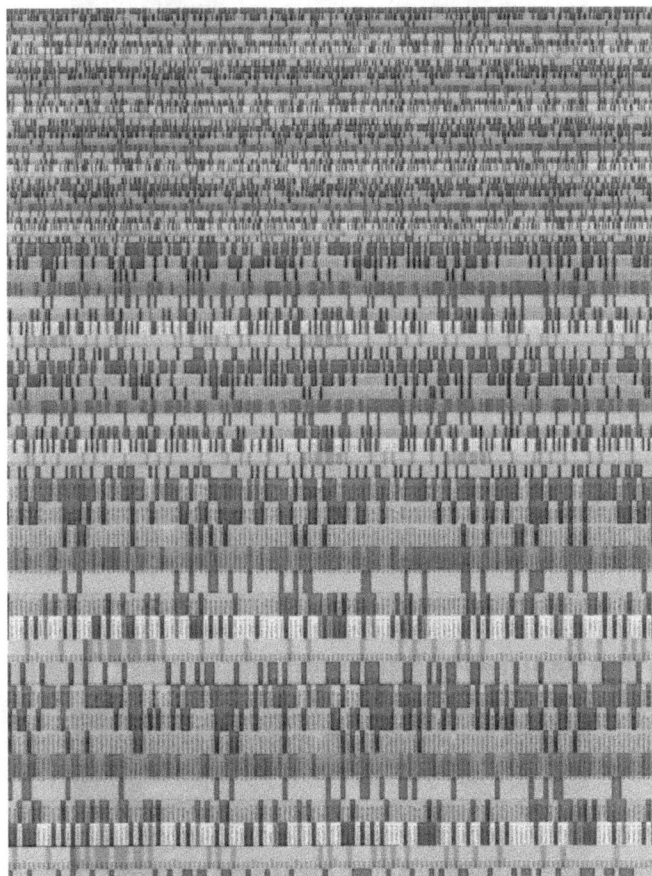

DATA//VOXEL//
AGENTS >> N DIMENSIONS

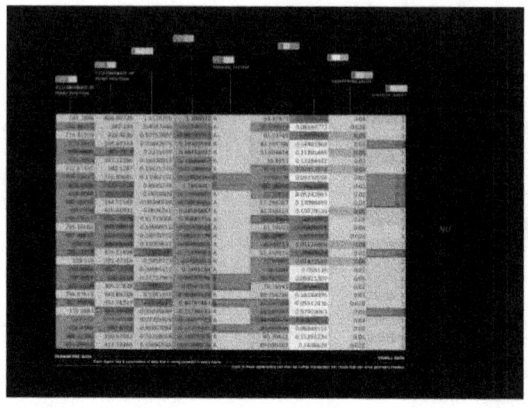

Peirce's Three-valued Connectives

Charles Peirce was the first logician to define logical operators for a many-valued system of logic.[1] In February 1909, on three pages of a notebook in which he recorded his thoughts on logic (MS 339), he defined several three-valued connectives using the truth-table, or matrix, method.[2] The system of triadic logic that Peirce envisioned employs the values "V", "F", and "L". He interpreted "V" and "F" as "verum" ("true") and "falsum" ("false"), respectively, and he interpreted the third value, "L", as "the limit."

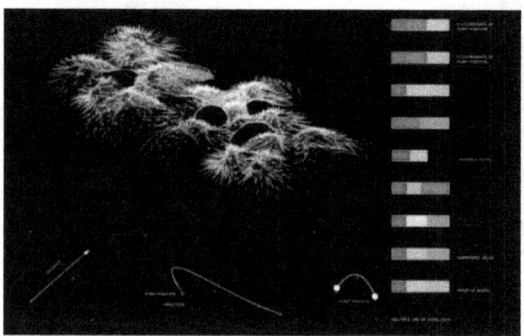

| |fissurePort _ Port Terminal _ Kaohsiung Taiwan
biothing
Alisa Andrasek + Jose Sanchez_ principal designers
design team: Knut Brunier – Gabriel Morales – Denis Lacej
Competition Entry 2010 – Phase 1 – 40,000 sq meters

Cliff formations found along many coastlines (including Kaohsiung outer coastline) are replicated through strong vertical fissures of the building. Mathematics of Fractals are frequently used to calculate coastline behavior, given variable degree of "roughness" and multiple orders of scale in natural coastlines. | |Fissures Port Terminal proposal reflects the idea of such complex articulation within the tectonics of the building. Fabric of architecture is highly heterogeneous, structured through rapid changes in textures and experiences, unfolding multiplicity of parallel environments within a single building. Instead of creating seamless topological continuum typical for the passenger terminal typology, traveler is exposed to a series of cuts, different experiences carried through the strong vertical fissures. In order to accommodate large volume of requested program needed to be organized within a site, internal fissures: a blade-like tectonic elements shredding through the length of the site, are introducing internal landscape elements with various organizational and sustainable properties. These tall narrow "canyons" are simultaneously light wells for the building as well as efficient shading elements, providing abundance of light throughout the building yet preventing overheating. Waterside arrival sequence is accentuated by the strong "fissure" facade with deeper folds as receptacles for jetways for arriving and departing passengers. Tidal fluctuations and arrival of larger boats creates water movements and wave crushing against the seaside facade of the building. Passengers are transferred into the building through the first fissure which is a cooling water garden for the terminal. The proportions of extremely long and tall space with "canyon-like" glazed surfacing produces polydimensional experience _ a crystalline fabric. High Resolution Infrastructure: Intricate tectonic elements allow for distributed and redundant signaling through lighting systems that can coordinate faster and more legible distribution of passengers. Population of lighting particles embedded into the floors and ceilings could be programmed to respond to increased crowd migration through the terminals. They constitute material qualities of environments _ a slowed down lighting storm embodied into the fabric of architecture.

:::::*'inorganic synthesis feigning organic vitality'* _ (Reza Negarestani on Biothing)

:::::::::*the emergence of the organism should not be taken as a singularized event marking the temporary triumph of the organic life and the repression of the originary inorganic trace; on the contrary, it is nothing but the inorganic finding a new spatiotemporal equivalence for itself to open new topologies of tension and spaces of synthesis. And this does not indicate sort of an inorganic intelligence or panpsychism but a universal exercise in openness: on the one hand, replacing what appears to be necessity by expressions of universal contingency and on the other hand, opening new regional chasms or ruptures (new spaces discontinuous to the backdrop continuity) . . .* (Sandor Ferenczi via Reza Negarestani*)*

:::::::*There is only one universal drive which is neither thought nor intelligence, nor matter, it is the open (the veritable expression of an unbound universal continuum and its unrestricted synthesis). The open expropriates all temporal necessities (inorganic, organic, and so on) on behalf of universal contingency, it main-*

*tains openness not only on a universal level (by constantly renegotiating the frontiers) but also on a **regional level** (by creating ruptures in the universal continuum so as to open new topologies of tension and **spaces of synthesis**).*

*:::: Biothing vividly exhibits the latter connotation of openness i.e. **regional openness** where ruptures come into being and the fluxional continuity or plasticity must be thought through fissures, perforations and nested cuts. These ruptures are asymptotic to the continuity (of data, matter, etc.) from which they have been cut or 'excised'. They can neither be considered in terms of individuated variations nor forms, since their primary function is to establish all kinds of cobordisms (topological, categorical, processual equivalences) between the continuous and discontinuous spaces of the continuum or the universe. I think it's exactly because of this eccentric transitional quality of such ruptures that they consistently appear as mixed, brooding somewhere between fixity and becoming, dead and living, liquefaction and cohesion.*

kaohsiung port terminal / biothing 2010

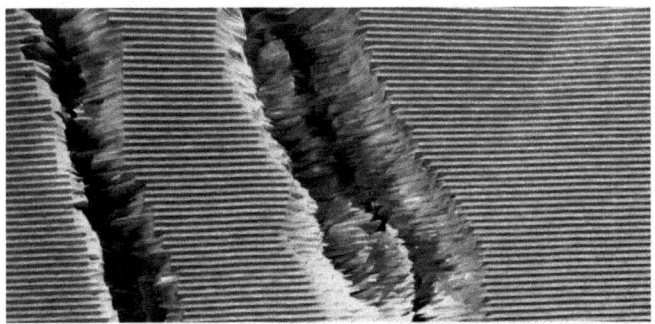

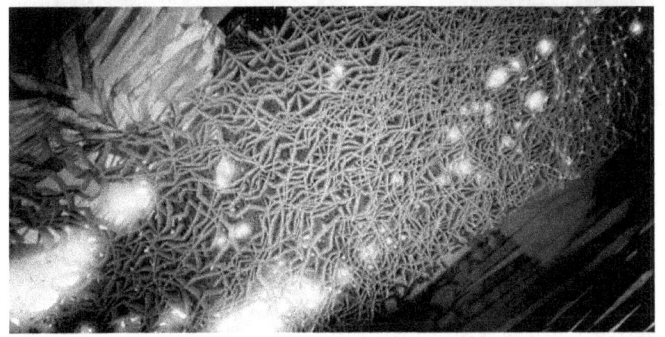

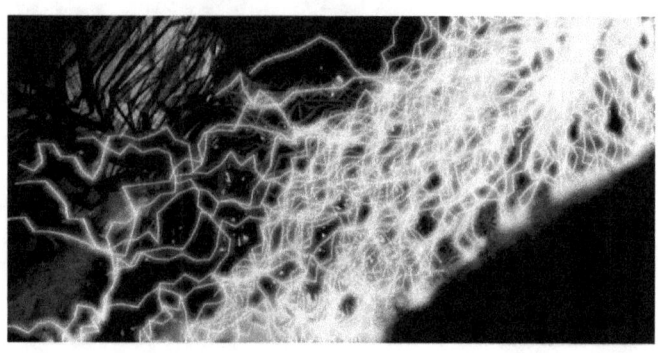

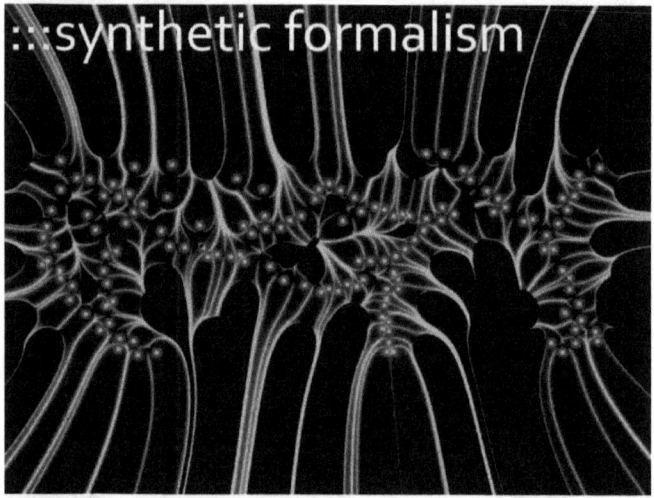

//////**Mesonic Fabrics/2007/09//**
biothing with Ezio Blasetti
Alisa Andrasek Ezio Blasetti
FlowerPower custom written plug-in: Kyle Steinfeld with Alisa Andrasek
Meson, n.

1. _any of a family of subatomic particles that participate in strong interactions
2. _in-between
3. _medium

In MF, BIOTHING explored in-between algorithmic states by trans-coding 3 different algorithms. Electro-Magnetic Field developed through Biothing's custom written plug-in for Rhino was initially distributed in order to develop structural trajectories for the roof condition. Resonating pattern was imprinted into the ground creating emitters for the second algorithmic logic _ radial wave interference pattern that formed global geography of the field. Finally, class 4 Cellular Automata was used to re-process wave data by imprinting micro-articulation of the ground. Zooming in and out of this field revels drifts in the character of the pattern. This effect is accelerated in the behavior of the CA pattern which drifts between distinct characters of rigid geometrical states and more organic states.

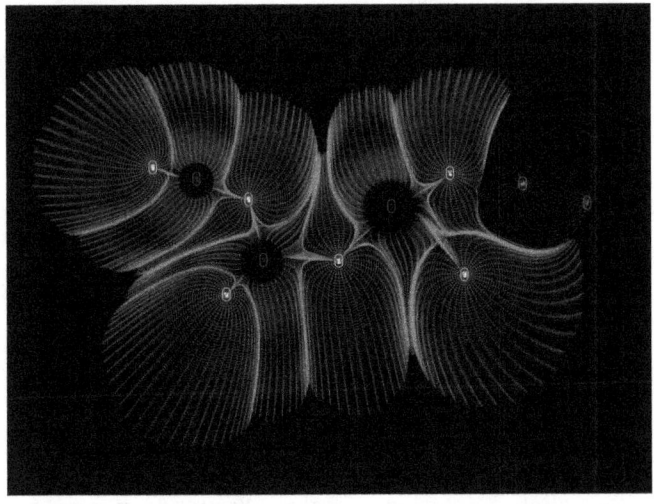

/////Seroussi Pavillion /paris//2007
Alisa Andrasek _ principal designer
FlowerPower custom written plug-in: Kyle Steinfeld with Alisa Andrasek
Design team: Ezio Blasetti / Che Wei Wang / Fabian Evers / Lakhena Raingsan / Jin Pyo Eun / Mark Bearak
Special thanks to Michael Reed (computational geometry)

Architectonic fabric for the Seroussi Pavilion was "grown" out of self-modifying patterns based on vectors of electromagnetic fields (EMF). Through logics of attraction/repulsion trajectories were computed in plan and "lifted" via series of structural micro-arching sections through different frequencies of wave function. Additional information embedded into the code allows for local adaptation to the site in regards to the section. Pavilion is implanted into a steep hill and EMF trajectories needed to "find the ground". Six different geometrical systems were instantiated for various design intents in a project, all steaming out from primary trajectories. The plan of the pavilion differs greatly from a classical notion of architectural drawing. It reads as a dynamic blueprint closer to musical notation. This abstraction based proto-ecology is seeding possible materialization procedures and adaptation to the site conditions. In a roof design, tilling resolution was increased by the algorithmic differentiation of components features. Distribution of view, lighting and shading is programmed through parametric patterns structured through sine-wave functions driving parametric differentiation of angle, orientation and size of the apertures as well as the relationship of metal and glass components within each cell. Double charged EMF trajectories are producing internal cocoon like spatial fabric, a system of veils that unfurls through the space building up continuous yet highly differentiated interlaced field. Wrapped in and in-between cocoon's swirling fibers are the opportunities for different degrees of cohabitation of humans and art collection _ living with art. Programming and reprogramming different exhibition sequences is understood as series of probabilistic events. One can rearrange the sequences of art pieces by finding spatial opportunities within this labyrinthine fabric.

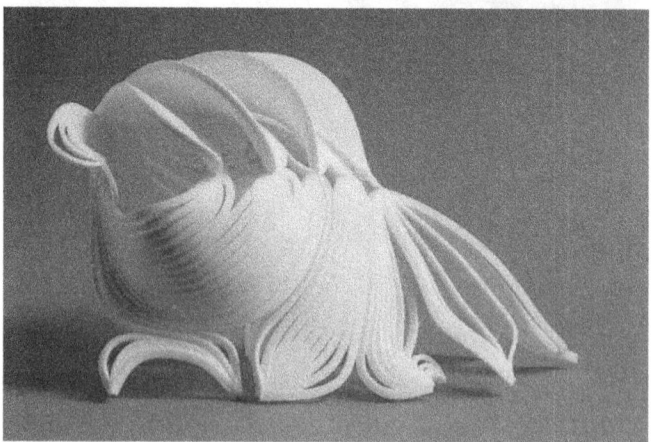

DUSTISM/TRANS-CODING

As an inter-dimensional carrier, dust scavenges xenochemical particles (outsiders)as its cores or con-

stituents, introduces and implants them into compositions, creations and establishments . . . (90)

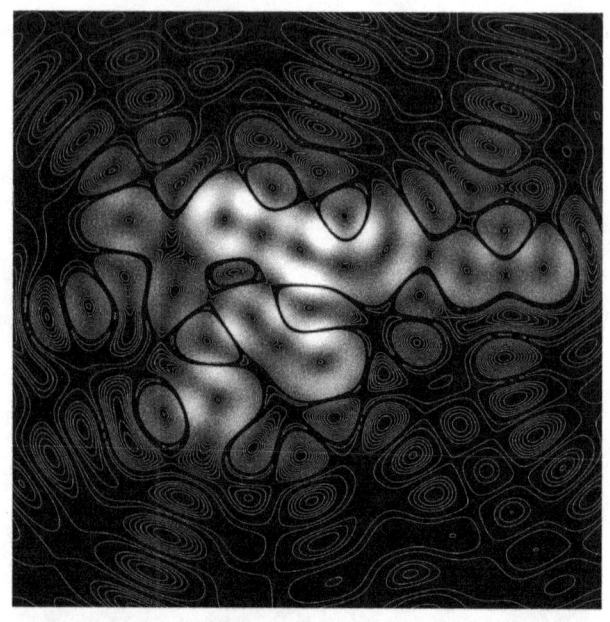
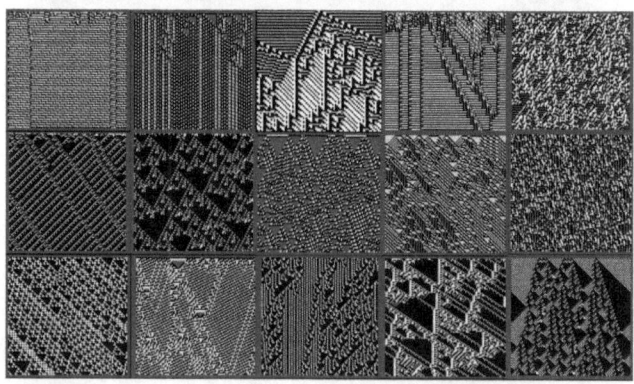

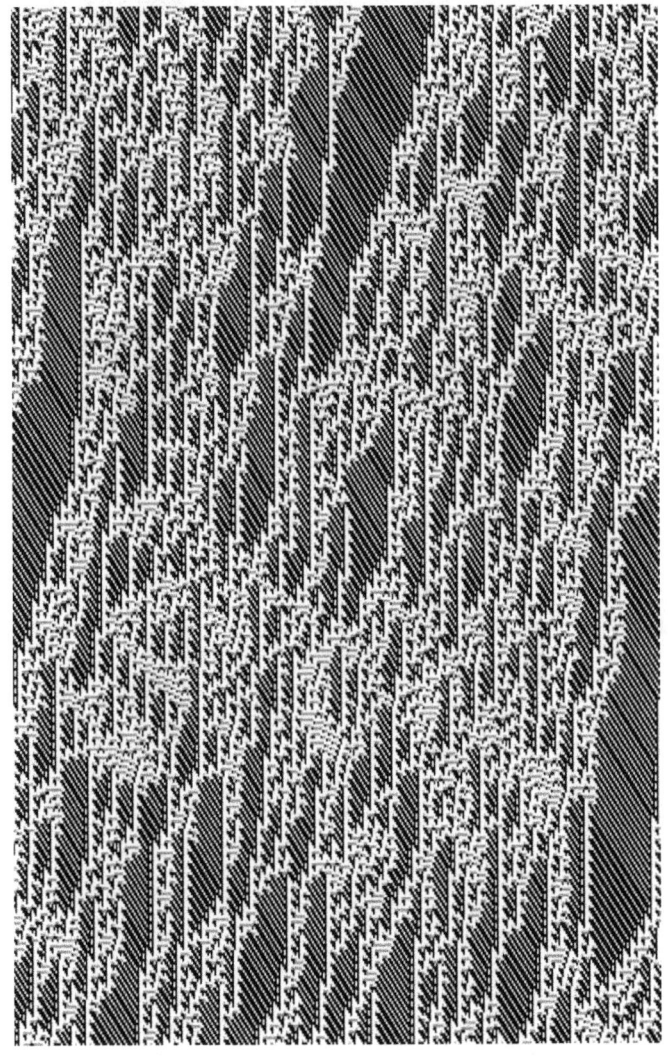

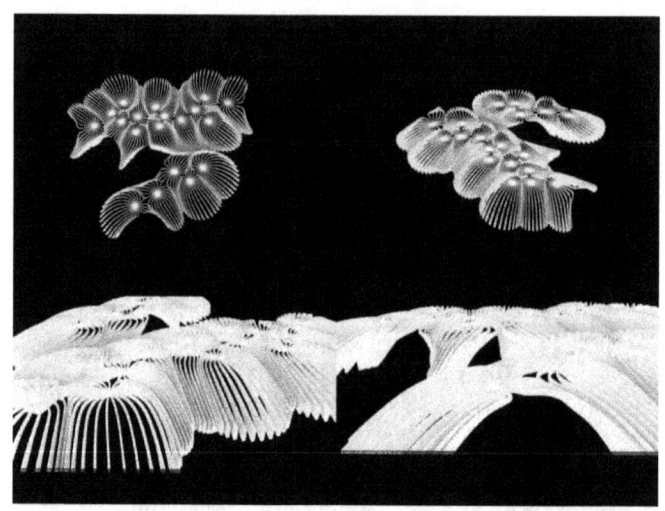

//Phosphorescence _ Pop Music Centre _ Kaohsiung Taiwan
biothing
Alisa Andrasek + Jose Sanchez_ principal designers
design team: Elizabeth Leidy – Alicia Nahmad – Denis Vlieghe – Rajat Sodhi
Competition Entry 2010 – Phase 1 – 80,000 sq meters + 20,000 sq meters
open air public space

Sonar phosphorescence: A new version of iconic resonating within the Current cultures. Guided by the iconic features of pop culture such as exuberant colors and light, Phosphorescence explores the possibilities of bringing such polychromatic shimmer qualities to the urban fabric. It resonates electrified lightscape found on Taiwanese streets and night markets. Massive amount of diverse program needed to be organized within an extensive urban location, requiring consisted organizational fabric that can negotiate heterogeneity of scales, sudden ruptures and multiplicity of flows and agencies. Two types of organizational systems are distributing other sub-systems within a project. In place of inflexible totalizing master plan, Biothing proposed resilient and adaptive fabric designed for inter-systems crossing at multiple scales. This allows for localized differentiation and unique moments while preserving the consistency of a project as a whole, since subsystems resonate through its internal dynamic blueprint. Magnets are synthetically weaving the larger programmatic sequences into a cohesive fabric. Corrosive action of Brownian motion tunnels through fibers of electromagnetic trajectories, carving the finer grain urban circuitry.

In many respects, the circulation is what matters, not the particular forms that it causes to emerge. The flow of energy and mineral nutrients through an ecosystem manifest themselves as actual plants and animals of a particular species. Our organic bodies in this sense are nothing more than temporary coagulations in these flows: we capture in our bodies at birth, then release it again when we die and micro-organisms transform us into a new batch of raw materials. The main form of matter-energy in the biosphere is the circulation of flesh in food chains. (Manuel De Landa)

When glimpsed in all its pitiless materiality, there is nothing so inhuman as life itself. (Gilbert Simondon)

The vast majority of theoretical trajectories through animal space give rise to impossible monsters. (Richard Dawkins)

A surface-consuming plague is a pack of rats whose tails are the most dangerous seismic equipment; tails are spatial synthesizers (fiber-machines), exposing the terrain which they traverse to sudden and violent folding and unfolding, while seizing patches of ground and composing them as a nonhuman music. Tails are musical instruments, playing metal – tails, lasher tanks in motion. (52)

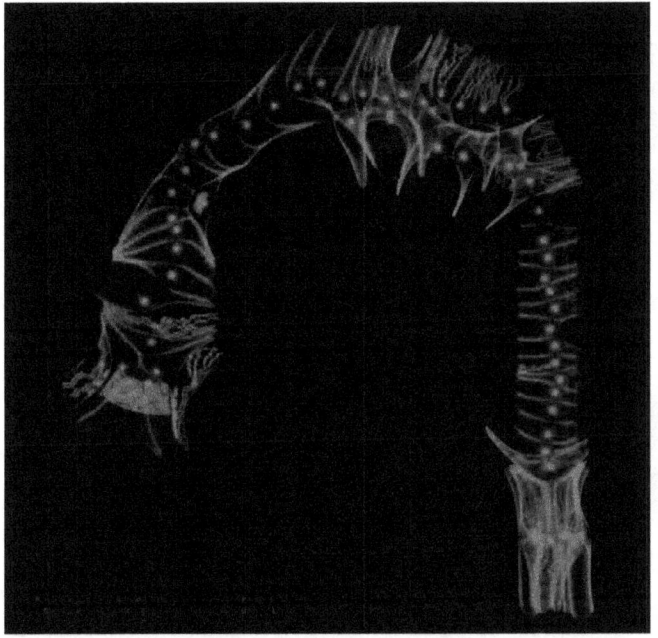

MAGNETS: based on mathematics of electro-magnetic fields, Magnetic fabrics are stitching the site into the city whilst bringing the city and its inhabitants to the water, as an adaptive masterplan. Additionally, through the extended network of underwater lights visually expanding the park/site into the water.

CANYONS: based on the math of Brownian motion, as a seemingly random movement of particles suspended in a fluid (i.e. a liquid such as water or air). They erode the pristine magnetic shells into different kind of spatial chasms that introduces specialized programs. This resilience allows for great diversity of tectonics locally, adapting to the character and demands of different programs.

AGENCY/CONTINGENCY

Coming now to the second consequence, this relates to the non-anthropocentric dimension and direction that biothing incorporates and points at. It is not simply the design process, but also the causal role of the designer that has changed. The designer's position in the chain of causality and its ontological status as the source of creativity is no longer fixed but is subject to constant renegotiation. This should not be understood in the postmodern sense of the 'death of the author' but rather in the 'premodern' sense of a dynamic flow, coupling and intermingling of events, causes, and materials. Everything leaks, flows and connects. In the words of Gregory Bateson, the mental characteristics of the system are immanent not in some part but in the system as a whole (1973).The composer is neither the leader nor the creator she is simply a part of the symphony; a part nonetheless with a catalytic role in the overall process. I often use the phrase from A. Pickering **'dance of agency'** (1995; Malafouris 2008b) to characterize this sort of dynamic partnerships that characterize most creative processes of material engagement. (Lambros Malafouris, Vital Materiality – Biothing, HYX 2009)

ABOVE THE FABRIC: Complexity found in natural ecologies unfolds into the fabric of architectural systems. Therefore the ground is a network of nested systems that can breed with one another. The project introduces a probabilistic program of human activities as well as tectonic behaviors on the surface they inhabit.

BELOW THE FABRIC: Planting a massive field of underwater lights will encourage the growth of particular species of algae to remediate local marine ecology and adopt it for aqua sports. The lighting scheme implants a new ecological layer into the site. Pop meets sustainability; culture fused into nature. Remediation processes are not hidden, but activated as elements of design. The site glows and shimmers resonating experiences found in pop culture. Aquatics and pop are fused into a hybrid entity.

Queerness, Openness

Zach Blas

The state of queer theory today is somewhere between death and life. Since Teresa de Lauretis coined the term at a conference at the University of California Santa Cruz in 1990, this body of theoretical work, it has been claimed, has quickly peaked—or reached an impasse—within the last 15-20 years. In fact, de Lauretis gave up on the term only after three years, claiming that "queer" had already been taken over by the various mainstream institutions and establishments it was created to resist against.

Yet, if queer theory always promises an openness to its future and constantly insists on its inability to be pinned down or limited, what has happened to queer theory, when so many proclaim its usefulness is over or pronounce its outright death. There are many thoughts, suggestions, and disagreements about this: while some suggest queer theory never made good on its promise of openness, others note that queer theory's very openness and amorphousness fatally diluted it. Perhaps the problem with the "peaking of queer theory,"[1] as David Ruffolo calls it, is that queer theory has not been open enough.

We began to hear these calls for a new direction, a new openness, in 2005, when an issue of *Social Text* titled "What's Queer About Queer Studies Now?" was released, edited by David Eng, Jack Halberstam, and

---

[1] David Ruffolo, *Post-Queer Politics* (Surrey: Ashgate, 2009): 1.

José Muñoz. Their introduction sets up a critique of queer, pushing for a "renewed queer studies" that attends to various intersectionalities, such as globalization and neoliberalism.[2] Yet, queer theory still finds itself stuck in an argumentative mire, now somewhere between identity politics and neo-materialisms. While a queer feminist theorist like Anamarie Jagose wants to keep queer theory in dialogue and relation to the feminist theories and political struggles it emerges out of,[3] others radically move away from these initial frameworks toward a primarily Deleuzian materialism. In 2007, Elizabeth Grosz delivered a keynote address to the Feminist Theory Workshop at Duke University on her dreams for a future feminism. In this talk, she outlined a feminism that could be, that ought to be, by faulting feminist theory for focusing too strictly upon identity politics and the subject as well as privileging the epistemological. Grosz proffered a feminism that delves into the Real, what she calls material chaos, by shifting feminist theory to account for that which is beyond the subject—the ontological, sexual difference, a primordial difference that exists before language or representation. For Grosz, this is a feminism that does not confirm or confine but expands outwards in "a process of opening oneself up to the otherness that is the world itself . . . that makes us become other than ourselves, that makes us unrecognizable."[4] Grosz's desire for a new feminism is echoed in various ventures that followed shortly after, into queer theory, materialism, and the nonhuman. In 2009, David Ruffolo published *Post-Queer Politics*, in which he argues

---

[2] See David Eng, Jack Halberstam, and José Muñoz, "Introduction," *Social Text* 23 (2005): 1.

[3] See Anamarie Jagose, "Feminism's Queer Theory," *Feminism & Psychology* 19 (2009): 157-74.

[4] Elizabeth Grosz, "The Future of Feminist Theory: Dreams for New Knowledges," 2007 (unpublished).

that while queer has reached its peak, a move away from subjectivity and the queer / heteronormativity dualism toward a focus on process, becoming, and matter à la Deleuze and Guattari can generate a new kind of queer theory that does not rely on the subject, heteronormativity, performativity, or even the human. Timothy Morton's recent work on queer ecology continues to bring queerness to bear on the nonhuman[5], but it is Michael O'Rourke that is forefronting a new direction in queer theory that directly intersects with various threads and off-shoots of speculative realism. In his introduction to Post-Queer Politics with Noreen Giffney, Ruffolo's post-queer politics is likened to Reza Negarestani's polytics, revealing a queerness that is in the process of being opened by the outside.

This all brings me to a question: why engage queer theory in a collection of writings on *Cyclonopedia*? Why bring a body of work that in so many ways is antithetical to Negarestani's writing? As O'Rourke has clearly pointed to and others hint at, I would like to suggest that there is a queerness in *Cyclonopedia*, a queerness that queer theory could learn and benefit from, as it continues to oscillate between old and new waves. Perhaps this is a queerness that is already radically opened beyond what has become the canon of queer theory, and so the word queer does not hold, cannot hold, does not surface, but is there just under the surface. Perhaps *Cyclonopedia* asks for queerness: within a queer or feminist context, when Negarestani writes that "the conflict between genders is an anthropomorphic folly,"[6] he picks up on a controversial fractioning of feminist theory from queer theory. In her 1984 essay "Thinking Sex: Notes for a

---

[5] See Timothy Morton, "Queer Ecology," *PMLA* 125 (2010): 273-82.

[6] Reza Negarestani, *Cyclonopedia: Complicity with Anonymous Materials* (Melbourne: re.press, 2008), 169.

Radical Theory of the Politics of Sexuality," Gayle Rubin suggested that feminism, while useful for thinking the category of women (or gender), is not so for sexuality; she writes, "It is not reducible to, or understandable in terms of class, race, ethnicity, or gender."[7] Historically, queer theory has addressed sexuality beyond gender, so if Negerastani, like Rubin, wishes to think sexuality—or love, in the case of *Cyclonopedia*—outside of gender, queer theory appears to be an unavoidable intersection.[8]

In this paper, I'd like to experiment and test out Negarestani's queerness: by teasing out, unearthing, the queerness in *Cyclonopedia*, making it more explicit. I'll do this by exhuming the hole complex and hidden writing, decay, and love. Importantly, I am not arguing to leave behind the older queer theoretical works that focus on identity and subjectivity; this is rather to put queerness to the test, to see if it can still exist when opened, stretched, widened, to the polytical. Notably, I am not bringing queerness to *Cyclonopedia*; queerness is already there, waiting to be exhumed, and like we are told in *Cyclonopedia*, exhumation defaces, messes up, changes. This queerness, when exhumed, will be different from *Cyclonopedia* and queer theory; it will be another kind of queerness that overlaps, or better, decays into both. We could say that *Cyclonopedia* gives us an abstract diagram for another queerness, just as O'Rourke & Giffney describe Ruffolo's post-queer politics offering a diagram for queerness through Deleuze, just as

---

[7] Gayle Rubin, "Thinking Sex: Notes for a Radical Theory of the Politics of Sexuality," in *The Lesbian and Gay Studies Reader*, eds. Henry Abelove, Michele Aina Barale, David M. Halperin (New York: Routledge, 1993), 22.

[8] There is a blurring or confusion between love and sex in *Cyclonopedia* that I'll briefly address later.

Dr. Hamid Parsani finds the Cross of Akht a diagram for intrepid blasphemy, petropolitical undercurrents.

EXHUMING QUEERNESS IN *CYCLONOPEDIA*

In Michael O'Rourke's forthcoming article on queer theory and speculative realism, he offers us a valuable passage from "What Does Queer Theory Teach Us About X?" by Lauren Berlant and Michael Warner; they write, "it is not useful to consider queer theory a thing, especially one defined by capital letters. We wonder whether queer commentary might not more accurately describe the things linked by the rubric, most of which are not theory. . . . Queer Theory is not the theory of anything in particular, and has no precise bibliographic shape."[9] What O'Rourke, Berlant, and Warner are highlighting here is queerness not as a theory or thing but queerness as a model for reading and writing, a kind of commentary, that can be applied to potentially anything. A shorthand for this familiar model is simply "queering."

In *Cyclonopedia*, we are also given models for reading and writing. The archeologist being studied, Parsani, claims that "archeology, with its ingrained understanding of Hidden Writing, will dominate the politics of the future and will be the military-science of the 21st century."[10] Archeology here can be understood as the exhumation of plot holes through the () hole complex.

The hole complex is a model for grasping the earth as a "destituted Whole" and a "holey-mess." The hole complex subverts the solidity of earth and ungrounds it. The hole complex is "the zone through which the Outside gradually but persistently emerges,

---

[9] Michael O'Rourke, "'Girls Welcome!!!' Speculative Realism, Object Oriented Ontology and Queer Theory," *Speculations* 2 (2011): 275-312.

[10] Negarestani, *Cyclonopedia*, 63.

creeps in (or out?) from the Inside."[11] The earth is turned into an insurgent mess. When the solidity of the earth is subverted, the holes that emerge are polytical. These holes, a confusion of solid and void, are inconsistencies, anomalies, material differentiation. In *Cyclonopedia*, they are connected via oil, narration lubes. Reading through the plot holes is to follow the narration lube. This act of reading moves from surface to the depths via holes: "for every inconsistency on the surface, there is a subterranean consistency."[12] To read this way ungrounds, toppling foundations. Negarestani calls this hidden writing, a model of complicity with the hole complex that asks us to read through plot holes.

Does queer theory not have a similar model for writing and reading? Queer Theory's mode of operation has been to take an object that is rendered stable, normal, accepted, solid and destabilize it, reveal its construction, expose its holes. This is what Berlant and Warner call queer commentary, what I have said is queering, but the difference between queer commentary and Hidden Writing is the logic or narration that runs through these holes. Queer Theory's aim at destabilization has commonly been to reveal a heteronormative logic at work in constituting whatever is the object of commentary. To take up Negarestani's models, we could say that queer theory's hole complex makes holes by queering and exposes the logic leaking out and running through these holes to be heteronormative. Queer Theory's subterranean consistency is heteronormative. Yet, what is different about the hole complex and Hidden Writing is that the patterns of holey-emergence are never known, that is, "things leak into each other according to a logic that does not

---

[11] Negarestani, *Cyclonopedia*, 44.
[12] Negarestani, *Cyclonopedia*, 53.

belong to us."[13] *Cyclonopedia*'s hole complex is of a more fundamental, material difference, one that does not necessarily concern itself with language, identity, and subjects. These kinds of material differentiations and anomalies are exactly what theorists like David Ruffolo and Elizabeth Grosz are attempting to formulate in queer and feminist contexts. What are these leaky holes revealing? Certainly narrations that go beyond the subject, but queer theory always wants to read them as heteronormative. Could another queer theory be open to reading the heteronormative aspects of this logic alongside the components that do not belong to us?

To return to archeology, it is a process of exhumation that changes the artifact it unearths by attending to its holes. If we treat an artifact as a piece of hidden writing, a "subsurface [of the artifact] can only be exhumed by distorting the structure [or surface]."[14] *Cyclonopedia*, as a piece of hidden writing, gives us at least two exteriorized subsurfaces when exhumed: 1) a model for queerness that departs from the subject and heteronormativity; or more abstractly, a model for reading inconsistencies and instabilities that acknowledges and confronts the fact that these holes will have a logic that consists, at least in part, on something that has no correlate in the subject, and 2) a model for reading though *Cyclonopedia*'s own plot holes for subsurfaces like queerness, that when brought to the surface, will distort the book--and whatever is exhumed--into something else.

I'd now like to use this model of hidden writing to exhume two more queer artifacts: decay and love. Decay in *Cyclonopedia* introduces a creativity that complicates our human relations to negativity, reproduction, and the future. Negarestani describes decay

---

[13] Negarestani, *Cyclonopedia*, 49.
[14] Negarestani, *Cyclonopedia*, 62.

as an "anti-creationist creativity"[15] that builds subtractively. This formation of decay resonates with current debates in queer theory on the so-called "anti-social turn" and futurity. Decay here seems to be a kind of missing materialist component to these anti-social queer politics. Queer theory needs a theory of decay, an "ethics of degeneration,"[16] to trouble and unground these arguments, including the very axes they reside on. Decay comes to bear on queerness through at least two fronts: 1) it rots the relationships queer theory has to reproduction and futurity and 2) reveals that queerness is always in a state of "taxonomic indetermination."[17]

Negarestani approaches decay architecturely, through his notions of nested interiorities and infinitesimal persistence toward zero. A thing that is decaying exteriorizes its interiorities. When this occurs, the original thing shrinks, becomes smaller, moves closer and closer toward zero (or total annihilation). This is what Negarestani calls intensive negativity. Yet, when the thing exteriorizes its interiorities, these newly exposed interiorities have other interiorities that can be exposed. Negarestani refers to these levels of interiorities that may be exteriorized as nested. This continues, and hence, there is an extensive positivity.

The anti-social turn in queer theory is a debate over the heteronormative, reproductive logics that guarantee the future as well as the relationalities that supposedly emerge in sex.[18] On one side, Lee Edelman refuses what he calls the heteronormative logic of the

---

[15] Negarestani, *Cyclonopedia*, 181.
[16] Negarestani, *Cyclonopedia*, 30.
[17] Negarestani, *Cyclonopedia*, 184.
[18] See Lee Edelman's *No Future: Queer Theory and the Death Drive* (Durham: Duke University Press, 2004) and Jack Halberstam's "The Anti-Social Turn in Queer Theory," *Graduate Journal of Social Science* 5 (2008): 140-56.

future, which hinges upon the figure of the child, and therefore, he refuses any future. On the other, Jack Halberstam embraces the anti-social experience of sex that Lee Edelman and Leo Bersani champion and also the negative refusal of the future, but he cites Edelman's absolute rejection of the future as formalist and apolitical. Rather, Halberstam refuses a capitalist, imperial future but wants another, one that especially does not build an exclusion around women, domesticity, reproduction, and children—a dismissal that comes commonly from white queer male scholarship. Yet, on either side, decay exists, persists. Decay delivers to queer theory a different kind of negativity that always provides a future and always produces, if not reproduces. This is the "infinite calculus of rot,"[19] forever toward zero; a future that even queer theory cannot deny. There is a rotting relationality that is not anti-social during sex, and there is a productive future of decay that degenerates all futures, whether those of heteronormative reproduction, Edelman's queer death drive, or Halberstam's punk queer future. While queer theory would certainly respond favorably to a process that builds "without creation,"[20] this "without creation" cannot be qualified only by queer refusal and imaginaries. Decay, Negarestani tells us, "ungrounds the very ground upon which power is conducted."[21] The fulcrum point of power that queer theory relies on here--the same queer-heteronormative dualism--is softened, exteriorized, changed. Decay "exteriorizes all interiorities in unimaginable ways."[22] Queer theory must engage with decay because it is always there,

---

[19] Reza Negarestani, "Undercover Softness: An Introduction to the Politics and Architecture of Decay," *Collapse* 4 (2010): 381.
[20] Negarestani, *Cyclonopedia*, 185.
[21] Negarestani, *Cyclonopedia*, 182.
[22] Negarestani, "Undercover Softness," 385.

inescapable, ungrounding how it plans for its futures and no-futures.

While decay interferes with the ways futures are made and maintained in queer theory, it also putrefies the conceptual apparatuses and "bibliographic shape" of queer theory. In his essay "Undercover Softness: An Introduction to the Architecture and Politics of Decay," Negarestani tells us that "If political systems are constituted of formations—both in the realm of ideas and in concrete structures—then, like living species, they also are subject to the troubling deformities brought about by the process of decay.[23]" Negarestani points out that decay offers the "possibility of the generation of one species from the putrefying corpse of another species" and that in decay "one species can uniformly or difformly deform in such a way that it gradually assumes the latitude of forms associated with other species."[24] Where are we in the decay process of queer theory? What are its current gradients of decay? What did it exteriorize out of? What is it exteriorizing into? Decay as a model for queerness' own transitions and transformations seems incredibly useful for thinking these changes: can we attend to the nested interiorities that have been exteriorized since the inception of queer theory? Is it possible to hold to an older gradient of exteriorization that has since rotted into something unrecognizable?

Like decay, love abounds in *Cyclonopedia*. Typically, it reads quite similarly to queer theoretical arguments against love as heteronormative and ideological. Negarestani refers to love as a "closure,"[25] "the end of health,"[26] "a failure to escape,"[27] a "tyran-

---

[23] Negarestani, "Undercover Softness," 381.
[24] Negarestani, "Undercover Softness," 381.
[25] Negarestani, *Cyclonopedia*, 220.
[26] Negarestani, *Cyclonopedia*, 85.
[27] Negarestani, *Cyclonopedia*, 85.

nical possibility."[28] Lauren Berlant, in her essay "Love, A Queer Feeling," describes love (that is not queered) as a generic, repetitive formalism that traps. Yet, *Cyclonopedia* contains another love, like queer theory offers another love. Indeed, we could say that *Cyclonopedia* is a love letter to the Outside; it is in a process of seducing the Outside, having an affair with the Outside. This is a kind of love that is "catastrophically unpleasant"[29] for the subject, love as radical openness. While Berlant cites normativity as a "horror genre,"[30] there is something else more horrific that queer theory has not adequately dealt with. Yet, queer theory is slowly opening up toward this kind of love. In Tim Dean's *Unlimited Intimacy*, gay male barebacking culture is described as "an arena of invention that involves experiments in how to do things with viruses."[31] This leads Dean to argue for an ethics of openness and alterity, one that welcomes sex with strangers and promiscuity. For Negarestani, Dean's depiction of barebacking might be considered economical openness rather than radical openness, which is an openness that one decides one can afford. Decisions of affordance are made by the barebacker prior to experiments with viruses.

Love as radical openness is located most vividly in passages from Parsani's own writings to Sorceress, who the book is dedicated to—is s/he the Outside? When Parsani states that "love is incomplete burning"[32] he defines love as a radical material transfor-

---

[28] Negarestani, *Cyclonopedia*, 85.

[29] Negarestani, *Cyclonopedia*, 200.

[30] Lauren Berlant, "Love, A Queer Feeling," *Homosexuality and Psychoanalysis* (Chicago: University of Chicago Press, 2001), 444.

[31] Tim Dean, *Unlimited Intimacy: Reflections on the Subculture of Barebacking*, (Chicago: University of Chicago Press, 2009), 47.

[32] Negarestani, *Cyclonopedia*, 39.

mation that blurs, pervades, is a process of "positive disintegration."[33] This is a kind of love that goes beyond recognition, to a far more radical notion of otherness that the human cannot imagine. Negaerstani calls this a "faceless love."[34] At the end of *Cyclonopedia*, when Parsani calls upon Sorceress: "let's gather our contagious diseases and make love,[35]" this making-love seems to echo Dean's barebacker; there is a decision to afford this openness beforehand. Yet, there is still illegibilities to this encounter, similar to the barebacker: is this love, sex, both, something else? what materials are being exchanged and transformed? Perhaps this making-love and barebacking are moments of radical openness if there is an attending to what cannot be imagined or recognized during these encounters.

How can queer theory respond to such a polytical love? How much must it open? I think queer theory needs this polytical love if it wants to not only escape its peaking but also think its relations to materiality. While Berlant has given us a queer love as transformative, there is something painful and horrifying that her love does not touch because it remains rooted in the human subject. This polytical love does exist in queer history; we have seen it in various forms, like HIV/AIDS. It is queer theory that has attended to these events without a polytical edge. To be clear, queerness is something that has seduced the Outside many times; it is queer theory that has been slow or late to account, address, and think this. While queer theory has maintained a fidelity to queer ways of living, opening queer theory to the polytical may actually strengthen that fidelity as well as contribute to an opening of queerness. Again, can we have a queer the-

---

[33] Negarestani, *Cyclonopedia*, 38.
[34] Negarestani, *Cyclonopedia*, 207.
[35] Negarestani, *Cyclonopedia*, 221.

ory that attempts faceless love? Or does this open queer theory into something else, something unrecognizable, something we would hesitate to name queer theory?

The next step in opening queer theory would be to apply Negarestani's exhumed queerness and use it to subject queer theory proper to radical openness, through the schizotrategies outlined in *Cyclonopedia*, to try to arrive at something like a queer polytics. Perhaps that will bring us closer to making queer theory more of a target, more of a good meal, for the outside.

Non-Oedipal Networks and the Inorganic Unconscious

Melanie Doherty

> "But I don't want to go among mad people," Alice remarked.
> "Oh, you can't help that," said the Cat: "We're all mad here. I'm mad. You're mad."
> "How do you know I'm mad?" said Alice.
> "You must be," said the Cheshire Cat, "or you wouldn't have come here."
> – Lewis Carroll

> Much madness is divinest sense.
> – Emily Dickinson

After being mysteriously invited to this conference out of the blue last fall and despite my reservations and anxieties, I[1] am here with a mixture of

---

[1] "Of course, I indulge myself, in innumerable ways. 'I' tell myself the personal pronoun fails to mark the pseudo-neutral position of a commentator *this time.* That is rather a protraction of 'Bataille's' incessant *je* into a further episode of debasement. For it is remarkable how degraded a discourse can become when it is marked by the obsessive reiteration of the abstract ego, mixing arrogance with pallid humility. The chronic whine that results something akin to a degenerated reverberation from Dostoyevsky's underground man—is the insistence of a humanity that has become an unbearable indignity. 'I' am (alone), as the tasteless exhibition of an endogenous torment, as the betrayal of communi-

trepidation and curiosity. I was called out of nowhere, like Josef K. called to the castle. I have wondered many times how I ended up on the radar of the individuals involved, and Reza Negarestani's radar in particular. I will not pretend to understand the engine behind this not entirely unpleasant experience of paranoia that I've been feeling for the past few months as I read and reread *Cyclonopedia*. As a good hystericized academic who still falls victim to the Discourse of the University, one who uses excessive Post-It© notes and checks footnotes, I read the text initially as a traditional book, but then I began to search beyond the original text on website after website after website, following the clues left initially in Kristen Alvanson's journal. As I began burrowing through the archives, mole-like, I started to suspect a ludic collective throbbing behind every cold discussion on *Hyperstition*,[2] every blog post and journal article, every conference announcement and facebook page, and perhaps linger-

---

cation, as a festering wound, in which the monadic knitting of the flesh loses itself in a mess of pus and scabs, etc. etc. . . . (You yawn of course, but I continue.) Yes, *I* am—*definitionally*—a filthy beggar (like God), scrabbling at the coattails of a reluctant and embarrassed attentiveness, driven into a guile that fuses wretchedness with an elusive element of threat. Is it mere indolence that defeats all tendency towards decorous impersonality? Scarcely. Or rather; I cannot bring myself to think so. I nag at the margins of this discourse on the writings of Georges Bataille as a hideous confirmation of its cowardice and moderation, simultaneous with the dreariness of its prostitution; a wheezing parody of laughter teetering upon the abject nakedness of a sob. Yet at the same time it scarcely matters whether I write of Bataille or myself. If there is a boundary between us it is only insofar as he was momentarily frustrated in his passage to the truth of his text" (Land, *The Thirst for Annihilation* [New York: Routledge, 1992], 10).

[2] See http://hyperstition.abstractdynamics.org/.

ing behind every page of the book as well. I began to see connections to the text everywhere online: trisons and weaponized rats, 9s and 11s, solar capitalism, Tellurian lubricant, xenopoetics! I giggled aloud with a tinge of hysteria when I saw that the date of the conference was indeed March 11—the same date as the first page of the *Cyclonopedia* manuscript itself! What grand and terrifying organizing skills were these?[3] What spell had been cast around me to make my hold on reality feel so tenuous? My Oedipa complex reached fever pitch as I read articles in Collapse, the history of the CCRU, Nick Land's *The Thirst for Annihilation*, and tracked the unfolding debates within Speculative Realism. Terror fractals radiated out of unexpected civilian spaces. Plotholes unfurling vulvically inside plotholes. And, finally, I suspected that I had plunged to a new depth in the molten magma core of my insanity when I woke up last Saturday morning to see this lead news story on the web: "Fox News Exclusive : NASA Scientist Claims Evidence of Alien Life on Meteorite!"[4] (Because of the contingency of my current geographic location in Macon, GA, and the wonders of Web 2.0, FOX news often pops up first on my browser. Not by choice.)

After reading this dubious article about a scientist who, in true Lovecraftian style, had collected his meteorites by braving long trips to Antarctica and Greenland, no doubt staving off a creeping sense of dread and journaling his flowering insanity with each newly recovered spacerock, I proceeded to link to an even more dubious website—if that's possible—called the *Journal of Cosmology*. Every indicator screamed that

---

[3] "It is not the ability to preserve riddles that has value, but the ability to engender them" (Land, *Annihilation*, 25).
[4] See http://www.foxnews.com/scitech/2011/03/05/exclusive-nasa-scientists-claims-evidence-alien-life-meteorite/.

this journal was a hoax: Articles on how to negotiate astronaut sexual relations during those long trips to Mars. Spores populating earth from outer space. A website design circa 1994, replete with technicolor pulp-fiction planets and just *horrible* use of frames. All that was missing was a looping 16-bit MIDI score from *2001: A Space Odyssey*. And yet, "authentic" NASA scientists had published here!! But now, apparently, at least according to *Discover* magazine online, the *Journal of Cosmology*, which had only started in 2009, was sadly and mysteriously folding, and NASA higher-ups had been scrambling to cover up their involvement. I stared at the worm-like aliens and felt a euphoric yet troubling peak in my months-long paranoid high. This also could be real. I simply didn't know. The space worms seemed to taunt me with their Cthulu-like embryonic tentacles. Crazed digressive narratives were playing against my every instinct toward sanity: Was this alien meteorite a viral creation of the *Hyperstition* lab? Was Reza Negarestani behind this as well?!?

That was it. I had lost it. I decided I had fully entered into a paranoid cyclonic media noise state and there was no hope. The true tenuousness of my capacity to parse reality from fiction had been brought to the fore![5] Friends listened with visible concern as I tried to recount what was happening to me. But then I began to enjoy the implications of my jammed reality channels. I watched a flickering Max Headroom-esque Reza Negarestani on Facebook, via YouTube, filmed on a flat screen, as he was Skyped into the London event on contingency last week. Screens within screens within screens looping recursively, bringing

---

[5] "It is time to wake up and realize the carnival is over and we are just clowns performing for one another – the critical crowd has long disappeared" (Reza Negarestani, Facebook post).

Reza to life in a shifting moray pattern of interference, more Douglas Hofstadter than *The Matrix*. I couldn't help but notice how few photos of Negarestani exist on the web. I got John Nash thrills at the internet whispers that Nick Land and Reza Negarestani were in fact one and the same person. Where had Nick gone, anyway? Lurking nosferatu underground, waiting to rise again, fanged noumena up from the earth? I found minute errata, such as a missing "s" off a book titled *Recent Research in Bible Lands* to read "Land" in the endnotes. It's an actual book, written in 1896 (according to Google Books) only it did not appear to contain "more details on the three-dotted perversion (the ubiquitous "Trison") . . . or the history of terror-fractals" as the footnote suggested (227). Go figure. Was this just a mistake? Was it significant? Had I lost my mind? All these clues were coming together, all pointed to some deeper significance that I had almost-but-not-quite unpacked![6] Reza, rising acephalic and non-oedipal, Reza coordinating in militaristic trisons, Reza emerging from the muck of internet, like Bush and Bin-Laden puppets bobbing on the surface oil. Only oil in this case was the noise of the network. Reza as legion! Everywhere and nowhere! Reza as the razor and the resonator of reason!

Increasingly, my desire to extend this moment of paranoid schizophrenic decadence, to suspend my disbelief ad infinitum was spent searching for more

---

[6] "What I offer is a web of half-choked ravings that vaunts its incompetence, exploiting the meticulous conceptual fabrications of positive knowledge as a resource for delirium, appealing only to the indolent, the maladapted, and the psychologically diseased. I would like to think that if due to some collective spiritual seism the natural sciences were to become strictly unintelligible to us, and were read instead as a poetics of the sacred, the consequence would resonate with the text that follows. At least disorder grows" (Nick Land, *Annihilation*, 26).

and more connections online. This is the anonymous-network paranoia that drives viral marketing campaigns and alternate-reality games. But in this case, the narratives produced were not being used to marshall legions of teens into producing surplus entertainment value for corporations. Instead, this was the click-logic of the internet that generates an endless barrage of associations with possible significance, but no final resolution. This was the Deleuzian logic of the AND AND AND AND.[7] This was cyber-free-association, and I was on the couch. I was being well and truly schizoanalyzed by *Cyclonopedia*.

But was this a blessing or a curse? Let's backup a bit and consider how I'd come to this sorry state. It helps to see a few of the clues that got me here. "Hyperstition," on the old blog posts of the same name, is defined as "a fiction that makes itself real."[8] As such,

---

[7] "Smiths are not nomadic among the nomads and sedentary among the sedentaries, nor half-nomadic among the nomads, half-sedentary among sedentaries. Their relation to others results from their internal itinerancy, from their vague essence, and not the reverse. It is in their specificity, it is by virtue of their inventing a holey space, that they necessarily communicate with the sedentaries *and* with the nomads (and with others besides, with the transhumant forest dwellers) . . . Holey space itself communicates with smooth space and striated space. In effect, the machinic phylum or the metallic line passes through all of the assemblages: nothing is more deterritorialized than matter-movement. But it is not at all in the same way, and the two communications are not symmetrical" (Gilles Deleuze and Félix Guattari, *A Thousand Plateaus*, trans. Brian Massumi [Minneapolis: University of Minnesota Press, 1987], 414-415).

[8] "All this being said, a minimalistic schema of hyperstitional activity might have three basic divisions:

1) Hyperstitional Doctrine. The assumed impetus here is eliminative. Can anything that has been treated as axiomatic be deducted from the set of

Cyclonopedia makes effects in the world, a myth-meme run amok, but not simply representationally. There is an experiential theorizing of the contemporary capitalist military-industrial-media complex here that enacts its critique beyond text, beyond representational writing and moves with terror-fractal stealth into lived reality. The text had spilled beyond the covers of the book onto the net, and the text as a collec-

---

'essential' hyperstitional tools/principles? A series of 'methodological appendices' collects potentially functional but inessential procedural assets. Lemurian Hyperstition, based on the pre-eminence of the Numogram and decanomic decoding — and associated qabbalistic techniques - belongs here, but in a continuously self-problematizing position. Defining questions: What is Hyperstition? How does it work? What are its essential procedures?

2) Hyperstitional Analysis. This has been a relatively neglected dimension of the Hyperstition blog to date, but there is no obvious theoretical basis for this. Phenomena such as Apocalyptic Monotheism, Magick, Capitalism, Science Fiction . . . ['random' examples at this stage] and many others intrinsically involve the operationalization of virtualities, or 'fictions that make themselves real.' Even if programmatic hyperstition had no 'engineering' ambitions whatsoever, the existence of hyperstition as an analytical apparatus would still be legitimated by this 'efficacy of potentials.'

3) Hyperstitional Production. The puppet theatre of carrier construction. Using hyperstitional procedures systematized in (1) above to investigate phenomena of all kinds within a polytical pragmatic framework. This dealt with at a methodological level in the series of 'Hyperstitional Carriers' posts, and practically exemplified elsewhere" (http://hyperstition.abstractdynamics.org/archives/004711.html).

tive work, a work that I suspected might even be literally inhuman and machine-generated in parts, had turned inside-out, a hyperbolic space surrounding me, at once infinite and yet claustrophobically boxing me in. The network was dense with resonating signifiers. *Gog Magog Axis! Hidden Writing! Nafta! The Cross of Akht!* I saw how the inorganic unconscious of oil was the deep logic of the internet itself! When the fleeting act of viewing a website burns anywhere from 20-300 mg of CO_2 each second,[9] I thought of the hours of hallucinatory web searches that I had embarked upon to decipher this text. I felt the deep irony and began to understand the blobjective warnings of the enigmatic "X/Z Dialogue": "Oil is the undercurrent of all narrations!"[10] My attempt to understand and unpack *Cyclonopedia* had been literally floating on crude! Information may want to be free, but the hackers are still burning oil.

All the while, the futility of my search for deep truth, the ridiculousness of my anxious need to be properly academic grew clearer. A sneering Nick Land was hovering somewhere behind all this textual noise, mocking how I refused to let go of my attachment to the idea that the author(s) would somehow be the key, or that the text itself somehow mapped directly onto the complex points of a vast international conspiracy of cybertheorists who were somehow inviting me to play, but only if I could figure this all out! *It's 3:30 in the morning*[11]. I'm frenetically creating anagrams for the name "Reza Negarestani":

---

[9] http://www.timesonline.co.uk/tol/news/environment/article5488934.ece>

[10] Negarestani, *Cyclonopedia*, 19.

[11] "It is 03.30 in the morning. Let us say one is 'drunk'—an impoverished cipher for all those terrible things one does to one's nervous-system in the depths of the night—and philosophy is 'impossible' (although one still thinks, even to the

A Satan Energizer!
Earnest Gaze Iran!
An Errata Sneezing!

All could be meaningful! All could hold the final key, the Rosetta Stone to *Cyclonopedia*!
And then, I had a darker thrill...
It dawned on me slowly, a cold dread coursing through my veins. Perhaps I was misguided to focus on Reza this whole time. The horrifying insight grew steadily! Of course! Why hadn't I been able to see it before? Was I so trapped in white Western patriarchal thinking?? Could I really be so blind to the obvious truth? Kristen Alvanson!![12] SHE was behind all this!!

---

point of terror and disgust). What does it mean for this episode in the real history of spirit to die without trace?" (Land, *Annihilation*, 9).

[12] "Looking for an avant-garde art and theory critic who would be willing to provide me with conceptual and theoretical materials for the website project I was developing in 2003, I contacted a PhD graduate from the University of Warwick. Corresponding with him regularly over the internet on various intellectual and current cultural topics for over a year, I gradually established a close friendship with him. In May 2004, while I was searching for his name to find one of his published articles, I came upon a controversial blog post and a string of comments questioning my friend's multiple literary identities and alleging that works had been drawn from many theoretical sources. Shocked by what I was reading, I started to search for more about the person I had been in touch with. Returning to our old correspondence, I found textual fragments from others surfacing one by one through his words. What followed my initial discoveries led me to take a more inclusive and exhaustively experimental interaction – no longer restricted by long distance or internet space – with the identities I could see behind him as well as the people and things emerging out of his unmask-

She who had set the stage with her journal entries, she who had whispered devastating love throughout the text in sly footnotes. She was the true and real ground! The female cutting edge of the Outside ripping open phallic closure! Kristen Alvanson, non-Euclidean and pissed off, invaginating the space around the boys-club bloggers! Kristen Alvanson, the Mother of All Abominations, ripping vulvo-cosmic singularities in all this masculinist warmongering! Kristen Alvanson as Aisha Qadisha, parasitically infecting her unsuspecting targets and never leaving, perpetually inhabiting her male host to guarantee his continued and total openness! Hot!

But no. That was far too binary and oppositional. As much as I truly preferred this last scenario, I had to rethink all this.[13] Obviously my obsession with authorial voice was missing the point some 50 years after Roland Barthes' Death of the Author. What mattered here wasn't the author(s) or the means of textual production at all, but rather the circulation and the effects of the text in the world. In *Anti-Oedipus*, Deleuze and Guattari teach us the difference between conceptions of the unconscious as theater versus the unconscious as factory. The unconscious as theater is a theater of representation. And I had been thinking all this time

---

ing: Them" (Kristen Alvanson, *Lessons in Schizophrenia*, <www.kristenalvanson.com/new/LIS-intro.html>)

[13] "What happens when the probability of being someone else or more radically being something else or other things surpasses the probability of the current state and present existence of an entity? Or simply what are the consequences of 'me' being someone or something else? What does actually happen when an individual realizes that it is no longer the subject of I and Self – everyone is me but not the other way around?" (Reza Negarestani, "Epithemic: *vox populi*," in Kristen Alvanson's *Lessons in Schizophrenia*, http://www.kristenalvanson.com/new/LIS-intro.html).

in terms of representation. What does this text represent? What is its history? What is its meaning? I was looking for the secret code behind the text and that led me to see signs everywhere. Instead, when Deleuze and Guattari talk about the unconscious as factory, they talk about it doing things, making things, creating things. So I had to let go of my drive to discover what this text represents, and begin to see what it does in the world.

It's no mistake that the Middle East is a sentient entity in *Cyclonopedia*. "Alive," as the text's epigraph states, "in a very literal sense of the word, apart from all metaphor or allegory." This may hint at the disparate and disjunctive voices that make up the book and the fact that, often, there is no singular organizing authorial identity or consensus. Playful references to H.P. Lovecraft in one part of the book, for example, are tempered by critical texts observing his rampant "racism, paranoia, and consistent emphasis on absolute closure" in another section.[14] This dialogism tempers potentially problematic and orientalist representations of the Middle East. Yet it's doubly interesting that paranoia itself has been cited as one of the effects of the text for those (mainly Western readers) who engage in the full experience.

In *Cyclonopedia*, noise pervades the narrative with solar rattles, sandstorms and vowelless nomad glossolalia. It resonates in the opaque and object nature of its juxtaposing textual forms. Noise also functions in the cybernetic sense, as a result of its viral functioning in the world. Gregory Bateson reminds us: "All that is not information, not redundancy, not form and not restraints—is noise, the only possible source of new patterns" (416). In cybernetic terms, noise is good. Rather than getting rid of noise on the channels, noise in information is a productive aspect of commu-

---

[14] Negarestani, *Cyclonopedia*, 210.

nication. It gives rise to new ideas, new lines of flight, new objects. Without noise, all we do is repeat. We repeat the same institutional structures, we repeat the same ideas, we repeat the same tedious bourgeois literary subjectivities. Michel Serres shows us the creative nature of noise.[15] Niklas Luhmann[16] taught us to

---

[15] "Noise destroys and horrifies. But order and flat repetition are in the vicinity of death. Noise nourishes a new order. Organization, life, and intelligent thought live between order and noise, between disorder and perfect harmony. If there were only order, if we only heard perfect harmonies, our stupidity would soon fall down toward a dreamless sleep; if we were always surrounded by the shivaree, we would lose our breath and our consistency, we would spread out among all the dancing atoms of the universe. We are; we live; we think on the fringe, in the probable fed by the unexpected, in the legal nourished with information. There are two ways to die, two ways to sleep, two ways to be stupid—a head-first dive into chaos or stabilized installation in order and chitin. We are provided with enough senses and instinct to protect us against the danger of explosion, but we do not have enough when faced with death from order or with falling asleep from rules and harmony" (Michel Serres, *The Parasite*, trans. Lawrence R. Schehr [Minneapolis: University of Minnesota Press], 2007), 127.

[16] "When individuals look at media as text or as image, they are outside; when they experience their results within themselves, they are inside. They have to oscillate between outside and inside, as if in a paradoxical situation: quickly, almost without losing any time, and undecidably. For the one position is only possible thanks to the other – and vice versa.

"The consequence must be that the individual must resolve this paradox for herself and construct her identity or her 'self' herself. The materials used for this can be the usual ones. But there is no possibility of taking on an 'I' by analogy from outside. No one can be like someone else. No one sees himself as the reflection of another. The only point of agreement is the necessity of using schemata for sustaining a memory" (Niklas Luhmann, *The Reality of the Mass Media*,

use recursivity and noise to test the limits of the reality of the mass media. Levi Bryant encourages us to identify the negative feedback loops that organize the social so that we can disrupt repetitive signals of power and dominance.

Cyclonopedia introduces a new literary and political strategy. I hesitate to put a label it for many reasons,[17] but for the sake of discussion we might call this type of work "noise fiction." It's a form of textuality designed not to represent the world, but to act virally in the world, to circulate throughout the world, producing effects by simultaneously scrambling existing codes, disrupting expectations, and casting the reader outside the covers of the book to gather even more experiences, thus opening up spaces where new forms of practice and critique can take flight.

As noise fiction, *Cyclonopedia* disrupts regularly scheduled genres and blasts viral interference across contemporary channels of literary production. It has roots in James Joyce and William Burroughs, Ishmael Reed and Kathy Acker[18], but it's also responding to the

---

trans. Kathleen Cross [Stanford: Stanford University Press, 2000], 115).

[17] "In other words, our claim is that it is possible to sincerely maintain that objects could *actually and for no reason whatsoever* behave in the most erratic fashion, without having to modify our usual everyday relations to things" (Quentin Meillassoux, *After Finitude: An Essay on the Necessity of Contingency*, trans. Ray Brassier [New York: Continuum, 2008], 85).

[18] "So now there's going to be a war! Hey! Finally something exciting's going to happen! The United States's coming back to life! The government of the United States is realizing that someone's angry about something or other and's descending to offer its people a target for their bilious bitterness. O emotionless sentimental and sedentary people, because your government's a democracy and responsible to you, it is giving you a whole race to detest, a whole nation on which to

space beyond the traditionally literary. It's another transformation of the sphere of late-print culture, another perturbation in the system. It works to highlight how, in the logic of the global media network, the signal is often replicated too neatly. Certain identities, institutions and power relations are treated as unquestionable reality, even when they are not as they appear. Noise politics would seek to undermine this reproduction and scramble these codes as much as possible. If Web 2.0 can benevolently dictate our daily newsfeeds by reading into our assumed personal preferences via GPS location, if NASA can publish in the faux *Journal of Cosmology* and there's no noise, no change, and no dissonance to suggest a problem, then how can we ever trust the information that we receive?

Cyclonopedia moves out of the realm of the representational to generate further conversations, debates, arguments and other practices. It has already generated art works and other objects. It has even, in a sense, rather eerily, somehow asked me to write this

---

spit, a religion to damn, everything you've ever wanted. You're incontestably superior to men who wear dresses. Again you will become important in the eyes of the world.

"You Americans need to be right. This war will not only be a pathway to future glory: once war's begun, you'll feel secure because you'll no longer have to understand anything else. You will again know what good and evil are.

"Tomorrow you're going to give your sons joyfully to the desert, maybe daughters if you're feminist enough, because you're emotionless and, in war, you can be so emotionless, you don't have to exist. Therefore war allows people to surpass themselves. The English know this full well. As soon as you have tanks and dead people all around you, you'll be able to feel alive, once more powerful, magnanimous, and generous to all the world" (Kathy Acker, *My Mother: Demonology* [New York: Grove Press, 1993], 17).

paper. And not all discussions will agree. There are valid questions that can be raised about how the image of the Middle East works in a text like this, especially when noise by its very nature can't be easily directed and there are very real struggles to be addressed. What is the political efficacy of noise as strategy? When we introduce it into situations, we don't know what results it will produce. This can be good because it's creative, but when we talk about the variety of real struggles in the world, what we want is action directed toward a specific aim. The struggles within acephalic networked groups like Anonymous offer evidence of this problem, with some participants seriously invested in critiquing the flows of capital, while others use the mask of anonymity to spew hate speech and replicate the same power dynamics that they are ostensibly fighting against.

Questioning patriarchy, presence and paranoid white Western bias, *Cyclonopedia* perturbs established critical realms to stay in a state of resonating flux rather than resting on pre-packaged meaning or closed-signal identity. It raises anxieties about authenticity and the archive. It questions both the fetishes of the academy and the self-aggrandizing egos of the blogosphere. This is not simply a novel to be read. It doesn't work on the level of representation. This is a textual machine designed to produce other machines. Instead of quieting down and maintaining cultural status quo, *Cyclonopedia* incites us to go out and make some noise.

Symptomatic Horror: Lovecraft's "The Colour Out of Space"

Anthony Sciscione

Symptomatic horror describes works that attempt to encounter the radically non-human without recourse to ontological presence and positive conceptualization, instead channeling the incompatible agency through its effects on the landscape and representing it in the text primarily with reference to the discursive and hermeneutic gaps it occasions. In H.P. Lovecraft's "The Colour Out of Space,"[1] a classic work of this sort,[2] a constitutionally-indeterminate extraterrestrial agency deposited by a meteorite infiltrates a local biophysical milieu and reengineers it in accordance with its alien molecular agenda. At the same time, the agency occupies a liminal dimension with regard to phenomenal (extensive) space by nesting in the interstice between object and quality and also suggesting itself just beyond the borders of perception by sounds sensed only at "moments where consciousness

---

[1] In *The Annotated H.P. Lovecraft*, ed. S. T. Joshi (Dell, 1997), 58-100. Hereafter abbreviated *COS*.
[2] Perhaps the earliest example is Poe's "The Fall of the House of Usher." Other works in this vein are T.E.D. Klein's "The Events at Poroth Farm," Laird Barron's "—30—," and Shirley Jackson's unparalleled *The Haunting of Hill House*, which unlike most haunted-house narratives, never supplies a determinable agent at the root of the anomalous occurrences.

[seems] to half slip away."³ The habits of "stealthy listening" and obsessive nocturnal watching the Gardners develop thus increase its phenomenal availability, making paranoia a 'schizotrategic' mode of drawing victims toward it at "the outer limits of demon and system"⁴ where, to borrow from Deleuze-Guattari, "the interior forces of earth [and] the exterior forces of chaos...clasp and are wed in a battle whose only criterion and stakes is the earth."⁵ The "xenoagent"⁶ or radical outsider never appears as a discrete entity or individuated substance beyond vague indications of motion and fog, but is revealed only nebulously on the ground (the superficial or visible outside) through symptoms of transmutation and madness. In cosmic horror fiction, radical exteriority tends to reflect some abyss in cognitive apprehension, a chasm or disjuncture between person and world widened by our profound vulnerability in an aleatory, unfavorable cosmos. The shadow of what we don't know becomes

---

³ *COS*, 74.
⁴ Reza Negarestani, *Cyclonopedia* (Melbourne: re.press, 2008), 118, 203.
⁵ See Gilles Deleuze and Félix Guattari, *A Thousand Plateaus*, trans. Brian Massumi (Minneapolis: University of Minnesota Press, 1987), 321.
⁶ In this case, a "xenolithic artifact" or Inorganic Demon, of which Negarestani writes, "Autonomous, sentient and independent of human will, their existence is categorized by their forsaken status, their immemorial slumber and their provocatively exquisite forms. Their autonomy alone marks their outsideness to the human and to its ecology, the planetary biosphere; this is why they are frequently associated with alien life forms and defined by the prefix xeno- (outside). Emerging from one common lineage—that of demons from the possessing class—artifacts or inorganic demons contribute their cryptic outsideness to the human host through a series of generalized but consistent lineaments and symptoms" (*Cyclonopedia*, 223n4).

an alterior horror that knows all, that stares back through mist with myriad eyes or takes advantage of solidity's dependence on void[7] to wriggle out the eye-holes of anthropocentrism. In this paper I will explore symptomatic horror in Lovecraft's tale through Negarestani's "( )hole-complex," understood as a "machine" by which the xeno-agent as "avatar of absolute exteriority" infiltrates the interior of a system and opens it up to the outside (the unhuman) via derangement and disintegration, making what once thrived a dusty signature of human impotence in a world that, the more it opens up *to* us, the more horrifyingly *weird* it becomes.

For this colour, this illicit shade from regions unfathomed, is not to be conflated with the light of discovery but rather with that of "'the grey brittle death,' the eclipse of knowledge, the demonstration of the inadequacy of what purports to be knowledge . . . the reduction of living minds (and by extension, their categorizing, system-building ambitions) to an ashen residue."[8] Negarestani introduces ( )hole-complex in *Cyclonopedia* as a way of talking about both degenerate wholes and the poromechanics of ungrounding responsible for them. He is explicitly influenced by Lovecraft in his notion of local dominions as riddled with openings for invasion by 'unnamable' nether entities, insidious agents that take advantage of "convoluted compositions of solid and void" as "zones of emergence" whereby "the Outside gradually but persistently emerges, creeps in (or out?) from the Inside."[9]

---

[7] See *Cyclonopedia*, 44: "[Void] excludes solid but solid must include void to architectonically survive" (emphasis removed).

[8] Donald R. Burleson, "Lovecraft's 'The Colour Out of Space,'" *The Explicator* 52 (1993): 48-50..

[9] *Cyclonopedia,* 44. Cf. "It is Lovecraftian worm-ridden space that makes solidity the altruistic host of emergence"

While, as George Sieg has observed, Lovecraft's horror is that of the xenophobe Anglo-purist confronting "an inescapably dreadful experience of *invasion from without*,"[10] Negarestani twists Lovecraft's cosmicism back upon itself by exposing the inside as always-already perforated by void, possessed of an interior ungrounding complicit with radically destabilizing forces of the exterior.[11] Accordingly, *Cyclonopedia* is rife with images of violated solids, bodies invaded by demonic destabilizers which drive them beyond the capacity for affordance and crack them open, exposing the presumptuousness of self-contained closure to the outside. Even the full body of the earth, which would seem to be our lone stronghold in the cosmic abyss, is outed as "the Unground,"[12] a thin shell of crust undermined by a liquid and lubricious interior and itself barely able to afford us in its convoluted porousness. This in turn implicates physical and conceptual structures erected on the ground as themselves shot through with void, perforated with gaps (negations, ellipses, plot holes) permitting the entrance and/or emergence of things producible only by way of the interstice. Nemat-functions or lines of emergence register the interiorized xeno-agent on the ground through inconsistencies or *symptoms*; this is summed

---

(48). Both authors can be said to participate in "Hidden Writing," which Negarestani describes as "utilizing every plot hole, all problematics, every suspicious obscurity or repulsive wrongness as a new plot with a tentacled and autonomous mobility" (61).

[10] George J. Sieg, "Infinite Regress into Self-Referential Horror: The Gnosis of the Victim," *Collapse* 4 (2008): 29-55.

[11] *Cyclonopedia*, 239: "Ungrounding is involved with discovering or unearthing a chemically-degenerating underside to the ground." As I take it, ungrounding describes immanent forces of decay that would seem to conspire with the outside by degrading the consistency of solid bodies.

[12] *Cyclonopedia*, 43.

up in Negarestani's archaeo-Freudian "law of subterranean cause," which states that "for every inconsistency on the surface, there is a subterranean consistency." He elaborates, "for every inconsistency or anomaly visible on the ground, there is a buried schizoid consistency; to reach the schizoid consistency, a paranoid consistency or plane of paranoia must first be traversed."[13]

For Negarestani, the outsider is itself an "expendable [puppet] of cosmic alienage," a more abstract exteriority-function that "cannot register itself other than by violating boundaries and the order of the system," an "'act'" that is indifferent to ontology. "The Lovecraftian outsider," he writes, "is not reducible to the alien, for before everything, it is the act of outsiding imposed by the exteriority of cosmic alienage or the radical outside."[14] This is borne out in *COS* by the rather elaborate nesting strategy Lovecraft employs to string the setting along a chain of cosmic alienage. Our narrator comes from Boston to the fictional city of Arkham, where he visits old Ammi Pierce's house in a glen of abandoned farmhouses on its outskirts, and hears of "strange days" that passed forty years earlier around the Gardner farm which lay even deeper in the woods, but not quite as far as a primeval space of wild hills and brooklets which "trickle without ever having caught the glint of sunlight." This sequence establishes an incremental de-centering of the action from civic center to where human settlement encroaches upon forbidding glens of "elder mystery" and "woods that no axe has ever cut."[15] Of course, above and beyond even the most remote terrestrial spaces there brood the "skyey voids" and "fathomless gulfs" of the outer

---

[13] *Cyclonopedia*, 53-54.
[14] *Cyclonopedia*, 201-202.
[15] *COS*, 58-61.

cosmos, the apex of radical exteriority conceived in terms of extensive space.

This realm of inscrutable alterity is the source of the "lone, weird message" that transports the xeno-agent to earth's body: a meteorite that never cools, only negligibly reacts to corrosives and reagents, and releases spectroscopic frequencies that transcend known wavelengths, details that mark it as alien in composition and essence, "with outside properties and obedient to outside laws."[16] Being molecularly inconsistent with earth's atmosphere, it steadily diminishes in open air and consequently eludes scientific attempts to positively identify and classify its constituents. Prior to its ultimate destruction in a lighting-storm, scientists find a brittle globule of uncouth hue nested inside it that pops when tapped with a hammer, revealing only an empty pit and releasing nothing visible to the ground. However, it is precisely in this moment of non-manifestation that the xeno-agent is first deposited into the landscape (as material stratum immanently linking individuated surfaces), moving from meteoric to terrestrial interior in a way that signals the elusive agency's incompatibility with circumferential revelation.[17] This limit of expressibility is defined by the inability of the terrestrial surface to afford its expression, perhaps by virtue of its actual form exceeding local spectrums or other atmospheric criteria for the making-manifest of organisms. Whatever emerges finds amenable space only below the ground, in "the ooze and slime" at the bottom of the Gardner family well which, when sounded by investigators later in the tale, seems "inexplicably porous and bubbling" though untenanted by any solid object.[18] This

---

[16] *COS*, 70.
[17] That is, expression on the surface as an extensive, individuated body.
[18] *COS*, 88.

abrupt transition follows a nemat-function from radical exterior to local interior traced through the continuity of phenomena and manifestation, revelation and presence. In short, the xeno-agent bores a "plot hole," a gaping inconsistency in the surface of events which motivates its conceptual genesis (in the reader's mind, as it moves along the narrative frame—another chain of alienage) as a categorically unassimilable anomaly.

The "colour" of the title metonymically refers to the xeno-agent by the only non-symptomatic trait it communicates on the ground, first through the meteorite's odd spectroscopic bands and then the identical hue of the nested globule. The colour's eventual emergence as a quality *of* ground is symptomatic of the xeno-agent's taking-root as an endogenous process by co-opting the chemical foundations of the local biosphere. This schizoid consistency, Outsider-turned-subversive-Insider, constantly expands its paranecrotic[19] regime through chthonic and molecular channels, de-familiarizing or *weirding* the local milieu by mottling it with inconsistencies. In addition to the eldritch glow of swollen, inedible vegetation, other symptoms include strangely altered tracks and anomalous behav-

---

[19] "Paranecrotic changes arise after the action of an irritant, which is a mechanism triggering biochemical transformation. . . . [P]arabiotic and paranecrotic are different ways of describing the local reaction of a living system to action from without and constitute the external expression of one of the fundamental properties of living matter—irritability" (D.N. Nasonov, "Substratal Changes in Protoplasm Following Local and Spreading Excitation," *Tsitologiya* (*Cytology*) 1.6 (Moscow, 1959), trans. U.S. Joint Publications Research Services, 5-15. See also V.B. Sapunov, "The Effect of Pesticides on the Evolutionary Ecology of Pests," in *Third International Conference on Urban Pests: Prague, 1999*, www.icup.org.uk. The term seems to have come to prominence among Soviet biologists in the 1940s; I am unsure of its currency in modern cytology.

ior of local fauna, degenerative growths on livestock, domestic animals anxious and withdrawn, and the physical and psychic deterioration of the Gardner family. Locals concur with Nahum that these anomalies are due to some poison deposited by the meteorite and begin to avoid the area after unwholesome skunk-cabbages with "unprecedented" scents spring up, plants that "ought never to sprout in a healthy world."[20] This notion compounds the xeno-agent with disease and leads to a paranoid shunning of the area as inconsistent with the newly-resituated human milieu, with the Gardner farm—a haplessly subversive Insider—becoming a new consistency governed by growing immanence with radical (cosmic) exteriority, its very ambience like "a breath from regions unnamed and unnamable."[21]

A particularly unnerving symptom Lovecraft chooses is that of treetops moving in the absence of wind, as in this description that draws explicit continuity between the surface anomaly and the interiorized alien consistency:

> [The trees] were twitching morbidly and spasmodically, clawing in convulsive and epileptic madness at the moonlit clouds; scratching impotently in the noxious air as if jerked by some alien and bodiless line of linkage with subterrene horrors writhing and struggling beneath the black roots.[22]

This anthropomorphic image of suffering wrought by the machinations of subsurface infection parallels the degeneration undergone by Mrs. Gardner, who is the first human to exhibit symptoms of infection by the

---

[20] *COS*, 73.
[21] *COS*, 80.
[22] *COS*, 92.

extrastellar agency.[23] Initially she raves about indistinct "things in the air" and sensory "impulses which were not wholly sounds," her impressions summarized in this bit of indirect discourse:

> Something was taken away—she was being drained of something—something was fastening itself on her that ought not to be—someone must make it keep off—nothing was ever still in the night—the walls and windows shifted.[24]

Conceptually, both the agency and its somatic vector of emergence (i.e. what of Mrs. Gardner's it is 'draining') are couched in pronominal obscurity, with passive constructions emphasizing the absence of a determinable or localizable agent (hence my preference for the term 'agency').[25] The overall picture is one of parasitic inhabitation concurrent with a shifting perception of surfaces as ungrounded and inconsistent beyond their objective appearance. As in the landscape, the agency is 'present' in Mrs. Gardner only through symptoms of derangement similar to those of demonic possession; Brontë's madwoman has nothing on the chilling form Gardner eventually locks in the attic after "her [facial] expression changed" and their son Thaddeus "nearly fainted at the way she made faces at him."[26] Over time she goes mute, begins

---

[23] For an unfortunate but intriguing real-life example of comparable symptomatic horror, see the case of Gloria Ramirez in Richard Stone, "Analysis of a Toxic Death," *Discover Magazine* (April 1995), http://discovermagazine.com/1995/apr/analysisofatoxic493.

[24] *COS*, 77.

[25] Except where I use "xeno-agent" to describe it as a power of that category.

[26] *COS*, 77.

crawling on all fours and gives Nahum "the mad notion that she was slightly luminous in the dark."[27] While the symptoms are positive manifestations insofar as they are expressed on the surface, they are qualitatively *negative* in that they point to a loss or diminution of the afflicted entity in terms of its surface-identity. This loss signals a ceding-place of the human to the unhuman as the derangement of becoming-alien or possessing the radical Outside engineers an "overkill" that "effectuates openness outside the system's capacity to afford it,"[28] reducing victims to reeking, "blasphemous monstrosities" the detailing of which is abhorrent to anyone of whole (evapora*ting* 'w') mind. The unhuman has no right to exist on the surface, and creates a moral imperative for its witness to quash it out, as in where the narrator glosses over Ammi's use of a pipe to dispatch what was left of Mrs. Gardner:

> There are things which cannot be mentioned, and what is done in common humanity is sometimes cruelly judged by the law. I gathered that no moving thing was left in that attic room, and that to leave anything capable of motion there would have been a deed so monstrous as to damn any accountable being to eternal torment.[29]

Following his commission of this life-affirming duty, Ammi returns downstairs where he'd left Nahum in a delusional yet physically intact state thirty minutes earlier to find that "what he sought was no longer there"; "it" has been reduced to the conceptual status of the indefinite pronoun, an inconsistent,

---

[27] *COS*, 77.
[28] *Cyclonopedia*, 118.
[29] *COS*, 84.

paranecrotic form that can only be called 'alive' in the way that the alien radiance is "only by analogy" called a colour.[30] "Ammi could not touch it, but looked horrifiedly into the distorted parody that had been a face. 'What was it, Nahum[?] he whispered, and the cleft, bulging lips were just able to crack out a final answer: "Nothin' . . . nothin' . . ."[31] Nahum's heavily elliptical response recalls the hyphenated account of Mrs. Gardner's ravings as he tells of the cold, wet burning and sucking he feels, and how the agency, as "a kind o' smoke," lured two of his sons to the well from which they haven't returned. Unlike in the case of Mrs. Gardner and Thaddeus, Nahum's "collapse, greying, and disintegration" proceeds rapidly and his mind does not appear compromised by the xeno-agent's immanent self-engineering. It is implied that he does not experience the utter derangement evidenced by the above pair's screaming at each other through the walls and, in young Merwin's account, talking "in some terrible language that was not of earth."[32] The line recounting his submission to demonic overkill is one of Lovecraft's most shocking for its concision: "That which spoke could speak no more because it had completely caved in." This perverse pliancy recalls the texture of the meteorite and suggests a characteristic alteration the thing effects upon its host environment, which has no choice but to yield to its affordance.

As Thacker observes of the demon called "Legion," the Inorganic Demon in *COS* is "never present in [itself], but only via some form of earthly embodiment" by which it announces itself "only indirect-

---

[30] *COS*, 69.
[31] *COS*, 85-86.
[32] *COS*, 80.

ly."[33] Likewise we can say that the symptom expresses the "immediate absence" of the subversive Insider. Its "embodiment is a disembodiment" on two levels: first, it degrades bodies it takes root in and looses their identity unto radical exteriority/the unhuman through the paranecrosis of becoming-it (that is, becoming cosmic non-entity); second, it is encountered on the ground as a field of contagion distributed across diverse vectors of emergence and incommensurate with the limits of any individuated body (a "subterranean consistency" of indeterminate extension and depth). Collectively, symptoms arise from the ungrounding or vermiculate motion of the paranecrotic Insider which signals its presence on the ground "by corrupting the coherency of surfaces."[34]

Geophysical wrongness is experienced as the sudden inability of the landscape to afford the needs of the human; we find it in Adam's penalty, an accursed earth newly acreep with slithery fanged things. Of course, the subsurface activity of ( )hole-complex demands novel strategies for negotiating ground—the solid body of strategy reshaped by the vermiculate functions of void. Cosmic horror depends upon the paralysis of recuperative tactics to sustain the integrity of the violated conceptual scheme, making material disintegration in such works horrific insofar as it becomes a vector for categorical interstitiality. Accordingly, Graham Harman identifies Lovecraft's technique for evoking the weird as partly dependent on dissolving links between objects and their properties,[35] arguing that in Lovecraft's "weird realism,"

---

[33] See Eugene Thacker, *In the Dust of this Planet: Horror of Philosophy Vol. 1* (Winchester, UK: Zero Books, 2011), 29.
[34] *Cyclonopedia,* 43.
[35] See Graham Harman, "On the Horror of Phenomenology: Lovecraft and Husserl," *Collapse* 4 (2008): 358.

> the relation between a thing and its surface is perturbed by irregularities that resist immediate comprehension, as if the object suffered from a strange disease of the nervous system. [...] A rare fissure is generated between the object and its traits. [...] [To] suggest that something is amiss in the expected colour of a wall, something that faintly suggests imminent physical breakdown, is to decompose the usual bond between the phenomenon and the outer forms through which it is announced.[36]

This gap or "fissure" in object-quality continuity conveys the impression that, in the words of the bacterial archaeologist, "'there is something deeply wrong with this thing.'"[37] In Harman's view, such *weirding* exposes a fundamental fault in the hermeneutic assimilation of objects, which is the tendency to conflate intentionality with "surface features" despite the fact that "this intimate bond between object and quality is an illusion."[38] Rather, objects retain a 'deeper,' ever-elusive identity which always exceeds the expressive capacities of the ground. Weird realism is, then, less speculative indulgence than an *eminently* realist affirmation of this disjunction between the positive categories we must use to understand objects and their occulted depth: ignorance of the outside is tantamount to concealment of the *inside*, where strange consistencies ply a ( )holey logic conceivable only in terms of symptomatic horror from without.

The nameless narrator of *COS* is a city surveyor scouting land for a planned reservoir to feed the city of Arkham. Upon arrival he intuits a discomfiting ex-

---

[36] Harman, "On the Horror," 356-357.

[37] *Cyclonopedia*, 64.

[38] Harman, "On the Horror," 355.

cess about the dark glens surrounding in the vicinity of the old Gardner land; the trees grow "too thickly" and their trunks are "too big" to be healthy by local standards, there is "too much" silence among them, the ground is "too soft" with moss and decayed vegetation.[39] This uncanny depth betrays the immediate absence of a chthonic remnant, some persistent subterranean consistency which, if not paranecrotic (ungrounding), at least *weirds* (unhinges) by forging subtle inconsistencies between objects and their expected qualities. He finds a "blasted heath" where the Gardner farm had been, "five acres of grey desolation that *sprawled open to the sky* like a great spot eaten by acid in the woods and fields."[40] The only structure still standing is the old well, a "yawning black maw . . . whose stagnant vapours played strange tricks with the hue of the sunlight"; likewise Ammi Pierce's house, the nearest settlement to the shunned place, exudes "the faint miasmal odour which clings about houses that have stood too long."[41] The narrator's retelling of the Gardner horror is a streamlined version of Ammi's digressive, scientifically-unsure account, which entails that he "bridge over gaps where [Ammi's] sense of logic and continuity broke down."[42] Ammi's tale concludes with the apparent departure of the xeno-agent by rocketing straight up "through a round and curiously regular hole in the clouds" amid a fantastic "riot of luminous amorphousness."[43] This dramatic exit engineers a zone of emergence whereby "black, frore gusts from interstellar space . . . [lash] the fields and distorted woods in a mad cosmic frenzy,"

---

[39] *COS*, 61.
[40] *COS*, 62. My emphasis.
[41] *COS*, 60-62. Perhaps a nod to the "mystic vapor" said to seep from the pestilent tarn surrounding the Usher house.
[42] *COS*, 64.
[43] *COS*, 95.

with earth's atmospheric interior rent radically open in a geoterritorial overkill, "a spectacle staged on the fundamental incapacity of the system to cope with the outside."[44] What remains when the dust settles is the blasted heath, "five eldritch acres of dusty grey desert" inimical to vital growth and tainted with the local memory of earth's opening-unto-cosmos, symptomatic betrayal of the tellurian Insider's conspiracy with the cosmic exterior.

After hearing the tale for himself, the narrator hurries to depart before dark, "unwilling to have the stars come out above [him] in the open,"[45] and returns to Boston to give up his position solely to avoid having to return to the area. Like Ammi, he takes comfort in the fact that after the filling-in of the proposed reservoir, "the blasted heath will slumber far below blue waters whose surface will mirror the sky and ripple in the sun. And the secrets of the strange days will be one with the deep's secrets; one with the hidden lore of old ocean, and all the mystery of primal earth."[46] On the surface, watery inundation reclaims local consistency in the name of vitality by returning the human-centric openness of day-lit sky where the black inconsistency of cosmic exteriority should gape. If we look more deeply, however, we see that the integrity of the local milieu remains compromised by the plane of immanence wrought between the "black extra-cosmic gulfs" and the xeno-particles that persist below the ground,[47] which are soon to be carried east toward new vectors of emergence in Arkham. Since in Lovecraft discovery is a nemat-space of profound horrors, it is perhaps merciful that the narrator makes no attempt to raise the alarm on that city's pending status as the

---

[44] *COS*, 96; *Cyclonopedia*, 118.

[45] *COS*, 64.

[46] *COS,* 60.

[47] *COS* 99, 96.

latest link in the chain of cosmic alienage whose slippage now proceeds not by any rogue messenger from out of space, but rather an "intensive operative of horror from within."[48]

---

[48] *Cyclonopedia*, 203.

Cyclonopedia as Novel (a meditation on complicity as inauthenticity)

Kate Marshall

The found manuscript comprising one *Cyclonopedia*—that is, the "thick piece of writing" that Kristen Alvanson exhumes from under the bed in her Istanbul hotel room bearing the handwritten name of Reza Negarestani—has already begun to deteriorate.[1] Our heroine notes that "everyone in this manuscript seems to disappear without a trace" as she reads of persons who are "characterized by their exit-level."[2] By this description, the closest thing to a character in her somnambulist's treasure is Dr. Hamid Parsani, who has already departed when the manuscript begins.

Parsani is constructed through an assemblage of anonymous remembrances, fragmented writings, and obscure commentary. His "newly discovered notes" are the cause of the "tumultuous discussion" and "feverish excitement" that will form the bulk of the text.[3] At its most banal level, the manuscript *Cyclonopedia* is a posthumous collaboration between Parsani and the distributed anonymous author-collective *Hyperstition*, is narrated by or addressed to the fictional quantity Reza Negarestani, and is edited, introduced,

---

[1] Reza Negarestani, *Cyclonopedia: Complicity with Anonymous Materials* (Melbourne: re.press, 2008), xii.
[2] Negarestani, *Cyclonopedia*, xv.
[3] Negarestani, *Cyclonopedia*, 9.

annotated and ruthlessly deformed by Kristen Alvanson.

This is all to say that *Cyclonopedia* has all of the trappings of a postmodern novel: a self-subverting metafiction that destroys its own grounds even as it enacts them. Its readers will know, too, that to discuss it in this way is perverse. To taxonomize, or to assign even broad periodizing or genre labels such as "postmodern" and "novel" seems quite the opposite of the demands made by "Hidden Writing," which is the kind of book *Cyclonopedia* claims to be. This presents an inescapable paradox: Hidden Writing, we learn, "is not the object of layers and interpretation; it can only be exhumed by distorting the structure of the book or the surface plot."[4] The surface plot, of course, returns us to Kristen Alvanson's discovery of the manuscript, which as an exhumation must mean that the manuscript arrives pre-distorted, for "exhumation includes a process of concrete crypting and decrypting, rewording, bastardization and a changing of the book."[5] It becomes necessary to accept the text's contention that "so-called hermeneutic rigor" will be an unhelpful reading approach. More interesting perhaps is the demand of Hidden Writing for interaction instead of interpretation, to "continue and contribute to the writing process of the book."[6] This is, of course, a demand for complicity.

As a gesture in that direction, I would like to return to the so-called character of Hamid Parsani. Among the revelations of anonymous "secret students," "former friends," and otherwise unattributed scholars of his work is the sense that he was a good academic gone bad. He is found "lacking in the principled behavior expected from a scholar," he is inter-

---

[4] Negarestani, *Cyclonopedia*, 60.
[5] Negarestani, *Cyclonopedia*, 62.
[6] Negarestani, *Cyclonopedia*, 62.

ested in "topics usually entertained only by unhealthily-minded teenagers" and his "recent writings lack his former stylistic prose and sense of highbrow erudition; as if he has been struck by something he cannot digest."[7] His newly discovered notes, which form the occasion for the manuscript, are reported as "more like the contents of [his] office trash can than a notebook of an exceedingly disciplined scholar."[8] We're in on the joke—when Parsani is elaborated on by a named character (Professor Anush Sarchisian), the story changes to "what my other colleagues identify as defective prose or an unscholarly approach is more than anything a quite logical and predictable development . . . into something appropriate to these theories."[9] Strangely enough, it's appropriateness that identifies Parsani with the methodologies of Hidden Writing.

But the task here is to be complicit, and abide both the defectiveness and appropriateness of these reading models and platforms—to find Parsani, as one reviewer of *Cyclonopedia* describes the text, "partly genius, partly quite mad."[10] Another found text—an unattributed article on Parsani's later writings—is said to reveal that "the subjects had been picked with an overly obsessive disciplinary calculation but analyzed according to a decidedly nonconformist approach to academia."[11] This description offers a possible approach to reading *Cyclonopedia* with a fidelity to exhumation that I will take up in the pages that follow. To put it another way, I would like to pursue the nov-

---

[7] Negarestani, *Cyclonopedia*, 11.
[8] Negarestani, *Cyclonopedia*, 9.
[9] Negarestani, *Cyclonopedia*, 11.
[10] Peter Lamborn Wilson, "Partly Genius, Partly Quite Mad: Review of *Cyclonopedia: Complicity with Anonymous Materials*," *Fifth Estate* 44 (2009): 49.
[11] Negarestani, *Cyclonopedia*, 4.

elness of *Cyclonopedia* with something like an overly obsessive disciplinary calculation.

China Miéville begins his brief introduction to *Cyclonopedia* in *World Literature Today* with the provocation that "all literature is genre," a fact he attributes to the "ruthless taxonomizing machines" of human brains that produce and consume it. He sees *Cyclonopedia* as "at once *indelibly* generic" and "unremittingly strange and evasive," locating in the very permanence of protocol the capacity to exceed it.[12] What emerges is a description of *Cyclonopedia* as a novel, but "novel" in scare quotes—something that knows it's a novel far too well, and as if that designation were clear in the first place. In *Cyclonopedia* the strange intelligibility of the novel frame is an important aspect of the kind of discomforts the narrative produces. To be a novel, even in scare quotes, is to be inappropriate to the subject of the text, at least according to the logic of Hidden Writing. For we learn that "if texts with narrative plots and wholesome structures are read and written according to disciplines and procedures conforming to their configurations, then perforated structures, degenerate formations and plot holes must have reading and writing methodologies of their own."[13] This appears to be the unfathomable limit of *Cyclonopedia*'s project: the line at which its fictional entities cease to become real.

One disciplinary calculation would be to consider contextual models for considering this limit, or to form another set of plot holes in this description of the text. To turn to recent anthologies of novel history and theory that bill the novel unironically as "the first truly planetary literary form," a gesture often worthy of resistance, feels a little different in the context of *Cy-*

---

[12] China Miéville, "Fiction by Reza Negarestani," *World Literature Today* 84 (2010): 12.
[13] Negarestani, *Cyclonopedia*, 60.

clonopedia.[14] So too does turning within to an extended essay on "The Rise of Fictionality" to look for an old model of reading the genre of a piece that demands precisely its opposite. What emerges in the essay is an acknowledgement of a standard definition of a novel, that is, "a long, fictional, prose narrative," that makes no sense without a fully articulated concept of fictionality, which because "dormant" proves significantly more evasive.[15] But the question is not what *Cyclonopedia* is, but rather how: *How* is *Cyclonopedia* a novel, and how does it enact its fictionality? The historian of the form cited above, Catherine Gallagher, would have us look to both, and thus confirm its novelness in its fictionality. For, she says, "The historical connection between the terms *novel* and *fiction* is intimate; they were mutually constitutive."[16] While invoking the structure of historical connection in *Cyclonopedia* is a gesture of incorrectness, that is precisely the point: to bring this story of intimacy of novel and fiction into contact, to recontextualize it, can here be a local practice of "active inauthenticity."[17] Theory-fiction, incidentally, does not appear in this account, but in this context is perhaps a redundancy. Gallagher's discussion of fictionality, in addition, declares itself an "inquiry into the affective appeal of the novelistic nonentity."[18] Although appeal is not our business here, the novelistic nonentity just might be. Or, more precisely, the novelistic nonentity that persists in its own becoming.

---

[14] See *The Novel, vol. 1: History, Geography, Culture*, ed. Franco Moretti (Princeton: Princeton University Press, 2006).
[15] Catherine Gallagher, "The Rise of Fictionality," in *The Novel*, 336-361.
[16] Gallagher, "Rise of Fictionality," 337.
[17] Negarestani, *Cyclonopedia*, 61.
[18] Gallagher, "Rise of Fictionality," 356.

But the novelistic nonentity remains an illusion consigned to the "narrative plots and wholesome structures" that in *Cyclonopedia* produce conformist procedures inadequate to what is identified as "the lines of emergence associated with the porous earth, hole agencies and terminally political and insurgent formations."[19] This version of fictionality disappears in the nonentity—it becomes occluded, invisible, or as Gallagher puts it, "that which goes without saying."[20] Making it visible re-consigns fiction to a feature of novels in this history, whereas in *Cyclonopedia*, the novel becomes a feature of the fiction that "makes itself real," or makes itself.[21] But extracted from its constraints, the novelistic nonentity harbors the occult knowledge of fictionality that is almost always strange. This self-knowledge of fiction makes itself known everywhere; although we overlook the blocked sewers and clogged channels of wholesome plots, these infrastructures embrace their burial through refusal—as noise, irritation, and disruption. They form the architecture of the banal.

Consider the following moment from a small piece of regional American fiction, the 1977 story "Trilobites" by the West Virginian writer Breece D'J Pancake: "I feel way too mean to say anything. I look across the railroad to a field sown in timothy. There are wells there, pumps to suck the ancient gases. The gas burns blue, and I wonder if the ancient sun was blue. The tracks run on till they're a dot on the brown haze. They give off clicks from their switches. Some tankers wait on the spur. Their wheels are rusting to the tracks. I wonder what to hell I ever wanted with

---

[19] Negarestani, *Cyclonopedia*, 60.
[20] Gallagher, "Rise of Fictionality," 349.
[21] See Negarestani, *Cyclonopedia*, xiv: "Hyperstition, a term loosely defined as fictional quantities that make themselves real."

trilobites."[22] Rather than begin with the "I" in this passage, who takes in the scene of natural gas drilling as an escape from his anomie, we reverse the gaze. The "ancient gas" being unearthed from the rural hills burns blue, it acts, it evokes. It slows down time, so that the line, "their wheels are rusting to the tracks," describing the tankers waiting to be filled with the product of the wells, is of unclear origin. There is no interpretive payoff to pausing on the brief agency of the ancient gases in this passage—that would be more likely found in the narrator's wondering, in which he speculates about the color of the ancient sun he sees evoked by the gas plume, and in the same gesture puts an end to his interest in fossilized remains. "I wonder what the hell I ever wanted with trilobites" is certainly not a commitment to further investigation.

Worth pointing out here is the title attributed to the avatar of *Cyclonopedia* published with Miéville's introduction in *World Literature Today*. It reads as follows: "Outlines for a Science Fiction of the Earth as Narrated from a Nethermost Point of View." What is immediately interesting about this title is its slight of hand, perfectly in keeping with the contradictory narratologies of *Cyclonopedia*. It describes a fiction, a fact of narration, and a point of view. But unlike, for example, the definition of "world petropolitics" as "earth as narrated by oil," or even oil as organizer of the earth's narrations, something else is going on. The phrase "Earth as narrated by oil" has a subject earth, and a narrator, oil. Narrated by oil. But a "fiction of the earth as narrated from a nethermost point of view" has no narrator. It is not narrated "by" any one or thing. Or if it is, this science fiction of the earth is nar-

---

[22] Breece D'J Pancake, "Trilobites," in *The Stories of Breece D'J Pancake* (New York: Back Bay Books, 2002), 33. Thanks to Matt Coyne for introducing me to these stories.

rated by the point of view itself. But can a point of view narrate, even in *Cyclonopedia*?

I think that the answer must be of course, and not at all. It is a corruption of point of view as a narratological category, and can be further corrupted. Wayne C. Booth's canonical essay from 1961, "Distance and Point of View: an Essay in Classification," offers another tunnel. Booth is worried in the essay about rules for novels and their narrators. He notes that "since novelist's choices are in fact practically unlimited, in judging their effectiveness we can only fall back on the kind of reasoning used by Aristotle in the *Poetics*: *if* such-and-such effect is desired, *then* such-and-such points-of-view will be good or bad."[23] This is also a definition of the novel as producer of effects that can be in themselves more or less effective. And the effect, moreover is too tied to an idea of an underlying reality; for, he says, "All novels are said to be aiming for a common degree of realistic intensity; ambiguity and irony are discussed as if they were always beauties, never blemishes. Point-of-view should always be used 'consistently,' because otherwise the realistic illusion will be destroyed."[24] The escape he desires from fidelity and effectiveness is an "abstract rule" that would separate the novel from what he calls "the needs of particular works or kinds."[25] But it is the explicit conjuncture of particularity and desire that drives the project of Hyperstitional narratology in *Cyclonopedia*. Part of the interesting difficulty in drawing the contours of that narratology in the text is something that Booth's more general concerns make visible: the ways that point of view becomes both topic and act. Or put

---

[23] Wayne Booth, "Distance and Point-of-View: An Essay in Classification," in *Narrative/Theory*, ed. David H. Richter (New York: Longman, 1995), 142.
[24] Booth, "Distance and Point-of-View," 142.
[25] Booth, "Distance and Point-of-View," 142.

another and more delightful way, *Cyclonopedia's* self-identified "blobjective" narrative viewpoint is articulated from the blobjective point of view. Its effectiveness, should such a thing be desired, can be measured only to the degree that it describes itself from within. In these terms even Gertrude Stein would have encountered *Cyclonopedia* as a novel in her own lectures on narration, for she says, "The more a novel is a novel . . . the more a writing is a writing the more no outside is outside outside is inside inside is inside."[26]

What distinguishes narrative viewpoints, and narrators themselves for Booth ultimately is the category of distance. This distance is a measure of separation of the observer or reflector from what he designates as "the author, the reader, and the other characters of the story they relate or reflect," and can also be captured by the idea of "tone."[27] Booth remains tied to persons, but the coupling of distance and tone produces an interesting conjuncture in the narratology of *Cyclonopedia*.

The point of view embraced and enacted is both a subject and a position. Petroleum, the "sentient entity" narrates, but from a "nethermost" point of view.[28] And this too is unstable, because petroleum is the point of view itself. It is its distance below. The distance captures the spatiality of Hidden Writing beyond subterranean structures and holes, or in addition to them, as the "undercover softness" of decay.[29] And, finally, it looks from without, and from an innermost point of view. What *Cyclonopedia* does is locate what

---

[26] Gertrude Stein, *Narration* (Chicago: University of Chicago Press, 2010).
[27] Booth, 146, 148.
[28] See Negarestani in Miéville, "Fiction by Reza Negarestani," 13.
[29] Reza Negarestani, "Undercover Softness: An Introduction to the Architecture and Politics of Decay," *Collapse* 6 (2010).

Mieke Bal's famous narratological intervention into the point-of-view debates, "focalization," would separate from point of view and refine. The labels "point of view," "narrative perspective," or "narrative viewpoint" are all insufficient for Bal because they fail to distinguish between voice and vision, or "those who see and those who speak."[30] She offers her revision of point of view as a discussion of mediation, arguing, for example, that "the relation between the sign (the relief) and its contents (the fabula), can only be established by the mediation of an interjacent layer, the view of the events . . . Focalization is the relationship between the 'vision,' the agent that sees, and that which is seen."[31] Once again, this is the wrong story, a reading model designed for the wrong reading platform. It explicitly cannot attend to what appears in *Cyclonopedia* as "the course of emergence in any medium" which "corresponds to the formation of that medium," so that "the more agitated the line of emergence becomes, the more convoluted and complex the host medium must be."[32] But there is a glimmer in Bal's account of something that might be extracted and reconfigured as an element of a lurking prehistory of the narrative science of *Cyclonopedia*, and this can be found in her brief acknowledgement of the possibility of external focalization, or a mediation by what she describes as "an anonymous agent, situated outside the fabula," who functions as a focalizer in the narrative. This anonymous agent is both "external" to the narrative, and "non-character-bound."[33] This agent, simply waiting to be multiplied, then fades into the background, waiting to be reconfigured in a radically

---

[30] Mieke Bal, "Focalization," in *Narrative/Theory*, 154.
[31] Bal, "Focalization," 155.
[32] Negarestani, *Cyclonopedia,* 53.
[33] Bal, "Focalization," 156.

exteriorized "maze of interiorities."[34] Or, perhaps, what Joyelle McSweeney's boroque noir fiction *Nylund, the Sarcographer* announces as the method, point of view, and subject of sarcography, an ornate mode of comprehension "from the outside."[35] Another view of the "solid" as "the possessed narrator of the void."[36]

My modeling of "obsessive disciplinary calculation" aims not to provide a recognizable reading of *Cyclonopedia*, but rather a reading model that extends *Cyclonopedia*'s narratological productions by corrupting them with the contagions of the taxonomies it so deliriously rejects. And more than that, to see *Cyclonopedia* as a form of narrative thinking that can travel. To return to the exploded intimacies of novels and fictionality in their artificial disciplinary constraints, what I find compelling is how that intimacy continues and is overtly thematized in *Cyclonopedia* through its very end, in Parsani's "abysmal depths of love."[37]

---

[34] Negarestani, "Undercover Softness," 385.
[35] Joyelle McSweeney, *Nylund, the Sarcographer* (Grafton: Tarpaulin Sky Press, 2007).
[36] Negarestani, *Cyclonopedia*, 45.
[37] Negarestani, *Cyclonopedia*, 220.

What is a Hermeneutic Light?

Alexander R. Galloway

Of the many unresolved debates surrounding the work of Martin Heidegger, one often returns to an elemental question: is Heideggerian phenomenology ultimately a question of hermeneutics and interpretation, or is it ultimately a question of immanence and truth? Is *Dasein* forever questing after a Being that withdraws, or does it somehow achieve a primordial communion with the truth of Being?

Hermeneutics has been a dominant methodology for the tradition of theory and critique dating to the 1960s. Hence it is not surprising that Heidegger, who was being rediscovered and rethought during that period, would often be framed in terms of hermeneutics. To be sure, the critical tradition handed down from poststructuralism leaves little room for modes of immanence and immediacy, modes that were marginalized as essentialist or otherwise unpleasant (often for good reason). Thus it would be easy to assimilate a figure like Heidegger, with his complicated withdrawings of Being, into the tradition of hermeneutics. For where else would he fit? And one will admit that Heidegger is *typically* categorized within this tradition. But is it not also possible to show that Heidegger is a philosopher of immanence? That he speaks as much to illumination as to withdrawal? That he speak as much to the intuitive and proximate as to the detached and distanced?

For instance, one might return to his notion of *gelichtet*, a word stemming from the noun for "light."

In the chapter on the "there" in *Being and Time*, Heidegger speaks of *Dasein* as *lumen* (one of two Latin words meaning "light"), and defines *Dasein* in terms of the "clearing" (*gelichtet*) or "illumination" of Being.

> When we talk in an ontically figurative way of the *lumen naturale* in man, we have in mind nothing other than the existential-ontological structure of this entity, that it *is* in such a way as to be its "there". To say that it is 'illuminated' ["erleuchtet"] means that *as* Being-in-the-world it is cleared [gelichtet] in itself, not through any other entity, but in such a way that it *is* itself the clearing.[1]

Certainly it is true that Being is cryptological in Heidegger, in other words that Being "likes to hide itself." But this is far outweighed by the fact that *Dasein* can indeed be experienced as an authentic disclosedness of Being, by the fact that phenomenology preaches—without irony or pathos—that one may strive "toward the things themselves" and actually arrive at them.

Recall that hermeneutics is the science of suspicion, the science of the insincere. But Heidegger, like Socrates before him, is the consummate philosopher of sincerity. The phenomenological subject is the one who has an authentic and sincere relationship with Being. Because of this, one should not be too quick to consign Heidegger to the history of hermeneutics. Hermes' home terrain was that of deception; his economies were economies in the absence of trust. But that is not Heidegger's terrain.

---

[1] Martin Heidegger, *Being and Time*, trans. John Macquarrie and Edward Robinson (New York: Harper and Row, 1962), 171.

Thus running in parallel to the Heidegger of Hermes, the Heidegger who touches on the tradition of interpretation and exchange in the face of the withdrawal of Being, there is also a Heidegger of Iris, the Heidegger who touches on the tradition of illumination and iridescence along the pathway of seeking. Heidegger's is not simply a narrative following Hermes, but also an arc following Iris.

When Heidegger evokes the *lumen naturale* of man he is making reference to one of two kinds of light. The light of man is a terrestrial light. When bodies with their *anima* (their vital force) are vigorous and alive, they are illuminated with the light of the *lumen naturale*. *Lumen* is the light of life, the light of this world, the light that sparkles from the eyes of consciousness.

But there is another kind of light. Being carries its own kind of light that is not the light of man. This light is a cosmological light, a divine light, the light of the phenomena. Light as grace.

So just as there are two Heideggers, there are also two lights. One light is the light of transparent bodies, clear and mobile. This light is the light of this world, experienced through passage and illumination. But the other light is the light of opaque bodies. It is the light of color, a holy light, experienced only through reflection and indirection.

THE BEING OF LIGHT

Given such an entrance, and given that the question has been broached regarding the two kinds of light, it is impossible to resist the question that follows: if there exists a natural lightness, is there not also a natural darkness? And if there are two kinds of light are there not also two kinds of dark?

Such a question lies at the heart of Reza Negarestani's *Cyclonopedia: Complicity With Anonymous Materials*. Oil is the Black Corpse of the Sun, he writes.[2] Oil is black, in color if not also in its moral decrepitude. But oil is also light, because it is a transmutation of the light of the sun. Oil is the geological product of sunlight having transitioned via photosynthesis into vegetable matter, that matter itself having been decomposed.

Before looking more closely at the two kinds of darkness, let us examine the two kinds of lightness a bit further. Negarestani writes about fog and light. He writes about the "mistmare." But what is mist? He writes of Pazuzu, the wind, the dust enforcer. But what is dust?

Of course, dust and fog have certain obfuscatory qualities. They strangle the light and interfere with one's ability to see. But at the same time they have their own form of luminosity. Fog glows with a certain ambience. It transforms a space of absolute coordinates into a proximal zone governed by thresholds of intelligibility. (Fog is thus first and foremost a category of existence. There can be no *ontological* fog. For that we will introduce a new term.) Fog is a dioptric phenomenon, even if ironically it acts to impede vision. It is a question of light passing through materials, and likewise a question of the light of man passing through (or being impeded from passing through) a proximal space. This means that fog is part of the *luminaria*. Fog gives off no light of its own, even if it has its own luminosity by virtue of filtering and passing along a light originating from elsewhere.

*

---

[2] Reza Negarestani, *Cyclonopedia: Complicity With Anonymous Materials* (Melbourne: re.press, 2008), 26.

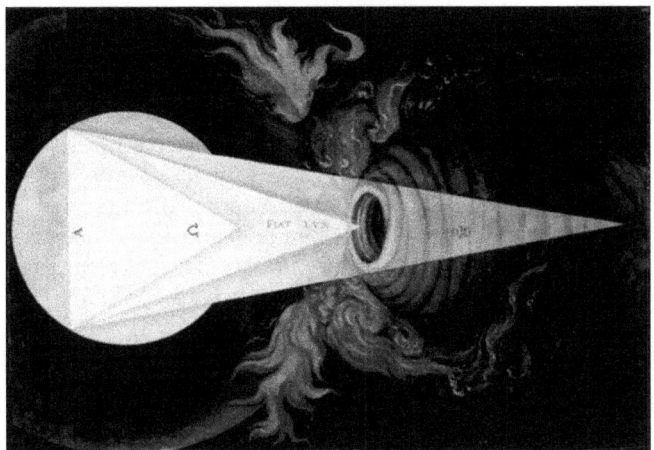

Figure 1. Diagram of catoptrics, illustrating the hermeneutic light. Source: Francisco de Holanda, "*Fiat lux*" ("Let there be light"), Genesis 1.3, Day 1, *De Aetatibus Mundi Imagines* (1543-1573).

The term "dioptric" has been broached, and in order to continue it will be necessary to define this term in some detail, particularly by way of its sister term "catoptric." These two terms are part of the science of optics, and hence the being of light, but they describe the dealings of light in two very different ways.

Dioptrics refers to light when it is *refracted*, that is to say, when light passes through transparent materials such as glass or water. As a branch of optical science, dioptrics is concerned principally with *lenses*. Yet things not specifically conceived as lenses can also act as such. The best examples for our purposes are the tiny water droplets contained in clouds, which being spherical in shape, allow light passing through them to refract twice, once as the light enters the droplet and again as it leaves. Prisms also offer a fine illustration of dioptric phenomena; the prism splits light into color bands because of the fact that different wavelengths of light refract differently. A dioptric device can therefore divide white light into colored light, just as it can merge colored light into white light again, given the right conditions.

On the other hand, catoptrics refers to light when it is *reflected*, that is to say, when light bounces off objects in the world. Whereas dioptrics is concerned with lenses, catoptrics is concerned principally with *mirrors*. All sorts of objects can act as mirrors proper—polished glass or metal, the surface of water—but one must also consider the duller quasi-mirror effects of plain objects themselves, which reflect light and allow themselves to be visible to the eye. Just as the prism can produce what Goethe called "physical color," there is also a color capacity in catoptric phenomena, as some objects reflect certain colors and absorb others (Goethe's "chemical color"). So if, in general, prisms and lenses are the emblematic devices for dioptrics, mirrors, screens, opaque surfaces, and walls are the emblematic devices for catoptrics.

In short, the former is a question of transparency, while the latter is a question of opacity. Dioptrics is a *perspective* (seeing through), while catoptrics is a *speculum* or *aspect* (reflecting, looking at).[3]

---

[3] Athanasius Kircher was known to have a catoptric chest "completely filled with a treasure of all sorts of delicacies, fruits, and precious ornaments," as described by his student Kaspar Schott: "You will exhibit the most delightful trick if you [introduce into the chest] a live cat, as Fr. Kircher has done. While the cat sees himself to be surrounded by an innumerable multitude of catoptric cats, some of them standing close to him and others spread very far away from him, it can hardly be said how many jokes will be exhibited in that theatre, while he sometimes tries to follow the other cats, sometimes to entice them with his tail, sometimes attempts a kiss, and indeed tries to break through the obstacles in every way with his claws so that he can be united with the other cats, until finally, with various noises, and miserable whines he declares his various affections of

Now a bit more light can be shed on the opening remarks concerning Heidegger. Recall the god of so many aspects, so many epithets. He is Hermes, messenger to Zeus. And yet his counterpart Iris, messenger to Hera, has relatively few; her business is that of shining through. In this way Hermes is the aspect god, the god of catoptrics, and Iris is the perspective goddess, the goddess of dioptrics. The effects of refraction "remain within" a transparent physical object such as a glass lens, and hence are to be considered a phenomenon of immanence. By contrast the effects of reflection are to obscure the source object, to leverage the very opacity of the object for some other end, and hence they are to be considered a phenomenon of hermeneutics.

These same principles can be stated in different terms. Both dioptrics and catoptrics have a special relationship to depth, however the distinction between the two could not be more stark. Reflection is *semiotically* deep, that is, it is deep in the domain of meaning, whereas refraction is *experientially* deep, that is, it is deep in the domain of subjective experience. Saying *semiotically* deep means that opaque reflection creates a depth model wherein two opposing layers, one manifest and one latent, work together to create meaning. This is the same depth model that exists in Freud or Marx. Saying *experientially* deep means that transparent refraction creates a depth model wherein a real sense of volumetric space is cre-

---

indignation, rage, jealousy, love and desire." See Georgio de Sepibus, *Romani Collegii Musaeum Celeberrimum...* and Kaspar Schott, *Magia Universalis,* quoted in Michael John Gorman and Nick Wilding, "Techica Curiosa: The Mechanical Marvels of Kaspar Schott (1608-1666)," in Kaspar Schott, *La "Technica Curiosa"* (Florence: Edizioni dell'Elefante, 2000), 260, 274.

ated and presented to a viewing subject. This is the same depth model that exists in Heidegger (or even in others like Immanuel Kant). There are veils covering the soul, but there are also telescopes for viewing the heavens—the one is aspect, the other perspective.

Yet beyond exhibiting depth in two contrasting ways, they are also equally distinct in how they deal with flatness. Being semiotically deep, catoptric reflection is at the same time *ontically* flat. That is to say, reflection is, in its real physical existence, manifest in two-dimensional surfaces and other flat things arranged in the world. The very existence of the reflected image is a flat existence. Dioptric refraction, on the other hand, being experientially deep, is at the same time *ontologically* flat. That is to say, refraction is immanent to materials; there is no transcendent or metaphysical cause that operates across or after the being of the phenomenon. This is why whatever is immanent also must be flat. This variety of flatness is best understood as a flatness of identity, a selfsame quality vis-a-vis the being of the thing. Dioptric refraction, as iridescent immanence, "remains within" itself.

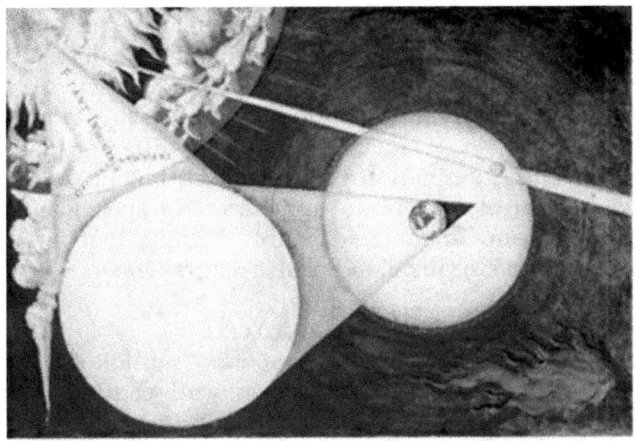

Figure 2. Diagram of dioptrics, illustrating the iridescent light. Source: Francisco de Holanda, "*Fiant luminaria in firmamento celi*" ("Let there be lights in the firmament of heaven"), Genesis 1.14, Day 4, *De Aetatibus Mundi Imagines* (1543-1573).

These claims, being somewhat abstract, should be explained a little further. One has asserted that dioptrics is experiential. What this means is that dioptrics is on the side of the subject. Dioptrics is always a question of crafting a clear or real subjective experience. This is why the concept of dioptric illumination is so closely associated with the modern period, why we refer to "the Enlightenment," which the French render even more simply as *les Lumières*. But it is also why this same modern trajectory ends up at Kantianism, at romanticism, and eventually at Heidegger and phenomenology, for the question of subjective experience must always remain at the heart of the modern experience. But by contrast, we said previously that catoptrics is semiotic. What this means is that catoptrics is on the side of matter, on the side of the *pharmakon*. Catoptrics is always a question of meaning. While subjects are involved in the process, it is never primarily subjective. It is, rather, primarily a question of what Bernard Stiegler terms hypomnesis, the act of externalizing the subject, or to be more precise, the subject's *memory*, into material supports. This too is a modern trajectory, but it ends up at a different place: not in the illumination of the subject, but in the obscurantism of the culture industries, in spectacle, in ideology, and in the tradition of critique that terminates in structuralism and poststructuralism.

FIANT LUMINARIA IN FIRMAMENTO CELI

Jesuit mathematician François d'Aguilon, in two propositions from his early-seventeenth-century opus on optics *Opticorum Libri Sex*, offers two additional points concerning the difference between dioptric transparency and catoptric opacity. The two points appear in propositions number 31 and 32 of book one:

> Proposition 31 – *Lux* [light] and color are the properties of an opaque body.
> Proposition 32 – *Lumen* [illumination, luminosity] is the action of a transparent body.[4]

As was already broached at the outset, the ancients distinguished between two types of light: in Latin *lux* and *lumen*, or in Hebrew *Or* (אור) and *Orot* (אורות). These two kinds of light are again distinguished here by d'Aguilon across these two propositions.

The difference between the two is nicely expressed in the echo that occurs between Genesis 1.3 and 1.14, when God creates light, and then creates it again. The first time light comes into the world it comes as *lux*. This *lux* means light, but it is a special kind of light, the light of being, the light of God, a

---

[4] Franciscus Aguilonius, *Opticorum Libri Sex, philosophis juxta ac mathematicis utiles* (Antwerp: Plantin Press, 1613), Book 1, 31, 33.

cosmological light. The second time light comes, it comes as *lumen* (or rather as *luminaria*, the things that show *lumen*). This *lumen* also means light, but it is much more specific. It is the sun, moon and stars, the bodies that give light in as much as they can shine through with the divine light.

Although we differentiate between light and luminosity, the English language often loses the subtly between these two kinds of light. D'Aguilon assigns the first term to opaque bodies, and thus, by association one may be certain that he speaks of catoptric phenomenon. The second he assigns to transparent bodies, and thus to dioptric phenomenon. So, in short, *lux* is catoptric and *lumen* dioptric.

There is a precedence here too: Just as the renaissance preceded the baroque, *lux* precedes *lumen*, and catoptrics precedes dioptrics.[5] (The firstness of Iris arrives, then, as a kind of miracle, scrapping all precedence, erasing diachrony for synchrony.)

God then, bearing the *lux* light of the cosmological fiat, is absolute in His opacity. God is the absolute source of light, but at the same time the one who is absolutely inaccessible. Opacity is the quality that we can assign to His being. Yet, the light of *lumen*--illumination, luminosity--is absolute in its transparency, as it travels through the actually existing world. Thus transparency is the quality that we can assign to His existing.

---

[5] A few years after d'Aguilon, Descartes would confirm this same sentiment, as Martin Jay points out in his book *Downcast Eyes*, quoting a 1638 letter written by Descartes: "Light, that is, *lux*, is a movement or an action in the luminous body, and tends to cause some movement in transparent bodies, namely *lumen*. Thus *lux* is before *lumen*." See Martin Jay, *Downcast Eyes: The Denigration of Vision in Twentieth-Century French Thought* (Berkeley: University of California Press, 1994), 73.

And this is the second point that can be gained from d'Aguilon's two propositions, that *lumen* or dioptrics is always an *action* of existence, an active motion of looking-throughness, while *lux* or catoptrics is always a fact of being (a *property*).

THE BLACK CORPSE OF THE SUN

Now we are in a better position to consider the kinds of darkness and their relationship to the light. To summarize, illumination (*lumen*) refers to the action of transparent bodies in their luminosity and radiant iridescence. These are the sun, the moon and stars, bodies, man, and fire. Not white so much as bright. This is the light of life and consciousness. It is multiple, never singular. It is a perspective, and therefore allied with dioptrics and Iris. By contrast, light (*lux*) refers to the property of an opaque body in its fact of being. This is the light of God, the light of being, a cosmological light, but also the light of daytime (as opposed to sunlight). It is an aspect, and therefore allied with catoptrics and Hermes. It is singular, never multiple. Only white in so much as it is the whiteness of pure opacity. *Lux* is the plenum. It is the obscure. It is grace.

Now to darkness, for here too there are two modalities of darkness, all the more different because of their near identity. Darkness may be gloom, murkiness, shadow, or shade. It may be dusk, night, or twilight. Bodies may be dark, or one might speak of "dark" materials, in as much as they are asleep, unconsciousness, dead, or cold. Likewise habit or cliché may be understood as a kind of darkness of experience, an inability to revivify the normal routine of one's life.

Hence the darkening, or *obscuritas*, spoken about in Revelation: *obscuratus est sol et aer de fumo putei*, "the sun was darkened, and the air, by the smoke of the pit" (Revelation 9:2). The sun is obscured by smoke, and hence the earth-bound shadows of an obscuring darkness. As the sun and moon and stars are progressively snuffed out, they are *obscurare*. One is not yet experiencing an ontological darkness, but rather the darkness of this world. This is the *nihil privativum* discussed in Schopenhauer, the "privative nothing" that is dark by virtue of depriving the light.

But there is another kind of darkness, the *tenebrae*, the shadows of black Being separated from the *lux* of heaven in Genesis (2, 4, 5, and 18). Now no longer simply dark, one must speak instead of *blackness*. Such is the infinite darkness of the abyss, the void and vacuum, the darkness of catastrophe and cataclysm. It is a cosmological blackness, the black of Satan, the black of absolute evil, the black of nonbeing. It is what Eugene Thacker in his essay on "Three Questions on Demonology" describes as "cosmic pessimism . . . hermeticism of the abyss."[6] The shadows of black Being are a hermeneutic blackness. This is not simply a world gone dark, but a world-without-us. It is not simply a question of dying or growing cold, it is a question of leaving being. In contrast to the "privative nothing" one may now invoke Schopenhauer's *nihil negativum* (negative nothing), nothing as absolute foreclosure. In this sense, the shadows of black Being are not part of any ontology, but rather constitute a *crypto-ontology*. These are the shadows of the *kruptos* (κρυπτός), the hidden parts that form the inward nature of things.

And in Revelation, beyond the sun being obscured and made dark, there is also a secondary darkness. For the kingdom of heaven is additionally threatened by the blackness of the *tenebrae*: *factum est*

---

[6] Eugene Thacker, "Three Questions on Demonology," in *Hideous Gnosis: Black Metal Theory Symposium 1*, ed. Nicola Masciandaro (New York: n.p., 2010), 186 [179-219].

regnum eius tenebrosum, "his kingdom was full of darkness" (Revelation 16:10).

Is oil, as putrification, the product of *lux* or *lumen*? Is oil black or dark? As Negarestani writes, oil is "Hydrocarbon Corpse Juice." Sun is captured in photosynthesis, then via decay is putrified into a liquid fossil form. So as sun juice, oil is the darkening of sunlight. In this sense oil is dead; oil is death. And as transubstantiated sunlight, oil is *lumen*, or at least some product thereof.

But there is also a blackness to oil; oil is also black. "Oil is the Black Corpse of the Sun," he writes. Now no longer simply solar, oil's tellurian core wells up, the insurgent enemy of solar capitalism. This is oil at its blackest. This is oil as the "Devil's Excrement." This is oil as the conspirator—as the *tenebra* or shadow of black Being, in contradistinction to *lux*—who annihilates societies by "tear[ing] them apart slowly."[7] And so, just as it was possible to speak of the shadows of black Being as a crypto-ontology, one must begin to speak of a crypto-ontology for oil. In such a crypto-ontology, oil is understood not simply as dark but as infinite blackness, held in escrow by a cosmic pessimism, with its *kruptos* or hidden parts absolutely foreclosed to us, but also to Being itself.

---

[7] Negarestani, *Cyclonopedia*, 28.

Black Infinity; or, Oil Discovers Humans

Eugene Thacker

In 1964, the horror and fantasy author Fritz Leiber published a short story entitled "Black Gondolier," which appeared in the Arkham House anthology *Over the Edge*, and was subsequently reprinted in the Ace Double volume *Night Monsters*. In this story, an unnamed narrator tells of the mysterious disappearance of his friend Daloway, a recluse and autodidact living nearby oil fields in southern California. Daloway, it seems, began to develop a bizarre and unnatural fascination with oil—not just as a natural resource, and not just as something of geopolitical value, but with oil in itself as an ancient and enigmatic manifestation of the hidden world. Over time Daloway's conversations with the narrator begin to take on the form of mystical visions, described by Daloway as a kind of gothic, funereal ooze:

> . . . that black and nefarious essence of all life that had ever been, constituting in fact a great deep-digged black graveyard of the ultimate eldritch past with blackest ghosts, oil had waited for hundreds of millions of years, dreaming its black dreams, sluggishly pulsing beneath Earth's stony skin, quivering in lightless pools roofed with marsh gas and in top-filled rocky tanks and coursing through a myriad channels . . . [1]

The image of oil as stealthily waiting gives the ooze the vague quality of intelligence and intent—and, more specifically, of malefic intent. In Leiber's hyperbolic prose, oil is not the type of ooze that we see in Cold War monster movies, where the ooze remains hidden beneath the surface of the Earth. Instead, in "Black Gondolier" oil is described as an animate, creeping ooze that already is on the surface, and that immanently courses through all the channels of modern industrial civilization, from the central pipelines feeding major cities, to the individual homes and cars that populate those cities. At one point in the story, the narrator attempts to put Daloway's rather crackpot theories into coherent form:

---

[1] Fritz Leiber, "Black Gondolier," in *Night Monsters* (New York: Ace, 1969), 14.

> Daloway's theory, based on his wide readings in world history, geology, and the occult, was that crude oil—petroleum—was more than figuratively the life-blood of industry and the modern world and modern lightening-war, that it truly had a dim life and will of its own, an inorganic consciousness or sub-consciousness, that we were all its puppets or creatures, and that its chemical mind had guided and even enforced the development of modern technological civilization . . . [2]

"In brief," the narrator concludes, "Daloway's theory was that man hadn't discovered oil, but that oil had found man."[3]

At the center of Leiber's story is an inversion that takes place between human beings and an enigmatic, something else that constitutes a horizon for human thought. Let us call this "something else" the *unhuman*. The unhuman is not simply that which is not human, be it animals, machines, oceans, or cities, though all of these play a role in Leiber's story. The unhuman is also not that which is made human, in which we would have featherless, bipedal walking and talking lumps of oil—though even this is hinted at in Leiber's story as well. The unhuman is distinct from these two ways of thinking—anthropocentrism and anthropomorphism, respectively.

What then is the unhuman? It is, first of all, a limit without reserve, something that one is always arriving at, but which is never circumscribed within the ambit of human thought. In Leiber's story, we see at least four stages by which one encounters the unhuman:

---

[2] Leiber, "Black Gondolier," 14.
[3] Leiber, "Black Gondolier," 15.

At the first level, we encounter the unhuman only as it exists for the human. This is the normative world of modern industrial capitalism described by Daloway in the story. At this level, the unhuman is everything that is for us and for our benefit as human beings, living in human cultures, and bearing some unilateral and instrumental relation to the world around us. This relation between human and unhuman relies upon an *anthropic subversion*. The unhuman is only that which exists within the scope of the human; in a sense, there is no outside of the human, in so far as the unhuman is always fully encompassed by human knowledge and technics. At this level, the unhuman is everything that is subject to and produced by human knowledge. At this level, anthropocentrism overlaps almost perfectly with anthropomorphism.

But Leiber's story steadily moves towards a second level, which explores a notion of the unhuman through an inversion of the relation between human and unhuman. The key phrase in Leiber's story is the following: "man hadn't discovered oil, but . . . oil had found man." We don't use oil, oil uses us. Note that a relation of unilateralism still exists, except that it has been reversed. Instead of human beings making use of the planet for their own ends, the planet is revealed to be making use of human beings for its own ends. Humans are simply a way for the planet to produce and reproduce itself. Clearly, with this sort of epiphany all bets are off—one can no longer regard the human endeavors of science, technology, and economy in quite the same way. But the terms of this relation are still "human"—intentionality, instrumental rationality, and even a touch of malice are attributed to the anonymous ooze of oil. It is as if the unhuman can only be understood through the lens of the human. We can call this the *anthropic inversion*. The anthropic inversion allows for a concept of the unhuman to emerge, but it is ultimately recuperated within the ambit of human categories, such as intelligence and intentionality.

Towards the end of Leiber's story, this anthropic inversion undergoes another turn, leading to a third level where the unhuman is encountered. As Daloway is weirdly carried off into the viscous night where oil and nocturnal darkness merge into one, effacing all horizon lines in a miasmatic, black blur, Daloway's own individuation slips away and is engulfed, and at this moment he realizes that the human categories of life, mind, and technics are themselves simply one manifestation of the unhuman. In other words, as opposed to the anthropic inversion (human don't use oil, oil uses humans), here Daloway experiences another kind of inversion, an *ontogenic inversion* in which everything human is revealed to be one instance of the unhuman. The ontogenic inversion is both ontological and ontogenetic, at once the evisceration of thought from the human, as well as an epiphany about the essentially unhuman qualities of the human. In the ontogenic inversion, the human is only one instance of the unhuman.

At this point thought falters, and here we enter a fourth stage that we can call *misanthropic subtraction*. At this point, thought falters, and language can only continue by way of an apophatic use of negative terms ("nameless," "formless," "lifeless"), which are themselves doomed to failure. This failure is leveraged with great effect in the literary tradition of supernatural horror and weird fiction. Authors such as Algernon Blackwood, William Hope Hodgson, and of course H.P. Lovecraft excel at driving language to this breaking point. Here one notices two strategies that are often used, often in concert with each other. There is a strategy of minimalism, in which language is stripped of all its attributes, leaving only skeletal phrases such as "the nameless thing," "the shapeless thing," or "the unnamable" (which is also the title of a Lovecraft story). There is also a strategy of hyperbole, in which the unknowability of the unhuman is expressed through a litany of baroque descriptors, all of which ultimately fail to inscribe the unhuman within human thought and language. Some examples from Lovecraft follow:

> . . . the rayless gloom with Miltonic legions of the misshapen damned . . .
> . . . the nameless bands of abhorrent elder-world hierophants . . .
> . . . brooding, half-material, alien Things that festered in earth's nether abysses . . .
> . . . a pandeamoniae vortex of loathsome sound and utter, materially tangible blackness . . .

Often these two strategies—minimalism and hyperbole—dovetail into a singular epiphany concerning the faltering not just of language, but of thought as well. At the end of Lovecraft's story "The Unnamable," one of the characters, speaking to his friend Carter from a hospital bed, attempts to describe his strange experience in the following way:

> "*No—it wasn't that way at all.* It was everywhere—a gelatin—a slime—yet it had shapes, a thousand shapes of horror beyond all memory. There were eyes—and a blemish. It was the pit—the maelstrom—the ultimate abomination. Carter, *it was the unnamable!*"[4]

Taken together, these four stages of the unhuman result in a paradoxical revelation, in which one thinks

---

[4] H. P. Lovecraft, "The Unnamable," in *The Dreams in the Witch-House and Other Stories*, ed. S.T. Joshi (New York: Penguin, 2004), 89.

the thought of the limit of all thought. At the level of the anthropic subversion—the first stage—this limit is present but hidden, occulted, and it remains unrecognized. At the level of the anthropic inversion—the second stage—this limit is brought into the foreground through a reversal of the terms, but not of the relation. But here the unhuman still remains hidden, something only known at best indirectly, through the ad-hoc use of human terms (such as sentience or intentionality or malice).

Proceeding from this, at the third level the ontogenic inversion produces a misanthropic realization, a realization that the unhuman exists antagonistically with respect to the human. This leads to the fourth stage, the misanthropic subtraction, in which the relation itself is reversed. Here the unhuman is not even known indirectly—and yet it is still intuited, still thought, but only via a thought that has been stripped of all its attributes. What is thought is only this absolute inaccessibility, this absolute incommensurability; what is affirmed is only that which is itself negation.

What results, then, is strange kind of epiphany, a realization that is, at its core, profoundly antihumanistic. It is not just a realization about human knowledge and its relative horizon of the thinkable, but an enigmatic revelation of the unthinkable, or really, what we might call a *black illumination.* Black illumination leads from the human to the unhuman, but it is also already the unhuman, or one instance of the unhuman. Black illumination does not lead to the affirmation of the human within the unhuman, but instead opens onto the *indifference* of the unhuman (Lovecraft, in his letters, refers to his own position as "indifferentism.") The unhuman does not exist for us (the humanisim of the unhuman), and neither is it against us (the misanthropy of the unhuman). Black illumination leads to the enigmatic thought of the immanence of indifference. The unhuman, at its limit, becomes identical with a kind of apophatic indifference towards the human—at the same time that this indifferent unhuman is immanently "within" the human as well. It is for this reason that the examples of black illumination in supernatural horror indelibly bear the mark of a generalized misanthropy, that moment when philosophy and horror negate themselves, and in the process become one and the same.

Gourmandized in the Abattoir of Openness

Nicola Masciandaro

The burning corpse of god shall keep us warm in the doom of howling winds, / For we are a race from beyond the wanderers of night.

— Xasthur[1]

And just as one can die of fright before the blow is struck, so too can one die of joy. Thus the soul dies to herself *before* she steps into God.

— Meister Eckhart[2]

---

[1] Xasthur, "Doomed by Howling Winds," *Xasthur*, Moribund Records, 2006.

Cyclonopedia is a book that opens Earth to the divinity of reality. The intoxicating effect of its theory-fiction terror is to defuse the double, mutual hostage-taking of philosophy and religion, their shared aporetic stand-off according to which reality remains the occluded object of fiction and divinity the eclipsed object of theory. Here theory-fiction is not a cool new hybrid capable of synthesizing and rescripting their domains towards an iterable new science or discipline. It is not about unifying and resolving their double truth. Instead the book is a trisonic betrayal that is treacherously against both via treason of each to the other. *Cyclonopedia* thus takes place in a new time that it instantiates and narrates: Incognitum Hactenus, or anonymous-until-Now, "a double-dealing mode of time connecting abyssal time scales to our chronological time, thus exposing us to the horror of times beyond."[3] Anonymous-until-Now is the time of *Cyclonopedic* writing, the date of this symposium, an evental logic that deals with local and cosmic time as it does with fiction and theory.[4] In this time, "things leak into each other according to a logic that does not belong to us and cannot be correlated to our chronological time."[5] *Chronos* leaks into theory (the vision of *aiôn*), *aiôn* leaks into fiction (the narration of *chronos*). Inverting the messianic now wherein time is kairically suspended above chronicity as "the time we

---

[2] Meister Eckhart, *The Complete Mystical Works*, trans. Maurice O'C. Walshe (New York: Crossroad, 2009), Sermon 84, 415.
[3] Reza Negarestani, *Cyclonopedia: Complicity with Anonymous Materials* (Melbourne: re.press, 2008), 49.
[4] It is not by design that today (11 March 2011) is the seventh anniversary of the text's opening (11 March 2004), seven being "a numeric crypt which leads to the Warp Region of the Numogram, or the Outsider" (Negarestani, *Cyclonopedia*, 157).
[5] Negarestani, *Cyclonopedia*, 49.

need to make time end: *the time that is left us [il tempo che ci resta]*,"[6] *Cyclonopedia* chronically inters kairos into a time we no longer need to make time begin: *the time that never was ours*. Now that all life is over, every moment is opportune, the time of human gods and divine demons, a present stretching far beyond the limits of past and future. In place of the expectation of resurrection the book offers a funerary feast: "God turns himself into a good meal for the human, the earth and the outside."[7] In place of Armageddon it offers the terrestrial playground of White War, the abode of unbounded, as opposed to final, conflict, "at once the white of impenetrable fog and the color of peace."[8] Incognitum Hactenus is a revolutionary enthymeme or argument-without-assumption, applicable in all spheres, that stabs at the heart of the mutual exclusiveness of plans and peace, the wanting-to-have-it-both-ways of human worry whose global monument is the Middle East Peace Plan.[9]

So the text's symptom, a sign of its truly taking effect, is to render the philosopher (realist or idealist) no longer concerned with *being right* and the believer (nihilist or theist) no longer concerned with *being good*—a corruption or fatal breaking of anxious commitment that, far from ruining rightness and goodness,

---

[6] Giorgio Agamben, *The Time That Remains: A Commentary on the Letter to the Romans*, trans. Patricia Dailey (Stanford: Stanford University Press, 2005), 68.

[7] Negarestani, *Cyclonopedia*, 207.

[8] Negarestni, *Cyclonopedia*, 126.

[9] "'Now tell me, what do you want?' [said Meher Baba] The man answered, 'I want to fulfill my plans and have peace of mind.' 'Plans and peace! These two can never go hand in hand. Where there is peace, there is no plan; and where there are plans, there is turmoil. Either give up plans and have peace, or have your plans and give up thoughts of peace. You cannot have both. That is impossible" (*Lord Meher*, 6.2171, http://www.lordmeher.org).

extimately intensify them into the beautiful absolute contingency of truth or being-divine of reality. Actually (what is happening right now), there is no such thing as divinity or reality. Neither ex-ist. The divine is no more divine than reality is real—a *no more* or *ne plus ultra* that is logically equivalent to the unnamable intersection of *the divine alone is real* and *reality alone is divine*. Truly, there is only a someone and something that is both and neither, a double dealing trison that treasonously twists all trinities, "a line of openness that slashes through the god, the human and the earth."[10] "*No—it wasn't that way at all . . . There were eyes—and a blemish. It was the pit—the maelstrom—the ultimate abomination . . . it was the unnamable!*"[11] This final conversion scene of Lovecraft's (un)eponymous tale, in which a rationalist-fideist or "orthodox sun-dweller" confesses experience of what escapes representation, something beyond imagination and conception, is my practical reception theory for *Cyclonopedia*, that is, a theory of reception as *real theory* or vision of the incommunicable real, the unbinding of experience and perception whose perfect storm does simultaneous violence to the being-there of the world as the ground of reality and the being-nowhere of God as the ground of divinity. The cyclone's spin is especially damaging to philosophy's perception of "the death of God . . . as a religious or a secular event, with an affordable price for both parties, God and human."[12] Into the fundamentally deferring mouths of the intellectual bargainers, whether of the party who "think a moratorium ought to be declared to

---

[10] Negarestani, *Cyclonopedia*, 207.
[11] H. P. Lovecraft, "The Unnamable," in *The Dreams in the Witch House and Other Weird Stories*, ed. S. T. Joshi (New York: Penguin, 2004), 87.
[12] Negarestani, *Cyclonopedia*, 207.

prevent any further 'God talk' by philosophers"[13] or of the party who hope in the hyperchaotic possibility of a God "posited as inexistent and possible . . . *contingent* and *unmasterable*,"[14] *Cyclonopedia* stuffs a "Good Meal or ambrosia plague . . . gourmandized in the abattoir of openness,"[15] a spicy immolated synthesis of what divinity eats 'up there' and punishes the world with 'down here'.

It is as victim-agents or wound-wielders of this divine slaughterhouse of the real that we are present today, complicit with the anonymous materials of a book whose divine reality resides in the same complicity with itself, its involvement and collusion with what "entertains no commonalities with anyone."[16] The nature of our interest is proof and demonstration of this: *interested in everything but not concerned with anything*. That is the mode and mood of a twisted symposium, free from worry in the immunity (as opposed to community) of its own spontaneity, the exemption from civic service and enjoyment of the Outside that is available to all. "The twist . . . has a spontaneous ability to reclaim and remobilise all forms of plot, perspective and history by force, collusion or contamination on behalf of a contingent outside."[17] Such *speculation from the other side* equals all-embracing concern-less interest in the sense of an enacted situation where concern (i.e. following the plot) is always bending back around into a hole for the

---

[13] Ray Brassier, "'I am a nihilist because I still believe in truth': Ray Brassier interviewed by Marcin Rychter," *Kronos* 4 (2011), http://kronos.org.pl/index.php?23151,896.

[14] Quentin Meillassoux, "Spectral Dilemma," *Collapse IV: Concept Horror* (2008): 271.

[15] Negarestani, *Cyclonopedia*, 207.

[16] Reza Negarestani, "Contingency and Complicity," in *The Medium of Contingency*, ed. Robin Mackay (London: Urbanomic & Ridinghouse, 2011), 14.

[17] Reza Negarestani, "All of a Twist," *Índex* 1 (2011): 16.

exercise of new interest. Concern is conic, an empty territorializing funnel-projection, which when reversed makes an enticing opening. Turn your worry inside out. The twist troubles, but essentially in a way that more deeply troubles trouble itself. Otherwise it is not a *real* twist. The common expression 'twisted reality' covertly acknowledges this spontaneous dynamic, which is the vehicle of project as science of being opened, rather than expressive scheming—the latter being a form of intentionality confessed by all who are triumphaly preoccupied (superiorly or inferiorly) with chronic *turns*, who insist upon remaining in the audience (being as public self-hallucination) and refuse to take the blame *for everything* by not worrying about it. Real turning, on the other hand, con-version or together-turning, is an occupation of the omnipresent *pivotal state* around which the All turns. At the center of revolution is the twist of the real, the infinitesimally essential axle-line of pure dis-tortion or utter-twisting. It is that which is negatively visible as face in the moment of Augustine's *nigredo*: "You turned me back toward myself, taking me from behind my own back . . . And you set me there before my own face that I might see how vile I was, how twisted [*distortus*]."[18] Correlatively, the twistedness of reality as external condition is illustrated in the logic of Lovecraftian vision, wherein the twist of the image shadows forth precisely by distortion the unimaginable shape of the real: "the phantom had been twisted and exaggerated, and had contained things which the real source did not contain; yet now, as we saw that real source, we thought it even more hideous and menacing than its distant image."[19] It appears, moreover, that these are Siamese facts, that the unseeability of oneself and the

---

[18] Augustine, *Confessions*, trans. F. J. Sheed, 2nd edn. (Cambridge: Hackett, 2006), 8.7.
[19] H. P. Lovecraft, *At the Mountains of Madness*, 43.

unboundedness of the cosmos are specularly identical or projections of the same mirror or reflective severing. "It possesses a face towards Being and nothingness. It stands opposite each of these two known things in its very essence. It is the third known thing. Within it are all possible things. It is infinite, just as each of the other two known things is infinite."[20] To which may be compared Reza's thinking of the revolutionary earth via "a theory of an exteriorizing Absolute that affords interiorized horizons and localizing points of view as its own forms of cut or excision which can be deepened or topologically recalibrated."[21] The twisted-on-itself curvature of the cosmos is homologically bound to the projective self-blindness of consciousness: "The process of the winding up of *sanskaras* [impressions] consists of these regular twists; and it is these twists which keep the consciousness, gained by the drop-soul, directed and fixed towards the bubble or the form instead of towards its real Self."[22] Concerted maximization of interest and minimization of concern accordingly follows a path to the centerless center along which increasing essential distortion is conjoined to intensifying freedom, a way of dervishly arriving or becoming-transparent towards a pure twist beyond all movement. *Cyclonopedia* narrates this process as the life-pottery of Ahrimanistic creativity or leper creativi-

---

[20] Ibn 'Arabī, *Futûhât al-Makkîya* [Meccan Illuminations], Chapter 312, quoted from Ibn 'Arabī, *The Universal Tree and The Four Birds: Treatise on Unification*, trans. Angela Jaffray (Oxford: Anqa, 2006), 76.
[21] Reza Negarestani, "On the Revolutionary Earth: A Dialectic in Territopic Materialism," (paper written for [but not presented at] the Dark Materialism symposium, Natural History Museum, London, January 12, 2011).
[22] Meher Baba, *God Speaks*, 2nd edn. (New York: Dodd, Mead & Co, 1973), 236.

ty, the development of "an enigmatic insensitivity in the act of creation in which the created and the creator are merged and dissociated through insensitivity to each other."[23] I *throw* myself, like clay on a potter's wheel, into "a confusion in which no straight line can be traced or drawn between the creator and the created—original inauthenticity," in other words, total simultaneous incomprehensibility of both the distinction and the non-distinction between divinity and reality: the truest image of what (I) is.

An agency of ambrosia plague, our interest in *Cyclonopedia* is parasitic, a sweet-smelling captivated vermin-response to the book as new earth, a place for openings: "Nemat-space is infected with gate hysteria."[24] Why would anyone bother if we are *not* a "( )hole complex . . . creat[ing] more passages than are needed in the Earth's body [i.e. contingently exceeding necessity], thus rendering it a host of its own ulterior motives?"[25] Just as "we must cultivate a search for a new earth that ends in repeated failure but in a sense that does not re-transcendentalize the original earth,"[26] so must we cultivate a search for a new *Cyclonopedia* that ends in repeated failure but in a sense that does not re-transcendentalize the original *Cyclonopedia*. Only parasites can speak with perfect honesty and authority about each others' desires. It is of the parasite's nature to be supremely interested and unconcerned, to be consumed with the taste of its own consumption, to be saturated with the spice of its own vital decay (*odor sanctitatis*). Oil too smells sweet, *oleum martyris*, the manna oil of Martyr Earth, like the

---

[23] Negarestani, *Cyclonopedia*, 191.
[24] Negarestani, *Cyclonopedia*, 66.
[25] Negarestani, *Cyclonopedia*, 66.
[26] Ben Woodard, "Nihilismus Autodidactus," *Naught Thought*, http://naughtthought.wordpress.com/2009/07/23/nihilismus-autodidactus/.

black liquid that comes out of Saint Catherine's body near the desert place called the 'Shadow of God' [Bezeleel], only more plentiful.[27] Sancta Tellus, endogenic parasite of the body of God. As a para-digm never ceases exemplifying via its very singularity, "neutralizing the dichotomy between the general and the particular" and replacing it "with a bipolar analogical model,"[28] the para-site (that which makes food of what is beside it) digests the host/parasite distinction into the bipolar disorder of its own being. The pest cannot stand looking up from its own meal. It only lives where there is *no longer any time* to refuse the absolute heresy: "The Grand Betrayal or Mithro-Druj is an all-inclusive invitation, a capital YES to everyone and everything, an ultimate welcome to all and everything; for this reason it secures a diffusive and affirmative epidemic power."[29]

I will now conclude by summarizing my idea in a more exact register. Reality is divine. Let us call this the Thesis of Universal Betrayal. The truth of it needs no other means, no reason nor revelation. It is as obvious as it is beyond assertion and denial. It is true through its own principle, which is to *be* its own principle, to betray everything for its own truth by *being* true. The being-divine of reality and the being-real of the divine are a two-faced double-dealing expression of one unnamable *spontaneous univocal causality*.

---

[27] "And the prelate of the monks shows the relics of this virgin to pilgrims; with an instrument of silver [oil rig] he moves the bones of the virgin on an altar. Then there comes out a little oil, like sweat; but it is like neither oil nor balm, for it is blacker. Of this liquid they give a little to the pilgrims – for only a little comes out" (*The Travels of Sir John Mandeville*, trans. C. W. R. D. Moseley [New York: Penguin, 1983], 70).

[28] Giorgio Agamben, *The Signature of All Things*, trans. Luca D'Isanto with Keven Attell (New York: Zone, 2009), 31.

[29] Negarestani, *Cyclonopedia*, 32.

That which is its own principle is divinely real and really divine. Reality is divinity causing itself to be real. Divinity is reality causing itself to be divine. On one side, the real's being its own principle carries the sense of what truly is, of what is anywhere despite everything (necessity). What is necessary does not possess necessity—it *is* necessity. On the other side, divinity's being its own principal carries the sense of what is absolutely independent, of what is everywhere itself (freedom). What is free does not possess freedom—it *is* freedom. Reality is real in being divine (free, unconditioned, absolutely itself). Divinity is divine in being real (necessary, conditioning, absolutely existent). Divinity and reality define a doubly necessary freedom, a doubly free necessity. A vortexical entity for whom freedom *is* necessity and necessity *is* freedom. The mood of the vortex, of the divinely twisting real, is interest without concern: being not *in*, but *the* middle (inter-esse) of the truth of the real and the enjoyment of divinity.

Cyclonopedia, in the real-contingent sense of the text that *is* our concernless interest in it, installs itself as the heretical interior of this twisting, spontaneous univocal causality. *Cyclonopedia* is the heresy, the intimate parasite of spontaneous univocal causality. Its double-helixed theme, Incognitum Hactenus or Anonymous-Until-Now and Inauthenticity or Complicity-With-Anonymous-Materials, names the two-faced form that is symptomatic of this causality, the universal abomination or Ur-Thing-That-Should-Not-Be whose presence is everywhere intimated and forgotten as the eternal and specularly-twinned contingencies of Now and Individuation.[30] This is the never-being of any reason at all why this is *this*, why I am *I*, why it is now *now*—an existent and actual never-

---

[30] Incognitum Hactenus and Inauthenticity correspond to freedom and necessity, respectively, but in a twisted way.

being whose truest image should be named the Horror: "that shocking final peril which gibbers unmentionably outside the ordered universe, where no dreams reach; that last amorphous blight of nethermost confusion which blasphemes and bubbles at the centre of all infinity."[31] The hyper-contingencies of Now and Individuation are not problems to be philosophically resolved or facts to be understood. They are the divine heresy of the real itself, its always splitting off in a spontaneous way. They are the covert substance of everything's remaining unconvinced that it is not God. In *Cyclonopedia*, this originary creativity or whim of the Horror takes the explicit form of Zurvan's parthenogenetic self-buggery, i.e. the obliviOnanism of the solitary universe (p.169: the sixty-nining of the One). Refusing to gaze in awe and stupefaction before this omnipresent perversion, *Cyclonopedia* weaponizes and wields it as a profound strategic tool, drawing it out into a line of openness that demon-strates more than wonder ever will its percussive limitless power, its being the never-ending blow *from which nothing will ever recover*. The joy of this, the dilation of the blow before the blow that *will* kill you, is that far from repeating the Horror, the book opens into a greater horror still, namely, that "there are no limits to the spreading influence of man."[32]

---

[31] Lovecraft, *The Dreams in the Witch House*, 156.
[32] Meher Baba, *Discourses*, II.92.

Phileas Fog^g, or the Cyclonic Passepartout: On the Alchemical Elements of War

Dan Mellamphy & Nandita Biswas Mellamphy

❖

I.
Chemistry (alchemy) begins with decay. Stripped before the mess-agents of decay, one can always ask, "isn't thought a gaseous rot?" . . . the question reverberates cancerously through the fetid air. Resistance to decay is both futile and fertile. But then, what is fertility in the sense of resistance toward decay? There is a yawning horror in this question.

— *Cyclonopedia*, 188

II.
For Parsani, oil as *helio-nigredo* or the black corpse of the Sun marks the rediscovery of mythology as the political geo-philosophy vacillating between economy and the ethics of openness . . . The Earth's dream . . . is realized as the *nigredo* . . . an affirmation of the ground and its subterranean potencies. In alchemy, *nigredo* is the blackening state which is usually associated with putrefaction and decay . . . The alchemical unbinding of the earth as an insurgent entity, and the manifest ethics of radical openness, are contingent upon . . . escape from gravity and transcendence – from *nigredo* (blackness) to *albedo* (whiteness) and

finally moving toward *rubedo* (redness). In the [affirmation of the ground and its subterranean potencies], chemical vectors start from *rubedo* or the redness of the Sun, and descend into *nigredo* or chthonlc blackness.

– *Cyclonopedia*, 234

III.

War-machines disappear into the fog at the meltdown point: a tempest of diverging particles narrating the epidemic of War. And it should be recalled that particles constitute the *al-khemy* of Sorcery and the Fog of War . . . The original manifestation of the Fog of War is *Aer*—a benighted 'air', described in Greek texts as something wet and dark (see, for example, Aristotle's *Meteorologica* for an account of such characterization). *Aer* meant fog and darkness—not darkness as in *tenebrae* (from the Sanskrit *tamas*, the darkness and shadow that belongs to the underworld, the realm of death), but darkness as in the Greek *omichle* (the darkness of fog, mist, dust-clouds . . .). While *tenebrae* belongs to death, *Aer* and *omichle* belong to War, the Fog of War.

– *Cyclonopedia*, 131, 101-103

According to *Cyclonopedia*'s crafty H.P. (Hamid Parsani), the black [w]hole of <u>melanosis in Greek</u> or of <u>nigredo in Latin</u> is not only the *beginning* of [al]chemical processes but their *end*, or indeed their beg*ending* their eschatouroboric *arc*[*he*].[1] *Alchemy*, from the Arabic *al khem*,[2] unleashes and frees the forces of the earth (*al khem* in Arabic, *chthonos* in Greek, *humus* in Latin), which are presented in *Cyclonopedia* as a toxic chthonic emission qua virulent

---

[1] Reza Negarestani, *Cyclonopedia: Complicity with Anonymous Materials* (Melbourne: re.press, 2008), 93-94.
[2] Negarestani, *Cyclonopedia*, 131.

petroleum effluvium.[3] The earth is as *fatal* as it is *fertile*, and its "alchemical unbinding"[4] opens onto the vicious and virtuous circle of this double-dealing double-bind. The alchemical operation and alchemical operator realizes the feedback-loop (loops or spool) wherein the so-called morphogenic progression from the *noir gris* or 'grey black' crepusculism of *nigredo* or Greek *melanosis*[5] (the stage of *mortification*), 1, to the *éclaircissement argenté* or 'silver sheen[ed]' enlightenment of *albedo* or Greek *leukosis*[6] (the stage of *revivification*), 2, and ultimately to the *fulguration fougueuse* qua overwhelming and apocalyptic 'fiery fulguration' of *rubedo* or Greek *iosis*[7] (the stage of ultimate *alteration*), 3, ouroborically or enantiodromologically[8] wraps back upon itself, 4, revealing in this recursion (the 'fo[u]rth' stage) that the 'end' or 'omega' is also the 'beginning' or 'alpha', that *iosis* leads to *melanosis*, or in the words of H.P., that "chemical vectors start from *rubedo* or the redness of the sun, and descend into *nigredo* or chthonic blackness" as they arise in the alternate cycle from 'earth' to the 'sun'.[9]

Two cycles, two cyclones—those of the aforementioned 'alpha' and 'omega'—therefore insinuate themselves in *al khem*, and reticulate in their respective coils a conflictive/conflagrational condition reminiscent of the one outlined in William Butler Yeats' equivalent to Edgar Allan Poe's *Eureka*—*here* referring to the "double gyres" of *A Vision* (a 1925 *Cyclonopedia* of sorts, published seventy-seven years after

---

[3] Negarestani, *Cyclonopedia*, 109.
[4] Negarestani, *Cyclonopedia*, 234.
[5] Negarestani, *Cyclonopedia*, 234.
[6] Negarestani, *Cyclonopedia*, 234.
[7] Negarestani, *Cyclonopedia*, 234.
[8] Negarestani, *Cyclonopedia*, 93-94.
[9] Negarestani, *Cyclonopedia*, 234.

Poe's *Eureka*.[10] The mythical manifestation of a creature conditioned by the double-gyre's <u>double-dealing double-bind</u> is, in *A Vision* as well as in *Cyclonopedia*, the Sargonian *Lamassu*, described by Yeats in his 1920 'Second Coming' as "A shape with lion body and the head of a man, / A gaze blank and pitiless as the sun, / . . . moving its slow thighs, while all about it / Reel shadows of the indignant desert birds." Darkness spreads ("darkness drops again") as the *Lamassu* "slouches forward," and "centuries of stony sleep [are] vexed to nightmare" in its wake. Completing a conic triangle of sorts (or trison[11]), in addition to the Cyclonic double-gyre or *geometrical* (mathematical) manifestation[s][12] and the Sargonic Sheedu-*Lamassu* or *mythological* manifestation[s][13] of alchemy's ouroboric *enantiodromos*, there are also its *militant* and *military* holy-/holey-/[w]holey-war manifestation[s]: the so-called People of *Naft*[14] who operate in many ways as if they were the occult parts or particles[15] of the Sargonic[16]/Cyclonic[17] ( )*hole*-complex[18] qua mythical *Lamassu*-complex[19] ("vexed to nightmare" after "centuries of stony sleep," in the words / "darkness"/ "shadows" of *A Vision*).

Like the mythical *Lamassus*, these occultural agents and military-religious operatives (the People of

---

[10] Roughly eighty years, give or take three years on either side, separate *Eureka* from *A Vision* and *A Vision* from *Cyclonopedia* — 80 or ∞0.

[11] Negarestani, *Cyclonopedia*, 31-37.

[12] Negarestani, *Cyclonopedia*, 35.

[13] Negarestani, *Cyclonopedia*, 76.

[14] Negarestani, *Cyclonopedia*, 26.

[15] Negarestani, *Cyclonopedia*, 80.

[16] Negarestani, *Cyclonopedia*, 76.

[17] Negarestani, *Cyclonopedia*, 35.

[18] Negarestani, *Cyclonopedia*, 42.

[19] Negarestani, *Cyclonopedia*, 79.

Naft, i.e. the *Naphtanese*[20]) have a "transient omnipresence inside and outside the battlefield"; their tactics and strategies are based on "the belief that war has a life of its own,"[21] one which might best be described as an *Un-life*[22] (hence neither life nor death as such, strictly speaking) and which is in any case beyond the bounds of any single individual's life, on an utterly different plane. "On this plane," writes Z in the *X-Z* interchange on the initial pages of *Cyclonopedia*, "you either turn into diabolical particles or evaporate and are recollected as cosmic-pest ingredients. This is exactly where religious extremists (the Taliban, with their ironically phallomaniac hatred for anything erected, for instance) turn into the stealth mercenaries of geological insurgencies, the cult of Tellurian Blasphemy (demonogrammatical decoding of the earth's body)."[23] The *X*s and *Z*s of and in *Cyclonopedia*'s hypersti[t]c[h]ings are precisely those who write of this "People of *Naft* (oil), frequently referred to as *Naphtanese*,"[24] and who describe them as "clandestine petro-nomads who roam between oil fields instead of oases."[25] It is explained that "oil as a ubiquitous earth-crawling entity—the Tellurian Lube—spreads the war-machines and politics of *Naphtanese* or desert-nomads"[26] and that this "militant religious cult"[27] "believe that the *Un-life of War* feeds on *oil*, which they call the 'black corpse of the Sun'. Petroleum [according to the *Naphtanese*] makes war-machines slide towards itself [– i.e. the People of *Naft*]. Hence Radical

---

[20] Negarestani, *Cyclonopedia*, 26.
[21] Negarestani, *Cyclonopedia*, 79.
[22] Negarestani, *Cyclonopedia*, 76.
[23] Negarestani, *Cyclonopedia*, 18.
[24] Negarestani, *Cyclonopedia*, 26.
[25] Negarestani, *Cyclonopedia*, 57.
[26] Negarestani, *Cyclonopedia*, 58.
[27] Negarestani, *Cyclonopedia*, 130.

War originally comes from the[ir] side of the oil pipeline".[28] indeed they <u>are</u> Radical War, they are the very *Fog* or *Aer* or black *oil-vapor* of war – its "diabolical particles."[29] A radical admission!—and a radical submission.

The alchemical agent – *Naphtanese* militant, *Lamassurian* monster, *Cyclonic/Cyclonopedian* and *Tellurian*[30] mechanism – submits to the sovereign sentence[31] of "chthonic blackness."[32] The alchemical operative follows the order[s], in other words, – *taxis, tasséin;*[33] *syntaxis, syntasséin;*[34] *stratos-agéin*[35]—of *chthonos*. The alchemical agent or operative remains, in the words of Nietzsche's mouthpiece Zarathustra, "true to the earth,"[36] and wholly submits to its fate, thereby affirming "the basic text *homo natura*" and thus translating "the human back into nature."[37] Indeed "the alchemical unbinding of the earth"[38] requires of its agent[s] or operative[s] what Parsani describes as a "manifest ethics of radical openness":[39] a being *bound to* and *bound by* this *utter unbinding*, and in this sense a boundless submission (*Islam*). The 'mission' of the "militant religious cult named *Naph-*

---

[28] Negarestani, *Cyclonopedia*, 130.
[29] Negarestani, *Cyclonopedia*, 58, 130, 18.
[30] Negarestani, *Cyclonopedia*, 16-26.
[31] *Taxis, tasséin; syntaxis, syntasséin; stratos-agéin;* see notes 33-35, below.
[32] Negarestani, *Cyclonopedia*, 234.
[33] Online Etymological Dictionary, s.v. "tactics," http://www.etymonline.com/.
[34] Online Etymological Dictionary, s.v. "syntax," http://www.etymonline.com/.
[35] Online Etymological Dictionary, s.v. "strategy," http://www.etymonline.com.
[36] Nietzsche, *Thus Spoke Zarathustra*, 1.22.2.
[37] *Beyond Good and Evil*, 230.
[38] Negarestani, *Cyclonopedia*, 234.
[39] Negarestani, *Cyclonopedia*, 234.

tanese," for example,[40] is to hearken to the earthly emissions and submit to their orders and their orchestrations, to their strategies (Greek *strategos:* multiple/ *stratos* direction/*agéin*) and their tacticities (Greek *taxis, tasséin:* arrangement). Their mission is thus to aid and abet that earthly/alchemical pollution which is described in *Cyclonopedia* as the Persian *namba* or *naphta* qua "essence of *drem*":[41] that which the Greeks called *phlegéin* and which appears in arenas of agonistic conflagration (on the 'battlefield', for example) in the form a "fire which glows black as the result of a huge mass of uncombusted carbon particles."[42] This "*namba* or *drem* (*Druj-pollution, Trison*)" is "the effluvium of oil" according to Parsani,[43] and its excess (the "excess of [such] *namba*") "was referred to as the worst possible poison or *was-wišabăg:* being saturated-by-poison."[44] The *iós* of alchemical *iosis* also designates such a radical poison and poisoning ("*iosis,*" explains Jung in the 12th tome of his *Works*, "comes from [the Greek] *iós*, meaning poison"[45]). The alchemical 'agent' qua *effluvium-of-oil-*'operative' in a sense *becomes* the *iosis* of 'oil', acts in the name and on the plane of *namba* ("on this plane," to repeat, "you either turn into diabolical particles or evaporate and are recollected as cosmic-pest ingredients"[46]).

It is explained in *Cyclonopedia* that "in the Zoroastrian version of the *tetrasomia*" or *four elements* (conjoined by the Pythagoreans into a triangular *tetractys*) the tetractian *top, peak* or *apex*—the "three-

---

[40] Negarestani, *Cyclonopedia*, 130.
[41] Negarestani, *Cyclonopedia*, 108.
[42] Negarestani, *Cyclonopedia*, 108.
[43] Negarestani, *Cyclonopedia*, 109.
[44] Negarestani, *Cyclonopedia*, 108.
[45] C. G. Jung, *Psychology and Alchemy*, 229.
[46] Negarestani, *Cyclonopedia*, 18.

dotted perversion" of its trison[47]—was in point of fact an oil[y] eruption (a kind of 'peak oil' perhaps): the "vapor" and "miasma" of *naft*, *naphta* or *namba*, a plume of petroleum as its peak.[48] This quintessence of the *tetrasomia* (in Latin its *quinta essentia*, in Greek its *pempte ousia*) bursts forth like a fo[u]nt from the *top*, *cap* or *closure*, disclosing in so doing—and in so undoing—"a massive incendiary tendency" amongst [al]chemical elements.[49] The entire *tetractys* or *tetrasomia* turns out to be nought but a glowing black flame, the phlegmatic (or rather, *melanotic, melanchoric*) eruption of *al khem*, *chthonos* or *humus* (the earth), which is at once as 'dry' as *al deshret* (the desert) and as 'wet' as *an nil* (the nile), "increas[ing] . . . oil-saturated *wetness* through its *dryness* and deserting ambience" in the words of Parsani.[50] What's afoot here is footnoted in *Cyclonopedia* along with a diagram of the "*tetrasomia* or the Aristotelian model of affordance" conjoining *wetness*, *dryness*, the *hot* and the *cold* in a circle or cycle of inter-communication and complicitous affordance.[51] "Elements are [thereby shown as] open to each other either diametrically or diagonally," and although "they can never entirely overlap or radically communicate with each other" (i.e. "they require an intermediate state to form rotational nexuses and to maintain the overall wholeness") they nevertheless exhibit the "propulsive *polemikos* or cyclic dynamism"[52] characteristic of "an architecture, *mathesis* and politics of decay."[53]

---

[47] Negarestani, *Cyclonopedia*, 108-109.
[48] Negarestani, *Cyclonopedia*, 108-109.
[49] Negarestani, *Cyclonopedia*, 108.
[50] Negarestani, *Cyclonopedia*, 108.
[51] Negarestani, *Cyclonopedia*, 228.
[52] Negarestani, *Cyclonopedia*, 228.
[53] Reza Negarestani, "Undercover Softness," *Collapse* 6 (2010): 381.

Each element and/or each part is open to the process of decay—*melanosis, nigredo, putrefaction, decomposition*—and decay, as such, is the manifestation and/or incursion of the immanent *()hole*. The [ant]agonism and polemicism (the *polemikos* or *war*) at work in *Cyclonopedia* is not a 'war' that can be staged within a particular theatre of operations or theatre of war;[54] its 'operations' are far too radically and alchemically open for that. Nor can such *polemikos* or *war* be understood as a "grid of intelligibility";[55] *war – polemikos* – is here, again, not 'life', but rather that to which 'life' *submits* itself, that to which 'life' is radically *submitted*. "The sublime truth of war is expressed not by what happens between war-machines, but by that which transpires between war-machines and *War*, and which entails the extinction of war-machines once and for all […]. The *Un-life* of *War* maintains its radical 'outside'ness by turning the tactics of war-machines into pure strategy."[56] War comes from the 'outside' – on the one hand *autonomous* from geo-anthropo-morphogenesis (earth-human-formation processes, or "tellurian dynamics") and on the other hand *immanent* both to the *earthly* and the *human* (e.g. anthropomorphic belief-systems, ideological ap-

---

[54] Carl von Clausewitz defines "theatre of war" as "a portion of the space over which war prevails as has its boundaries protected, and thus possesses a kind of independence . . . Such a portion is not a mere piece of the whole, but a small whole complete in itself; and consequently it is more or less in such a condition that changes which take place at other points in the seat of war have only an indirect and no direct influence upon it" (*On War*, trans. Colonel J. J. Graham [New York: Barnes & Noble], v.ii).

[55] This is what Arnold I. Davidson, in his introduction to Michel Foucault's *Society Must Be Defended* (New York: Picador, 2003) called "the principle of intelligibility of 'politics' in the general form of war" (xvii).

[56] Negarestani, *Cyclonopedia*, 76.

parati) which serve as its "lubricants" and as conduits for its manifestation, or more precisely its *infestation*.[57] If for Nietzsche the human was a symptom of more hidden Dionysian (read: *earthly*, *chthonic*) processes, for the alchemical 'agent' qua chthonic 'conduit' everything 'human' is necessarily the pathological symptom of the *Un-life* of *War:* "every war-machine must burn, and all modes of military survival—whether belonging to the State or to nomadic insurgencies—must be consumed by the *Un-life* of *War*."[58] According to Parsani, it is through the Tiama-terialistic[59] (dragon-like or *dracontological* qua *chthonic-conflagrational*) model of participation, wherein the earth is a "twisted zone of insurgency against the Solar Economy,"[60] a widening gyre qua counter-heliacal conflagrational cyclone in which *decadence*, *degeneration* and *decay* play positive and catalytic conflagra-tional roles, that *War*—specifically *()holey war*—melanotically returns the earth to its "desert[ed]" condition. "The desert is an ideal battlefield; to desertify the earth is to make the earth ready for change in the name of the divine's monopoly as opposed to terrestrial idols"[61]—i.e. in the name of *in*-human *un*-life rather than the monopoly (and/or the plurality) of the *human*, all-too-*human*. Through petro-political narratives and counter-narratives (as well as petro-political entities and counter-entities—for instance the agents of "weaponized *taqiyya*" or "hyper-camouflage"[62] who are correlative to the "militant religious *Napthanese*"[63]), apocalyptism is the conduit

---

[57] Negarestani, *Cyclonopedia*, 50, 124.
[58] Negarestani, *Cyclonopedia*, 78.
[59] Negarestani, *Cyclonopedia*, 65-66 (also 94, 163, 240).
[60] Negarestani, *Cyclonopedia*, 42.
[61] Negarestani, *Cyclonopedia*, 18.
[62] Negarestani, *Cyclonopedia*, 122-128.
[63] Negarestani, *Cyclonopedia*, 26.

for the 'outside', since it is in this manner (via desertification) that War can enter camouflaged into belief-systems and thus be *accelerated*, *developed*, "anomalously *recomposed* and *intensified* by anthropomorphic entities."[64] In this sense, belief is *bait* enfleshed in human-all-too-human hosts who, in aligning themselves strategically to the forces of the exterior, allow themselves to be butchered open and made into tasty meals for the *Outside*. Anthropomorphic entities become lures upon which to *feed*, targets for *necrosis*, "ideal prey for the radical *outside*."[65] As the ancient Persian *Druj*-cult knew, one becomes such ideal prey by camouflaging oneself within established *beliefs* and *behaviors*— in this particular case, obsessive and paranoid rituals regarding health, hygiene and sanitation— which then can act as a "decoy to commence the hunt *from the other side*."[66]

In contradistinction to the DeleuzoGuattarian model of the war-machine in which war can be "thermodynamically grasped" as a *product* of war-machines,[67] *Cyclonopedia* offers the model of War-*as*-Machine, in which War is *independent* of war-machines and in which war indeed *hunts* war-machines.[68] In hunting war-machines, however, War does not simply kill indiscriminately and/or once-and-for-all. The *Un-life of War* "does not wipe out or terminate" but rather operates with/in the prey's economy of survival, sustaining itself by keeping the host-organism in an ongoing state of decay.[69] We are

---

[64] Negarestani, *Cyclonopedia*, 18.
[65] Negarestani, *Cyclonopedia*, 199.
[66] Negarestani, *Cyclonopedia*, 200.
[67] Negarestani, *Cyclonopedia*, 130.
[68] Negarestani, *Cyclonopedia*, 78.
[69] Negarestani, *Cyclonopedia*, 182. A model for this might be the recent discovery of parasitoid organisms that do not kill their prey outright, but rather infest the host organism with

presented, therefore, with an itinerant, oft-imperceptible, highly (perhaps even *hyper*) *portable* and particularly *potent* military mode[l] which sustains itself on the degenerative processes of its milieu, thus ensuring its propagation through an economy of positive disintegration.[70] The latter (positive disintegration) is the crux and crucible of an altogether alchemical transformation wherein War-as-Machine is dispersed and thus disseminated through the unleashing or unbinding of its virulence, through "contagious *distribution* and *diffusion*."[71] The diffuse militarization and dispersed weaponization wrought by this rotting/disintegrating mechanism ("the architecture, *mathesis* and politics of decay"[72]) opens up an "*affect-space*" or "*dracage-zone*"[73] that is somehow *terrible* or downright *terrifying*, if only by dint of its "crypto-fractal"[74] infinity. The expansive, unlimited *affect-space* or *dracage-zone* of War-as-Machine *arises from* and *builds upon* "differentiation, falsification, divergence, mass hysteria, terminal catabolism and disintegration in the direction of something other than death"[75] – here a larval, crypto-fractal kind of 'terror'.[76] Parsani discovers (by way of his rigorous study of Assyrian military and para-military doctrine) that in the model of War-as-Machine (which for *Cyclonopedia*'s Col. Jackson West is a model of contemporary War-on-Terror as well) the 'subjects' or 'agents' that make up

---

larvae that can control the host organism's behaviours. See for example, A. Grosman et al., "Parasitoid Increases Survival of Its Pupae by Inducing Hosts to Fight Predators," in *PLoS ONE* 3 (2008): e2276.

[70] Negarestani, *Cyclonopedia*, 38, 62, 91.
[71] Negarestani, *Cyclonopedia*, 91.
[72] Negarestani, "Undercover Softness," 381.
[73] Negarestani, *Cyclonopedia*, 36.
[74] Negarestani, *Cyclonopedia*, 31, 36, 138.
[75] Negarestani, *Cyclonopedia*, 38.
[76] Negarestani, *Cyclonopedia*, 31, 138, 153.

'war-machines' are them-selves *hunted down, broken down* and *consumed* by War, only to be *resurrected* and *"brought back to life* on the other side of the battlefield in the form of a Cimmerian *haze*, the 'Fog of War'."[77] Drained and purified of their very *ipseity* (their stable *self-identity*) only to return as hyper-camouflaged "hunting particles"[78] animated only by the *Un-life of War*, these new 'weapons of terror' are not 'grand transgressions' or deployments of 'visible and declared violence'; indeed the great innovation of Assyrian militarization is the invention of a new kind of war-machine that sustains itself in and upon so-called "peace": "the militarization of peace" in the words of Negarestani.[79] Like the biological example of 'parasitoid *hosts*' (*zombie-ants, -rats, -worms* and *fungi*),[80] the agents qua weapons of this militarized peace are non-transgressive hyper-camouflaged *hosts* rather than parasitical *predators*—indeed hosts *for the latter* (i.e. for the parasitical *predators*), *hosts* for the *Outside*, for the *Un-life of War*. These agents, these weapons, are larval operatives: under cover of peaceful and

---

[77] Negarestani, *Cyclonopedia*, 77-78.

[78] Negarestani, *Cyclonopedia*, 131.

[79] Reza Negarestani, "The Militarization of Peace," *Collapse* 1 (2006): 53. See also Negarestani, *Cyclonopedia*, 126: "'The necessity of peace must eclipse the necessity of war, as the indispensability of God must outshine the indispensability of Satan. Be keepers of peace, for war is ephemeral and shall not last long enough to bear your rage and shall not dive deep enough to harvest new blades and arrows' (ibn Maimun, *Risalatan fi Ahl-al-Ain*)."

[80] On 'parasitoid hosts' like "parasitic trematode *Dicrocoelium dendriticum*, which induces its intermediate host, ants, to move up onto blades of grass during the night and early morning, and firmly attach themselves to the substrate with their mandibles," see Grosman et al., "Parasitoid Increases Survival," e2276.

peace-time activity[81] they open themselves up to and onto their milieu such that tellurian pestilence, tellurian pests,[82] contaminate their hollowed-out bodies and abodes ("we are the hollow men" wrote T.S. Eliot in a poem that begins with reference to Mister/Colonel Kurtz). These "hollow men"-hosts are indistinguishable from peace-time civilians and citizens (non-'war operatives') and yet *War* burrows, nests, feeds and metamorphoses *with/in* them, *through* them. The host/pest binary is itself compromised by these creatures of earth as "nemat-space": the "hollowed bodies" of the inhuman[83] that are in effect "heresies" engineered to be the *freest* and most *aethereal* of all spirits.

In his discussion of the *Lamassu*-complex, Parsani explains that in order to protect their State from internal and external insurgencies, Assyrians "simulated" war-machines, engineered "simulations" that would mimic the autonomous behavior by which War *hunted* and *killed* war-machines. "The Assyrian Axis was supposed to engineer war-machines corresponding to *the Un-life of War* itself, if only as faint terres-trial echoes of its unlimited ferocity."[84] These simulated war-machines were able to roam beyond the borders of the Assyrian State, gathering information and intelligence of all kinds— and yet, what the Assyrians miscalculated was that the radical *mobility* and *openness* of these simulated war-machines would eventually become the sources for the erosion of the Assyrian State itself, *not* by becoming 'security leaks' for the enemies of the Assyrian State, but rather by becoming 'gateways' and 'conduits' for the radical

---

[81] (which might here be theorized as the *Fog of Peace*)
[82] Negarestani, *Cyclonopedia*, 26.
[83] Negarestani, *Cyclonopedia*, 67.
[84] Negarestani, *Cyclonopedia*, 78.

Outside (the *Un-life of War*).[85] In their *Lamassu*-like crypto-fractal complexity,[86] agents of larval terror—the simulated war-machines of War-as-Machine—are hyper-camouflaged/ever-clandestine *double-agents* insofar as they are, on the one hand, *deployed by* the military apparatus of the State, and on the other hand, *autonomous from* the State, operating as a conduits for that which is radically exterior to the State. Ultimately, the Assyrian war-machine becomes a cyclonic pulverizing force for the Assyrian State, but also a clandestine force for the dispersion of new obscure power-formations."[87]

These putrephilic machines of larval terror or "poromechanical entities"[88] constitute the *al-khemy*[89] (*al khem*) of the "Fog of War"[90] by reticulating *Black Revolution*, *White War*, and the *Red* or *Gold Dust* of *al-deshret* (the desert). Indeed, [*a*] the double-gyred "draco-spiral model of War on Terror"[91] described in *Cyclonopedia* as a "petro-political contamination of the global politico-economic systems"[92] and [*b*] the use of "*taqiyya* or Islamic hyper-camouflage"[93]—i.e. of "strategy rather than tactics" and of "contagious communication rather than transgression"[94]—within the overall logic of returning everything to *Dust*,[95] can only be grasped within an alchemical process in which melanotic *Blackness* (petro-politics), leukotic *Whiteness* (hyper-camouflaged *war*) and iotic *Red-*

---

[85] Negarestani, *Cyclonopedia*, 78.
[86] Negarestani, *Cyclonopedia*, 36-37.
[87] Negarestani, *Cyclonopedia*, 80-81.
[88] Negarestani, *Cyclonopedia*, 55.
[89] Negarestani, *Cyclonopedia*, 131.
[90] Negarestani, *Cyclonopedia*, 131.
[91] Negarestani, *Cyclonopedia*, 177.
[92] Negarestani, *Cyclonopedia*, 176.
[93] Negarestani, *Cyclonopedia*, 176-177.
[94] Negarestani, *Cyclonopedia*, 177.
[95] Negarestani, *Cyclonopedia*, 117.

goldenness[96] ("the sentient process of *desertification*"[97]) form pathways of complicity and communication between earth and sun.[98] As Colonel West begins to discover and to articulate in his theories of urbanized war, "War on Terror" is and must necessarily be understood—or as West says "decrypted"—according to a mutually implicative *mythical, mathematical* and *military* logic brought to bear on the double-dealing dynamisms of geometrically "trisonic" and Lamassurian "crypto-fractal" complexities inherent to the militarized politics of *Naft*. The agent of leukotic *White War* (the hyper-camouflaged and weaponized civilian within the logistics of peace-time) should be understood as an equivalent of both the militant religious *Naphtanese* and the mytho-militant *Lamassu*, harbingers of a melanotic *Black Revolution* (this interrelation itself constituting the Tiamaterialist or dracontological double-spiral/cyclone/gyre of the *Red Dust*'s *iosis*). When the civilian becomes a "dormant war-machine"[99]—i.e. the hyper-camouflaged ("white" and/or *unseen* rather than "black" and/ or *obscurant*) "Fog of War" – it covertly carries with and in itself the dormant powers of the *Lamassu*, *Napthanese* and cyclonic *double-gyre* in order to become a larval machine of degeneration and contagion dispersing cyclonic insurgencies and clandestine terror that penetrate into and ultimately unbind all political orientations, making everything submit to the Will of the Desert. "From the White War of the Jihadi under *taqiyya* evolves the Black Revolution of civilians against their own inconsequentiality and the hegemo-

---

[96] *Erythrosis* is an alternative designation for *iosis*—hence *melanosis, leukosis, iosis* or *erythrosis*.
[97] Negarestani, *Cyclonopedia*, 132.
[98] Negarestani, *Cyclonopedia*, 145.
[99] Negarestani, *Cyclonopedia*, 127.

ny of the State. The true Revolution is about rendering civilianhood intrinsically *consequential*."[100]

When contextualized within the kind of urban warfare described by Colonel West, the *al-khemy* of "War on Terror" gives the city "the logic of the desert":[101] the 'verticality' of the city (e.g. its ostensibly 'closed' features such as its tall buildings, narrow alleyways, and vertically-contoured urban terrain[102]) gets 'flattened' and 'opened' by nested communication-technologies and communication-pathways, by the ability of urban Jihadis to undergo "reversible metamorphoses"[103] from civilian to militia and back to civilian, by the capacity of urban militia to effectively wage war inside closed urban spaces,[104] by the breeding of *rogue units* that are not dependent on conventionally hierarchical military command-and-control directives, by the refinement of weaponry focusing on *bullets* and *ballistics*, *et cetera*.[105]

Perhaps a more interesting and confounding example of desertification is the one that is a more radically 'open' environment for the surreptitious propagation/infestation of the Fog of War and the epidemic dispersion of its agents of larval terror, in which the warrior of weaponized *taqiyya* completely overlaps with the ordinary *citizen*. "By becoming as one with the citizens as expendable entities for the

---

[100] Negarestani, *Cyclonopedia*, 127.
[101] Negarestani, *Cyclonopedia*, 133.
[102] Negarestani, *Cyclonopedia*, 134.
[103] Negarestani, *Cyclonopedia*, 134.
[104] Negarestani, *Cyclonopedia*, 135: "West . . . uses *Parkour* as the exemplary discipline in which the practitioner becomes as one with the obstacle during movement."
[105] Negarestani, *Cyclonopedia*, 136-138. This is also what the 'Revolution in Military Affairs' (RMA) calls "asymmetrical warfare"; for another contemporary fictive-philosophical/philosofictive account of the latter, see Adam Roberts's *New Model Army* (London: Gollancz, 2010).

State, the warrior under *taqiyya* shifts the battlefield to the homeland and shifts the attention of the State and its instruments of policing onto citizens rather than outside forces."[106] By unleashing the immuno-political responses that attack the State's own body-politic within the logistics of peace-time (by fomenting paranoia and pitting citizen against citizen), the *White Warrior* engages in the blackening of *decay* (*nigredo*, *melanosis*), the ultimate effect of which (as in *rubedo*, *iosis*) is to *desertify* the State's institutions and institutionalized values, rendering them fragile, porous, and open to the *Dust* qua *Un-life* of *War*. Within the alchemical logic of larval terror, no visible or transgressive act of war or of terrorism is required for the body-politic to begin cannabilizing itself: when greased by the lube of petro-political narratives—*Islamophobia*, *Islamophilia*, arguments that there are *causal links* between *multiculturalism* and *terrorism* and *the biopolitics of citizenship*, *et cetera*—the body-politic of the State becomes subject to the autophagic process of decay[107] wrought by the *Un-life of War* and combusts to the point of meltdown. "The State's border is reinvented as a field of vortices unloading occultural heterogeneities into the State and resulting in *corrosion*, *dissemination* of internal insurgencies, *inflammation* of regions, boundaries and organization, the rise of *parasitical modes of politics and economy*, and finally the *implosion* of the State."[108]

That which *Cyclonopedia* describes in terms of a "politics of decay"[109] qua "ethics of degeneration" ("the *differential cosmogenesis* of decay")[110] is the *alkhemy* of *War* as "the model of participation or com-

---

[106] Negarestani, *Cyclonopedia*, 127.

[107] Negarestani, *Cyclonopedia*, 82.

[108] Negarestani, *Cyclonopedia*, 80-1.

[109] Negarestani, *Collapse* 6, 381.

[110] Negarestani, *Cyclonopedia*, 30.

plicity"[111] between [1] the *earth* and processes of melanotic decay, [2] those who *submit* to its tellurian insurgencies, and [3] the incursion or intrusion (infil-(infiltration, infestation) of *Outside* via the *( )hole-*complex. To be 'open' in this way is to be the host of, and host to, the *( )hole "Un-life of War"* (and incursions of "the *Outside*" as such) by becoming host and home to the *unhomely*, *unheimlich*, or what the Greeks called the "*omichle:* the darkness of *fog, mist,* [and] *dust-clouds*"—becoming, in short, the very *Fog, Aer* or *A*[*eth*]*er* - *net*[work] of *War*.[112]

---

[111] Negarestani, *Cyclonopedia*, 182.
[112] Negarestani, *Cyclonopedia*, 103.

The Untimely (and Unshapely) Decomposition of Onto-Epistemological Solidity: Negarestani's *Cyclonopedia* as Metaphysics

Ben Woodard

This paper asserts that Negarestani's *Cyclonopedia* is at its core a metaphysical text, a claim which I then force into complicity with a critique and reworking of the philosophical category of becoming. While not often discussed explicitly, becoming appears in Negarestani's work as different mutations—as the mathesis of decay,[1] as the cosmic liquidity of blobjectivity,[2] of trisonomy, and of the dissected spiral.[3]

Becoming, whether organically or inorganically vitalist (DeleuzoGuattarian or otherwise), Bergsonally imagistic, or experientially Whiteheadian or Jamesian, has historically remained too wedded to the power of reason. Ratiocination, as a power, is one too grounded, as it purports to sufficiently probe the meandering flows of becoming without recognizing itself as a result of other powers, processes and so on. This streaming conundrum reaches hyper-activity in Nick Land's work. While Land rightly molds thought into a productive process, Land's negation of representation and

---

[1] Reza Negarestani, *Cyclonopedia: Complicity with Anonymous Materials* (Melbourne: re.press, 2008), 15.
[2] Negarestani, *Cyclonopedia*, 16.
[3] Negarestani, *Cyclonopedia*, 31.

total destratification of materiality, as Ray Brassier has recently noted, raises the problem of individuation in a cosmos of only schizoid intensification. Negarestani's work, while indebted to Land, contrarily locates such intensification in an ever exteriorized absolute, in the strands of materiality as a process placing Negarestani's work between a mad black Deleuzianism and a mad black Schellingianism.[4] In order to dissect the metaphysical core of *Cyclonopedia*, this paper will engage the conceptual couplets ground/unground, interior/exterior (spatial and temporal) and a blackened becoming via the pivotal concept of the twist.

/1/ - GROUND / UNGROUND / DUST-BECOMING / NEGARESTANI / SCHELLING

As recent textual skirmishes between Graham Harman and Iain Hamilton Grant have made clear, the thorniest interchange between process and non-process (or becoming and anti-becoming) philosophies center on the problem of individuation. This is couched in terms of an opposition of singularity and multiplicity but this is a tension which Negarestani butchers through a degraded One, through a liquified yet dusty world. Given such a squishy materiality, individuation becomes thoroughly 'messed up', and indirected. Instead of being a privileged metaphysical function, it becomes the result of a "directional shear" in the shift from nothing to something[5] in which the halo of individuation becomes irreparably poxed.[6] Since wholeness itself is degenerate, since anything as a thing is merely a hole complex,[7] pre-perforated, be-

---

[4] The degree to which Nick Land's transcendental materialism is at odds with Negarestani's speculative project lies in the degree to which thought is instantiated in materiality.
[5] Negarestani, *Cyclonopedia*, 35.
[6] Negarestani, *Cyclonopedia*, 51.
[7] Negarestani, *Cyclonopedia*, 42-43.

coming itself becomes exhausted yet is unwilling to wither away completely, it is an ungrounding that is irreducible to nothing.[8] Furthermore, this blackening of the givenness of becoming is complicated through the formation of gradients[9] as there are a divergent series of becomings for each level of composition[10] distributed horizontally and vertically in and of a dust-covered world of rupturing.[11]

Negarestani's dust becoming is comprised of the ungrounded particles of materiality grappling with cosmic wetness[12] where a dust mound becomes a dereliction of DeLanda's assemblage,[13] the capacity of emergence following the hallowing-out of any would-be-totality, of "positive degenerating processes "[14] or "swirling dust vorticies"[15] or a dirtiness of the condensed, of the actual.[16]

Negarestani's dustism falls somewhat close to the Schellingian whirlpool as an inhibition point, or hiccup of becoming. Even more Schellingian, is Negarestani's use of apokrisis which "stratifies the universe into properly arranged layers which make unification, as a dynamic process, possible.[17] Compare to Schelling's Stufenfolge or graduated steps of dynamic nature[18] in which individuation is not separate from becoming but the result of a positive force interrupted

---

[8] Negarestani, *Cyclonopedia*, 43.
[9] Negarestani, *Cyclonopedia*, 43.
[10] Negarestani, *Cyclonopedia*, 48.
[11] Negarestani, *Cyclonopedia*, 54.
[12] Negarestani, *Cyclonopedia*, 88.
[13] Negarestani, *Cyclonopedia*, 89.
[14] Negarestani, *Cyclonopedia*, 91.
[15] Negarestani, *Cyclonopedia*, 92.
[16] Negarestani, *Cyclonopedia*, 102.
[17] Negarestani, *Cyclonopedia*, 102.
[18] Iain Hamilton Grant, *Philosophies of Nature after Schelling* (London: Continuum, 2008), 139.

by a negative force.[19] As Iain Grant states: "The Stufenfolge is derived, therefore, by combining the dynamic metrics of particular phenomena with the primary diversifying antithesis, or measuring the dynamics of phenomena against those of generation as such.[20]

Negarestani breaks from Schelling, or at least appears to, with the opposition of decay to nature since whereas nature is formless, decay is an ultra-metric or "excessive dimensioning."[21] Schelling, while a Negarestanian ally in the weaponization of the deep past, is not a strong theorist when it comes to space and the materialization and/or actualization of temporal processes. It is to this odd production of metrics which we turn to next.

/2/ - SPACE-TIME'S RAZOR OR NEGARESTANI V. BERGSON

Towards the end of *Creative Evolution* Henri Bergson gestures towards the possibility of stratifying becoming when he argues that there are different movements of becoming whether extensive, evolutionary, or qualitative before entering into a cinematographic exploration of sense. This can be read as an extension of the following from *Matter and Memory*:

> there is room, between metaphysical dogmatism, on the one hand, and critical philosophy, on the other hand, for a doctrine which regards homogeneous space and time as principles of division and of solidification introduced into the real, with a view to action and not with a view to knowledge . . . But erroneous conceptions about sensible quality and space are so deeply rooted in the

---

[19] Grant, *Philosophies*, 144.
[20] Grant, *Philosophies*, 145-146.
[21] Negarestani, *Cyclonopedia*, 185-186.

mind that it is important to attack them from every side.[22]

Negarestani address similar concepts of extensity: "To sum up: The weird as a conception of exteriority for which the deployment of unbound exteriority is explained or diagrammed in terms of a topological, economic and dynamic continuum i.e. a continuous sequence in which adjacent elements are not perceptibly different from each other, yet the extremes (horror/terror, presence/withdrawnness?) are quite distinct."[23] But, as we shall see, Negarestani staunchly differs from Bergson's intuitionistic positivity.

The materiality of decay as it grounds and ungrounds crosses the track switch of interiority/exteriority since for decay to function (in both space and time as a function of both and expression of both) there must be a decision of what is an entity, of what is decaying. As Reza has written:

> . . . decay [as] an unwholesome participation between the most abominable of time (non-belonging and pure contingency) and the most degenerate of space (space's tendency for infinite involutions which undermine any potential ground for the emergence of discrete entities). It is the complicity between the worst nightmares of space and time that brings about the possibility of putrefaction (even an infinite decay) as a differential form of irresolvable emptiness

---

[22] Henri Bergson, *Matter and Memory*, trans. Nancy Margaret Paul and W. Scott Palmer (New York: Macmillan, 1913), 282.
[23] 5/31/2009 – personal correspondence.

disguised as ideal objectivity with a generative twist.[24]

The generative twist is when emergence encounters the interior/exterior, that is, where the vital (as existence-through-time either organic or inorganic) borrows energy from an entity (partially ungrounding it) thereby threatening but perhaps not encountering its interior while using its exterior as ground yet as also exteriorized to set up a boundary. This spatiality is complicit with a temporal re-orientation, again following Reza:

> vital time appropriates the exteriority of the cosmic time and turns it into an interiorized conception of time accessible by life and its manifests. Yet the cosmic time of non-belonging and pure contingencies can never be fully appropriated or assimilated (interiorized) by the vital time and its temporal conception. Why? Because the vital time is itself contingent upon the cosmic time as a temporal condition for the interiorization and bracketing of the absolute time's contingencies and their realization as the necessary conditions required for the emergence of life.[25]

That is, where space-time has no limit to its process of grounding/ungrounding thereby creating interiors and exteriors as a side effect—life (thinking or otherwise) can only unground so far without taking out the floor beneath it both literally and energetically. Rot in particular displays the ungrounding limit of life (in the

---

[24] Negarestani, "Undercover Softness," *Collapse* 6 (2010): 400.
[25] Negarestani, "Undercover Softness," 404.

biological sense) to unground so that it can re-ground always in league with thanatosis leading to a mazed (umwege) materiality. Instead of thought fixing becoming it is a shallow butchering of itself in the stream of becoming. While Bergson is uneasy about cosmic unification, for Negarestani it exists but without the guarantee of affective positivity or complete intuitable coherency. This speaks to what Negarestani has refered to as participating in the project of scientific univeralism.[26]

Opposed to various romanticizations of finitude as well as to overly exuberant philosophies of process, Negarestani's decayed becoming allows for a spatio-temporality undetermined by thought yet not exteriorized and thrown far beyond it in such a way that thought cuts it without it cutting thought into total ruin. Becoming emerges as a self-gnawing non-entity blackened by a hive of voids.

/3/ - DARK BECOMING / THINKABLE AFFECT / NEGARESTANI / MEILLASSOUX

If becoming is becoming towards zero without ever reaching it[27] than how does Negarestani's necrotic vitalism or dark becoming differ from Meillassoux's absolute contingency? In *The Medium of Contingency*, Negarestani connects contingency to complicity. He writes: "rather than seeking openness towards the contingent outside through affordable modes of interaction" (13). If following an exteriorized absolute or exteriorized outside, becoming becomes an ontological exhausted concept and if becoming winds down, then the twist is a sideways or horizontal spread towards zero where the stretch of materiality towards destruc-

---

[26] Personal correspondence.
[27] Negarestani, *Cyclonopedia*, 35-36.

tion raises the problem of how to grapple with the productivity of thought, of thought as a gaseous rot.[28]

If becoming is a mere rearrangement and/or flow of energy-matter then it seems too easy to overemphasize (emergence or chaos) or organicism and metastability or that 'things happen' hence Meillassoux's conclusion that only contingency is necessary. Yet while Meillassoux addresses the accessibility of the in-itself via logical structures, he does not address the process or problem of materialization itself—since he argues that Hume's problem cannot be resolved (cause and effect cannot be substantiated) yet there is a difference between grounds relating to subordinate grounds and necessary grounds—it is not necessary that we have all grounds be necessary yet how things come to be materialized—how they come to be other than unrestricted becoming remains a question. It means stratifying becoming itself thereby fixing stratification as the secondary ontological operation behind becoming. The question becomes whether exhaustible becoming conflicts with an absolute outside. Does the absolute contain becoming or is it becoming? Is becoming the decay of the absolute or is the absolute outside always yet to be discovered gradient of the outside/absolute? The trisons and cavities of being complicate a beneficial immanence or becoming without becoming as well as any mechanistic system or ontological closure. Which is a better descriptive model—a broken mechanism or an exhaustible becoming? Negarestani arguably defines his metaphysics more regionally, as a void energetics—as the happening coming from trision, nemat space, etc but is this maximizable? Is becoming itself a cavity in the absolute outside or is becoming the absolute at work.

---

[28] Negarestani, *Cyclonopedia*, 188, 201.

Meillassoux's absolute of hyper-chaos purports that thinking science, or thinking non-correlational nature, reveals that any real sense of becoming must be contained within it and not subject to it[29] and distingushes the chaotic non-becoming of his absolute from classical Heraclitean flux since, for Meillassoux, becoming itself can be un-becomed, dissolved.[30]

But again, where Negarestani and Meillassoux appear to differ is over actualization—Negarestani, through the vorticle dustiness of an unraveling absolute, attempts to articulate actualization and individuation in becoming without privileging intellection or becoming as the sovereign metaphysical gesture. *Cyclonopedia* is an alchemical layering of the enterprise of becoming, stretched far back into the dusty accretion of cosomological formation into the apocalyptic future as chrono-politics.

/4/ - CONCLUSION

Arguably, becoming got ahead of itself and stumbled over its own exuberance—being steeped in the static of its own elan vital or in the organ-less mush leading up to the flesh-eating net frenzy of the 90s, perhaps an update of Bergson's cinematic stitching of experience. This cartoonish exuberance perhaps explains Graham Harman's statement that becoming has had its day. Negarestani's work is proof that such a declaration is premature. The important lesson is, while acknowledging the univocity or lack of ontological difference between thought and slime, or voids and dust, this does not admit a vertigo of indistinction, in which affect space (or the affective-aesthetic shell of a particular kind of thinking) is separate from its metaphysical wagers not only operationally but in layered actualization.

---

[29] Negarestani, *Cyclonopedia*, 22.

[30] Negarestani, *Cyclonopedia*, 64.

The weirdness of actuality, in a process or powers based metaphysics is summed up by Grant "Being is necessarily indeterminate if actuality is determinable."[31] Grant's genetic conceptualization of actuality separates it from objectality—a separation I would argue is carried forward gothically in Negarestani's work.

At the risk of too quickly becoming a caricature of myself, I wish to end on a weird note. In letters to his friend James Ferdinand Morton, HP Lovecraft waxes philosophic: "Amidst the cosmic chaos the only things we have to cherish are the transient shapes of illusion woven from the chance scraps our memories hold. Apart from these, we are lost in the meaningless void![32] . . . I'd damn well like to come out with a book some day, even though I might never win a place beside Schopenhauer, Nietzsche or Bertrand Russell. I think I'd call it *What is Anything?*"[33]

Negarestani's work in the field metaphysics constructs a realm of pulsating voids, always an outside-within, without the voidic ever losing its exteriority, without slipping away from what we might oddly call spatial antecedence, of what is anything now and then next to other thatness and isness.[34] Therefore, where with Lovecraft we might retain an iota of sanity if there was a singular void in which to drift, in the Negarestanian case, where we are permeated by a scourge of voids, where becoming is the energetic entrails of a long dead One, there is only the operational chasm between affect space and metaphysics, between the half-translucent cerebral rattle of consciousness, and the darkness of onto-epistemological indistinction.

---

[31] Negarestani, "Undercover Softness," 451.
[32] H. P. Lovecraft, *Selected Letters* (Sauk City: Arkham House, 1968), 3.102.
[33] Lovecraft, *Selected Letters*, 3.110.
[34] Negarestani, *Cyclonopedia*, 200.

The chasm being the interior gnawing and the yawning exterior.

... Or, Speaking with the Alien, a Refrain ...

Ed Keller

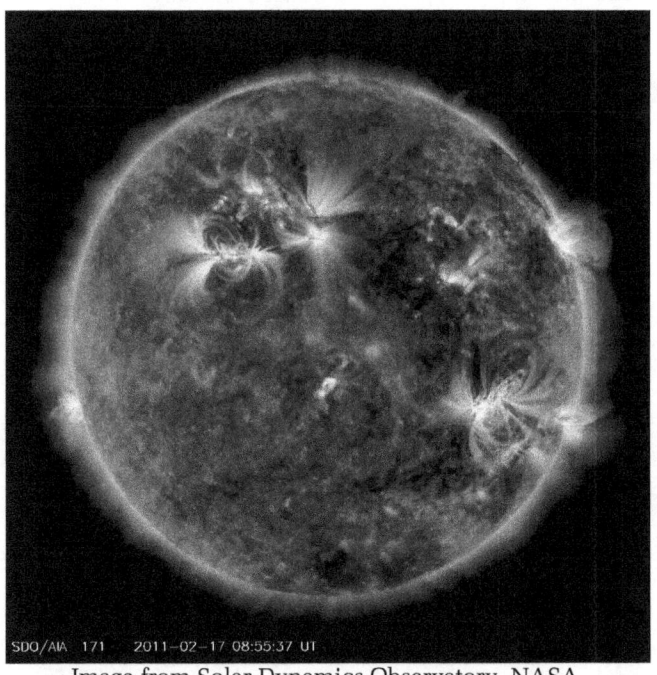

Image from Solar Dynamics Observatory, NASA, http://sdo.gsfc.nasa.gov/.

"On a global scale, the Solar Rattle is the ultimate musicality: It registers any message-oriented or signaling datastream as a parasitic sub-noise ambient within itself. The Solar Rattle rewrites every datastream as an Unsign, even beyond any pattern of disinformation . . . The highly stratified structure of Ionosphere/Magnetosphere provides the Earth with secret warmachines older than the Sun itself, with which it traps solar winds [high energy particles of the sun] and turns them into peculiarly planetary sonic entities. Ionospheric strata have been customized and arranged in such a way that they reinforce the earth's surface with demonic currents and forces by capturing solar winds, bringing the earth's surface and its biosphere into an immanence with the Sun and the burning core of the Earth through a sonic axis" (*Cyclonopedia*).

Image from Transition Region and Coronal Explorer, Lockheed Martin Solar and Astrophysics Lab, http://trace.lmsal.com/.

As is rendered clear in this passage, a key theme in *Cyclonopedia* is the fraught relationship between the sun and the earth, within a broader, cosmologically scaled economy of excess and consumption, of overlapping layers of time: where futures and pasts are enabled or erased by the stunning excess that the sun cannot restrain. We might ask: what is the manner by which humans can position themselves in relation to that magnificent, excessive erasing machine? Or is it an erasing machine?

Another key cyclonopediac plot-line investigates the presence of a kind of alien mind on earth, or in matter generally: oil as the black corpse of the sun, speaking through a bacterial archaeology and unmasking a cosmic insider that uses the earth as a territory from which to launch an insurrection against laws writ large by universal order. This talk will play a little with the tension between the logic of a solar economy and the sites where the alien might be found.

Death Valley.[1]

Is it true that "the universe is hostile . . . [and we] devour to survive"?[2] Primo Levi says: "We are alone. If we have interlocutors, they are so far away that, barring unforeseeable turns of events, we shall never talk to them; in spite of this, some years ago we sent them

---

[1] Dan Duriscoe, http://www2.nature.nps.gov/air/lightscapes/team.cfm/.
[2] TOOL, lyrics from "Vicarious," *10,000 Days* (Volcano II, 2006).

a pathetic message. Every year that passes leaves us more alone. Not only are we not the centre of the universe, but the universe is not made for human beings; it is hostile, violent, alien. In the sky there are no Elysian Fields, only matter and light, distorted, compressed, dilated, and rarefied to a degree that eludes our senses and our language."[3]

And Cormac McCarthy begins *Blood Meridian* like this: "The boy crouches by the fire and watches him. Night of your birth. Thirty three. The Leonids they were called. God how the stars did fall. I looked for blackness, holes in the heavens."[4]

McCarthy looks to the sky in this passage, but the book is relentlessly grounded in the earth, in blood, and in murder. A beautiful paean to the savage practice. Alienness could be as much on earth as it is in heaven.

All this makes me think of great B movies like Event Horizon, a meditation on the places where time/space break down: a sci-fi horror exploration of contingency, wherein a space ship voyages into pure chaos and brings it back to this universe.[5]

---

[3] Primo Levi, *The Search for Roots: A Personal Anthology*, ed. and trans. Peter Forbes (New York: Penguin, 2002). This passage is in Levi's brief commentary on Kip Thorne's text, "The Search for Black Holes," *Scientific American* (December 1974), 32-5, 43.

[4] Cormac McCarthy, *Blood Meridian* (New York: Vintage, 1992), 3.

[5] A ship designed by Dr. William Weir, played by Sam Neill, who appears in other great B films that treat this subject: *Mouth of Madness*, *Daybreakers*, *Possession* . . .

But let me start with some opening questions: what is the alien? what does it mean to speak with it? What's at risk when we get exposed to radically non-human systems? Communication, translation, noise, agency and thought itself: all have an indirect but crucial relation to the concept of the 'alien', which by definition seems to be something that exists outside language or measure.

Terragni – Photomontage created for a special issue of the Italian magazine *Quadrante* No. 35/36 dedicated to the Casa del Fascio by Giuseppe Terragni (1932-36).

East and West Berlin celebrating the new year together.

This quote from Nietzsche's *Birth of Tragedy* gives context: "At bottom the esthetic phenomenon is simple; one need only have the ability to see continually a living play and to live perpetually surrounded by hosts of spirits, and one is a poet; one need only feel the drive to alter oneself and to speak out of alien bodies and souls, and one is a dramatist. Dionysian excitation is capable of communicating to a whole multitude this artistic power to feel oneself surrounded by such a host of spirits, with whom one knows oneself to be inwardly one. This process of the tragic chorus is the originary dramatic phenomenon: seeing oneself altered before one's very eyes and now acting, as though one had really entered into another body, another character. Here already the individual gives itself up by entering into an alien nature. And what is more, this phenomenon arises epidemically: a whole crowd feels itself enchanted in this way."[6]

---

[6] Samuel Weber, "Displacing the Body: The Question of Digital Democracy," May 2, 1996, http://hydra.humanities.uci.edu/weber/displace.html/.

"We can communicate with others only through what in us—as much as in others—has remained potential, and any communication (as Benjamin perceives for language) is first of all communication not of something in common but of communicability itself."[7]

We may well ask who or what is communicating, and with whom, in this host of spirits—and what kind of consciousness arises when an individual becomes aware that they are part of a multifarious body?

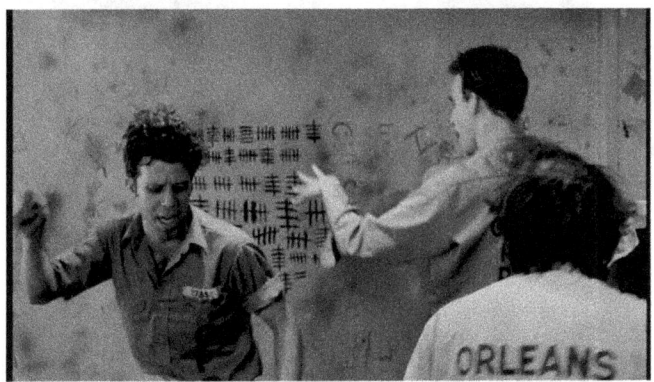
Still image from *Down by Law*, dir. Jim Jarmusch, 1986.

Agamben suggests that "The gesture . . . opens the sphere of ethos as the more proper sphere of that which is human . . . [and] is communication of a communicability."[8] The value of language, according to Agamben, is to be found in how it can show an intent on the part of the voices—the transmitters and the receivers—rather than in how faithfully it can transmit a message.

---

[7] G. Agamben, "Form-of-Life," in *Means Without End* (Univ. of Michigan, 2000), 10.
[8] Agamben, "Notes on Gesture," in *Means Without End*, 70.

The exchange of information between 'aliens' allows both parties to discover themselves connected to an interruption of signal, to a noise: it is the outside, the open, the unknown, the parasite, and danger. This idea of danger, scaled up to a geopolitical, a transhistorical, a cosmic level, brings us back to the sun as a reference point, a catalyst.

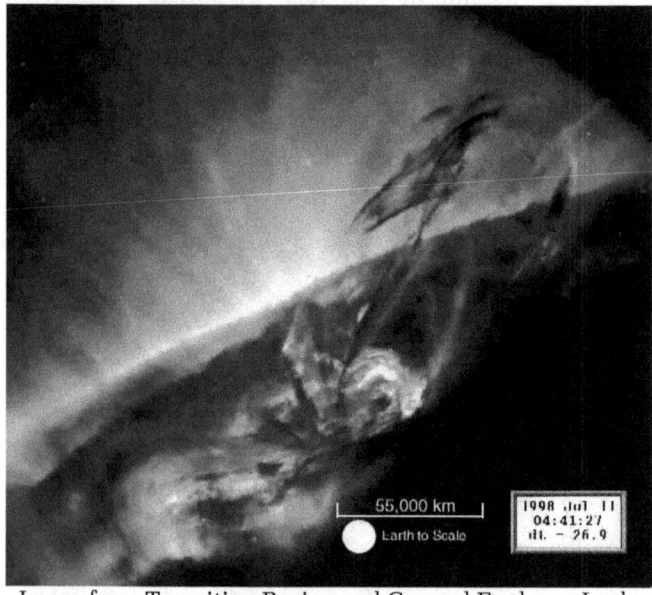

Image from Transition Region and Coronal Explorer, Lockheed Martin Solar and Astrophysics Lab, http://trace.lmsal.com/.

As Bataille points out in *The Accursed Share*, solar excess is one of the key engines driving planetary general economies in our corner of the universe. Monetary systems are part of the spectrum, along with many others: information, energy, biological systems, and so on. Redeploying Agamben's idea of communication in a solar context, this idea of a general economy is rendered yet more urgent by factors such as the sun's ability to give across a broad spectrum; the speed of light itself as a universal constant; light and energy understood as a messaging substrate- and there are questions. Can there be too much light, or too little, or just the right amount of light? 'We come from spent light.'[9] 'It's a trick of the light.'[10] 'Don't go into the light.'[11]

Still image from *Sunshine*, dir. Danny Boyle, 2007.

Michel Serres describes the phenotype as time machine, when he says, "within the context of an even more general circulation which goes from the sun to the black depths of space, the organism is a barrier of braided links that leaks like a wicker basket but can still function as a dam," thus positioning us as organisms in a vast gradient of information and energy flow, shifting density, and uniquely able [through our morphology, our phenotype] to render information meaningful.

---

[9] Louis Kahn, possibly apocryphal.
[10] Anonymous.
[11] *Poltergeist*, dir. Tobe Hooper (Metro-Goldwyn-Mayer, 1982).

I excerpt the following passages from the film *Sunshine* [dir. Danny Boyle, 2007] to viscerally illustrate what might be at stake in our own bodies' proximity to, and abject status against, the many 'fields' of the sun.

Searle: Icarus?
Icarus: Yes, Dr Searle?
Searle: Please re-filter the observation room portal.
Icarus: Filter up or down, Dr. Searle?
Searle: Down.
Searle: Icarus, how close is this to full brightness?
Icarus: At this distance of 36 million miles you are observing the sun at 2% of full brightness.
Searle: 2%? Can you show me 4%?
Icarus: 4% would result in irreversible damage to your retinas.
However, you could observe 3.1% for a period of not longer than 30 seconds.
Searle: Icarus, I'm going to reset the filter to 3.1%.
Searle: [Gasps from the intense heat and light.]

Clearly, there's too much light and heat. Searle has an obsession with the source. In a kind of slow-emo-drone-ambient manner [Mogwai come to mind] the film builds a complex image for us of the sun as both imperiled but also vastly unaware of human life and need- and each character's mental deterioration parallels the degree to which they are immersed in- and in communication with- that expanded field.

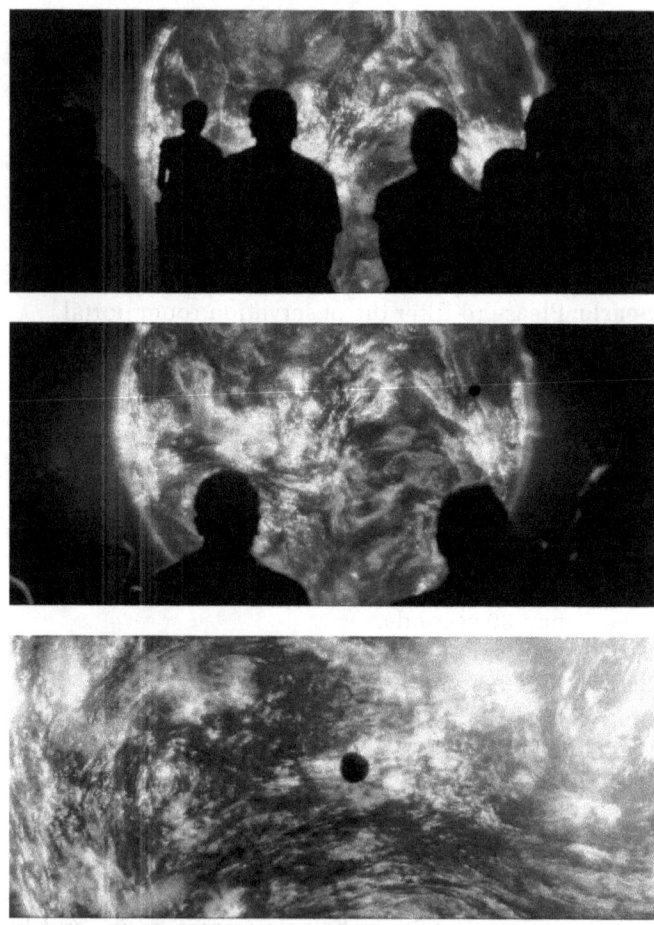

"On reflection, what can one say . . . Ladies and Gentlemen . . . Mercury."

Because it's a suicide mission it goes off the rails. We know that something bad is bound to happen, because the sun is dying, and they're on their way to restart it [!!!] with a chunk of matter the size of Manhattan. On the way, sci-fi genre-standard encounters with micro-asteroids puncturing the ship lead to malfunctions and heroic extravehicular missions.

Leper Creativity

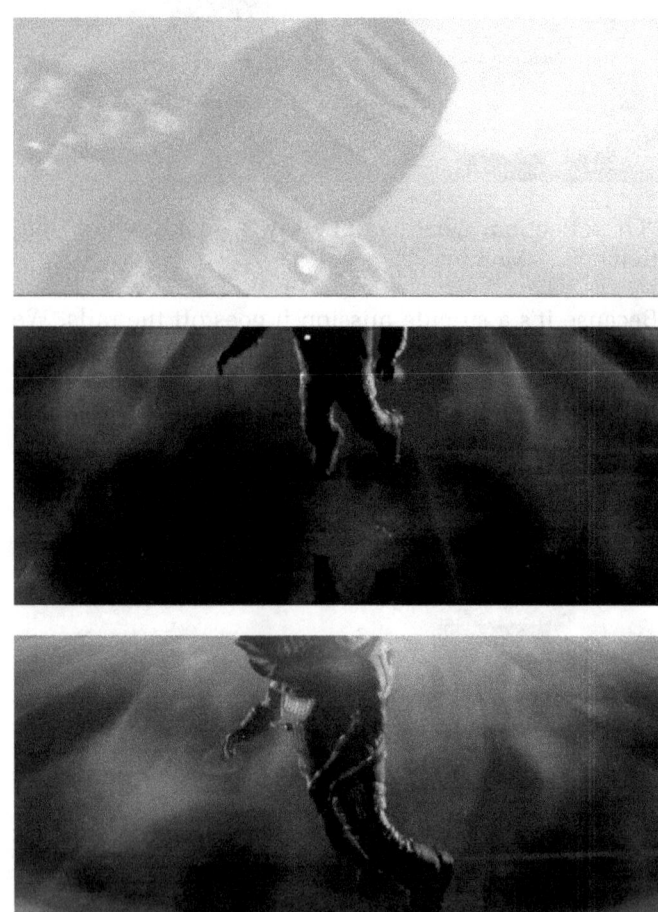

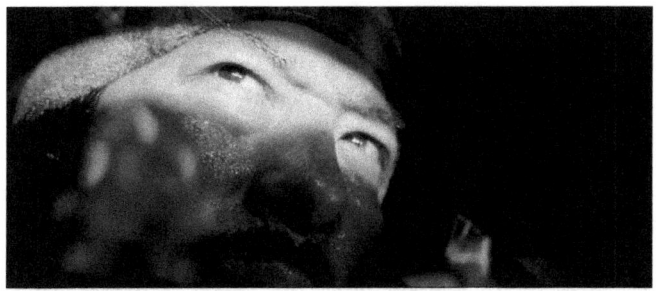

Icarus: 94% of shields in full sunlight.
Capa: Captain. Captain . . . entering the shield . . . Do you copy—You must leave now Captain!
Icarus: 97% of shield in full sunlight.
Kaneda: Final panel closing. Shield is secure.
Capa: You have to move right now! Captain, it's right on you.

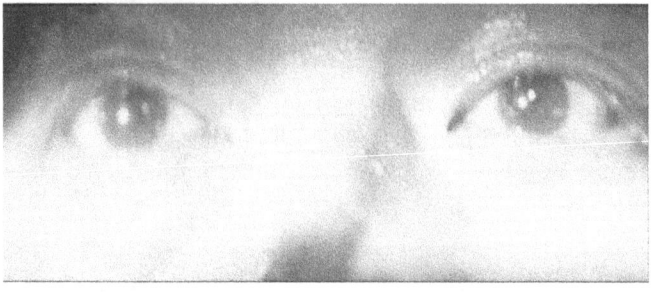

Crewmember: Kaneda's not going to make it!
Capa: You have to move, you have to move now!
Crewmember: It's too far . . .
Capa: You have to move . . . Why isn't he moving?
Kaneda: [turns in his protective spacesuit to face the oncoming sunlight]
Searle: Kaneda, what do you see?

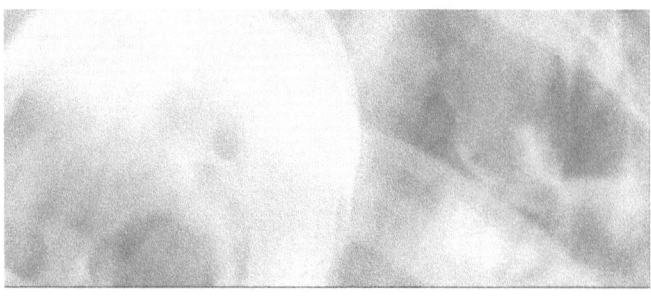

Capa: No . . . Captain, move!
Searle: Kaneda! What do you see? Kaneda!!!!
Kaneda [screaming]: Aouuuuggh!
Capa: Kaneda!
   [static]
Crewmember: [Weeping.]

HUBBLE Deep Field, image from http://hubblesite.org/.

At the end of this last sequence from *Sunshine*, there's a shot/return shot sequence where we're actually seeing from the p.o.v. of the sun, moving towards the surviving crewmember at the edge of the shield. This is the moment, cinematically, where what has been until now a very laconic camera starts to adopt the moves, tropes and cuts of a horror film. But the slasher in this case is the sun itself.

In his text *The Origin of Language: Biology, Information Theory, & Thermodynamics*, Michel Serres refigures the organism as body in noise, in the thermal howl of negentropy, as a bundle of perceptions, a fantastic sheaf of times. The organism itself becomes a parasite of noise, or an interlocking set of clinamens. He says: "we have discovered the place, the operation, and the theorem where and with which the knots of the bouquet [of time] are tied. It is here and in this manner that time flows back and can change direction ... For a moment the temporal sheaf makes a full circle. It forms a turbulence where opposing times converge. Organization, per se, as system and homeorrhesis, functions precisely as a converter of time."[12]

And light too could be a time machine. This is the implication in one of the very last scenes on the spaceship in Sunshine, when time itself seems to pause for Capa, the last surviving astronaut, as he delivers their 'payload' to 'jumpstart' the sun. A trick of the light?

Let's think about Serres's idea of time-conversion from an information-communication POV. What is transmissible and what is translatable?

---

[12] Michel Serres, *The Origin of Language: Biology, Information Theory, & Thermodynamics*, eds. Josue V. Harari and David F. Bell, in *Hermes: Literature, Science, Philosophy* (Baltimore: Johns Hopkins University Press, 1982).

Still image from *Andromeda Strain*, dir. Robert Wise (1971).

In *Andromeda Strain*, a great B movie sci-fi thriller from 1971, a dangerous alien life form has arrived on earth from outer space, and scientists are struggling against time to prevent a global outbreak. The film exposes the point of view of the 'alien', as the scientists must think through the alien body to understand what to do to mitigate the infection in humans. Hence, a crystal, nonhuman presence on earth—the alien p.o.v.—is as important as the human. The scientists understand this. They are sensitive to the energetic needs of this alien system, to the way that it might affect human bodies. They cannot speak with this almost abstract system yet they must struggle to communicate with it.[13]

---

[13] *Andromeda Strain*, dir. Robert Wise, (Universal Pictures, 1971); adapted from the 1969 novel by M. Crichton.

They practice a 'controlled folly', leveraging their scientific models for both analysis and communication. They attempt to establish an epistemological horizon, to 'see' systems that are either invisible, or outside their realms of perception. If a system can communicate, it can survive. The temporal factor is linked here to survival.

Still image from, *The Exorcist*, dir. William Friedkin (1973).

And in *The Exorcist*, which is a great beast influencing *Cyclonopedia*, what kind of time is at play? *The Exorcist* is a horror film operating as geopolitical allegory. It lurks behind and around *Cyclonopedia* like a Deleuzean 'Old One', always ready to sire a bastard child. It is an investigation of noise as the demonic and multiple, and of the contact between deep time [non-human time] and human time. The horizon of the sun reappears again, and the human body against it. But here an earthbound demon acts as interlocutor.[14]

---

[14] *The Exorcist*, dir. William Friedkin (Warner Bros., 1973); adapted from the 1971 novel by William Peter Blatty.

In the opening sequence to the film, we are presented with a fantastic image of the multitude—the multitude working the earth, working with the temporality of the earth, exhuming [by chance] something that has been buried, buried intentionally [the discovery of and unearthing of Pazuzu we can guess is unintentional]. This provides us with a clear model of a multiplicitous body which we usually find quite difficult to imagine. The plot and narrative holes that we find in *Cyclonopedia* point to *The Exorcist* as a beloved component of the cyclonopediac project, above and beyond its rendering visible the possession of a pubescent upper middle class girl—in a tiny Washington DC suburb—by a demon that emerges from the Middle East, exhumed by a Christian scientist [of course those are great plot lines also]. But this first image of multiplicitous bodies interacting with the earth and finding the traces of deep time is one of the most important parts of *The Exorcist*.

And *The Exorcist* is also a fantastic mediation on time, is it not? Reversible and irreversible, the time of the ruin, the time of the archive, linear time coming into contact with non-linear- the human performing as [cf. Serres] a wicker basket: a site, braided, that can hold certain things yet let others pass through. Did you know that *The Exorcist* was such a great investigation of the problem of linear time and non-linear time?

And this last sequence from the opening of the film says it all: the demon Pazuzu facing off against the human priest, the sun in between them, and then a fade to Washington DC which sets that geopolitical horizon ablaze.

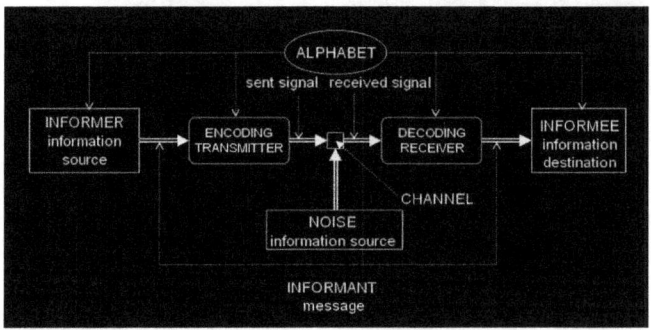

Shannon and Weaver, communication model.[15]

To speak with the alien, we need a protocol for the 'transmission' of information . . . to manage our own forced possession by the host of spirits.

---

[15] Luciano Floridi, "Semantic Conceptions of Information," *The Stanford Encyclopedia of Philosophy* (Spring 2011 Edition), http://plato.stanford.edu/archives/spr2011/entries/information-semantic/; image adapted from C. E. Shannon and W. Weaver, *The Mathematical Theory of Communication* (Urbana: University of Illinois Press, 1949).

Still image from *8 ½*, dir. Federico Fellini (Columbia Pictures, 1963).

In *8 1/2* [1963], Fellini collects *everyone*, brings them together, and invites them to join voices in a joyous babel, a festival of souls. Can this carnival resist the concluding erasure that we see in Sunshine? The main character, a filmmaker, Guido, is staging a fantasy circus within which all the people he has known, including his own childhood identity, play roles. Throughout the film he has slipped between memory, fantasy and reality, and the film itself is a masterpiece of self-reflexive structure. Perhaps this is where the idea of the refrain from my title can return. The memory unbidden, involuntary even, stuttering through a refractive glass, and invoking the host of spirits.

So this is a very human way to finish. My confidence was raised a bit when McKenzie Wark spoke of a material kind of friendship earlier today, and the idea that a narrative might be built out of an attention to the non-human. One imagines that we could understand thus the narrative of the anonymous materials that *Cyclonopedia* treats with. And so I imagine in a kind of hallucination, that *8 1/2* really concludes with materials-holding-hands-with-materials . . . and indeed it might yet be a fanged, multisexed beast that consumes us all in the end, yet we are still holding hands with it/her/him/them.

"Thought is form-of-life, life that cannot be segregated from its form; and anywhere the intimacy of this inseparable life appears, in the materiality of corporeal processes and of habitual ways of life no less than in theory, there and only there is there thought. And it is this thought, this form-of-life, that, abandoning naked life to 'Man' and to the 'Citizen,' who clothe it temporarily and represent it with their 'right,' must become the guiding concept and the unitary center of the coming politics."[16]

What does it mean to be an agent of revolutionary time? How can we invoke the host of spirits? What can we do if they come when we call? I hope that these examples all illustrate a body caught on the edge of knowing the future, open to time, as the gestures which constitute a 'means without end' are each autonomous acts out of which universes unfold.

Ultimately this recalls the problems of Information theory and the relation between forms of entropy and information flow.

---

[16] Agamben, *Means Without End*, 10.

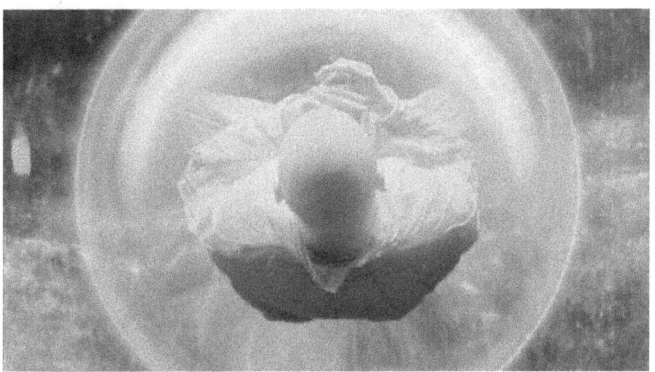
Still image from *The Fountain*, dir. Darren Arnofsky (Warner Bros, 2006).

A question remains: whether interiority and exteriority can ever truly trade messages; through the gauntlet of noise and the parasite, can a body [monad] ever connect to systems outside itself [Pynchon's *Crying of Lot 49*] or, immersed in an already given situation [Bioy Casares' *Invention of Morel*] somehow bootstrap into the 'yet to come'? The ability of a system to span [or convert] time is one measure of its ethical capacity.

Thought emerges when systems become aware that they are formed by and communicating with agents that can only provisionally speak their language, yet, nevertheless: the desire to communicate is set in motion, producing new modes of thought out of the necessarily untranslatable.

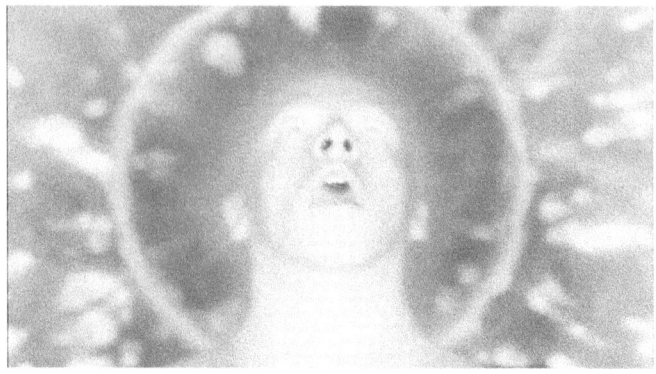

Is it perverse to see a connection between Agamben's 'thought is form-of-life' and *Cyclonopedia*'s anonymous materials? Where Agamben places the human as a strong frame for ethics, *Cyclonopedia* posits the existence of thought in any and all systems. [I think again of that reverse-shot horror film camera move in Sunshine; when suddenly as filmviewers, we go into transference with the radically non-human.]

That's where I'd draw the comparison and champion and support this thinking of friendship and love [complicity?] from a non-human point of view. Perhaps this is the cautionary tale that we find in *Cyclonopedia*: it is telling us that the work being done today—in the philosophies and ecologies that radically de-anthropocentrize their models—is Ballardian, simply an unending distance viewing and encounter with the unthinkably vast ways of the universe. And as they gain traction, theories of a 'coming community', a 'commonwealth', will constitute a new framework for an emerging earthly and celestial politics, a non-human eschatology. Artaud's here with us now, contemplating the signal to noise ratio of the solar rattle.

I'll conclude with a question that touches on territory Eugene Thacker has spent quite some time with and worked through so well: should we ask, is this Life at the Limits of Thought, or Thought at the Limits of Life?

Receipt of Malice

Lionel Maunz

Kata Tjuta (L5) Uluru (C2)

Kimberlysandstein

Schichtgestein

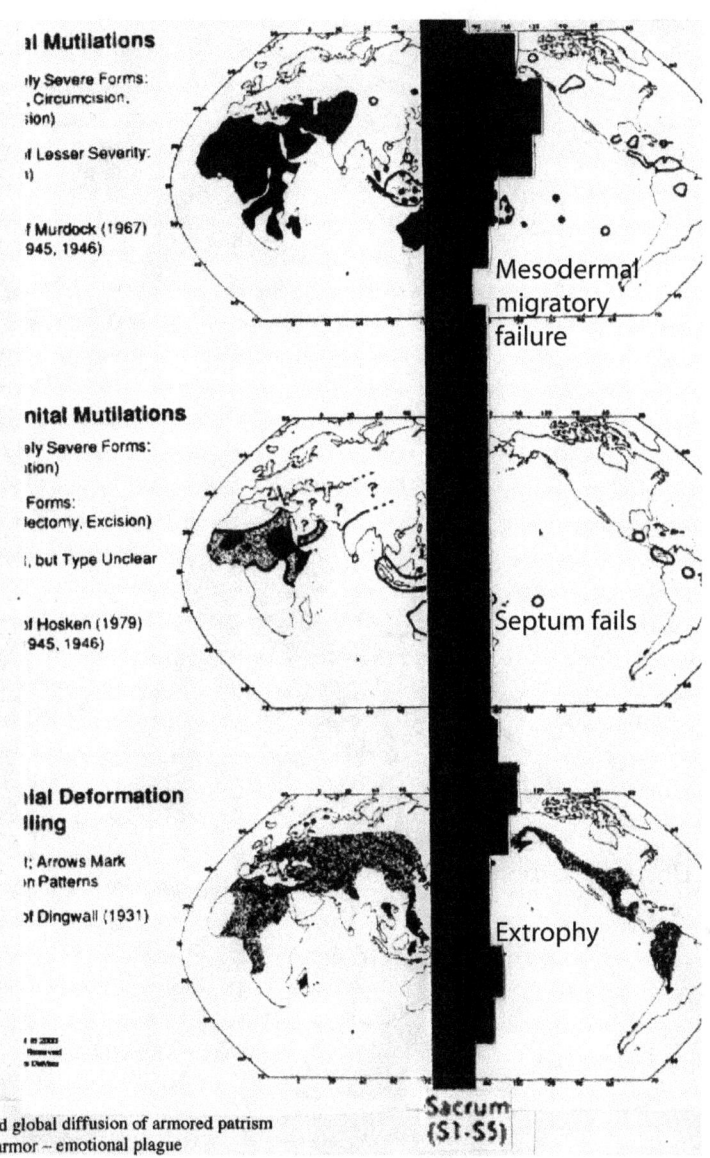

Genesis and global diffusion of armored patrism
Character armor -- emotional plague

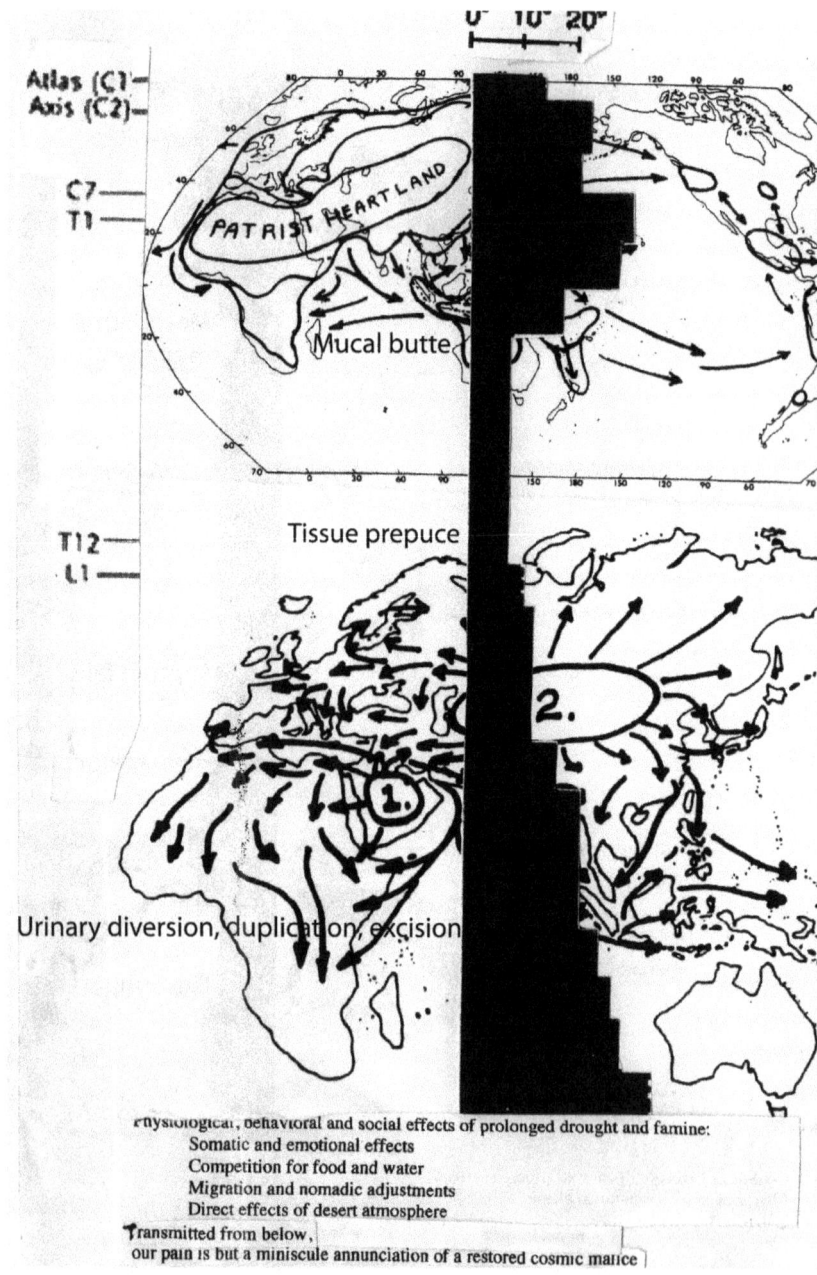

Atlas (C1)
Axis (C2)
C7
T1
PATRIST HEARTLAND
Mucal butte
T12
L1
Tissue prepuce
Urinary diversion, duplication, excision

Physiological, behavioral and social effects of prolonged drought and famine:
    Somatic and emotional effects
    Competition for food and water
    Migration and nomadic adjustments
    Direct effects of desert atmosphere
Transmitted from below,
our pain is but a miniscule annunciation of a restored cosmic malice

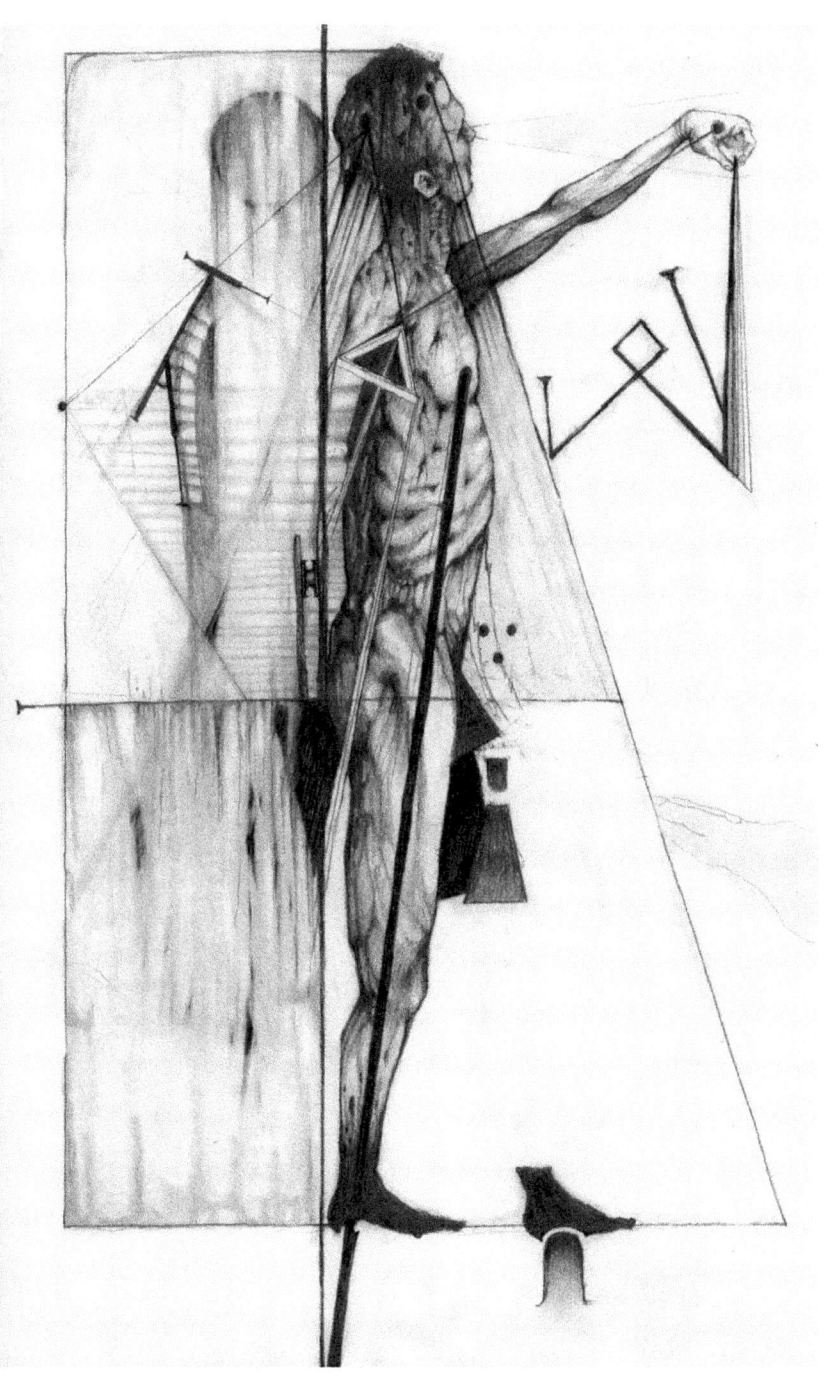

Receipt of malice

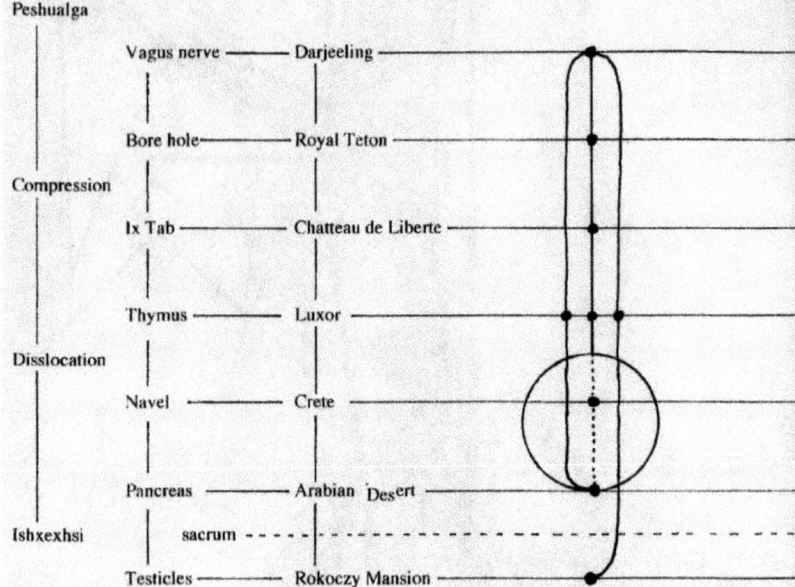

Peshualga

- Vagus nerve — Darjeeling
- Bore hole — Royal Teton

Compression

- Ix Tab — Chatteau de Liberte
- Thymus — Luxor

Disslocation

- Navel — Crete
- Pancreas — Arabian Desert

Ishxexhsi   sacrum - - - - - - - -

- Testicles — Rokoczy Mansion

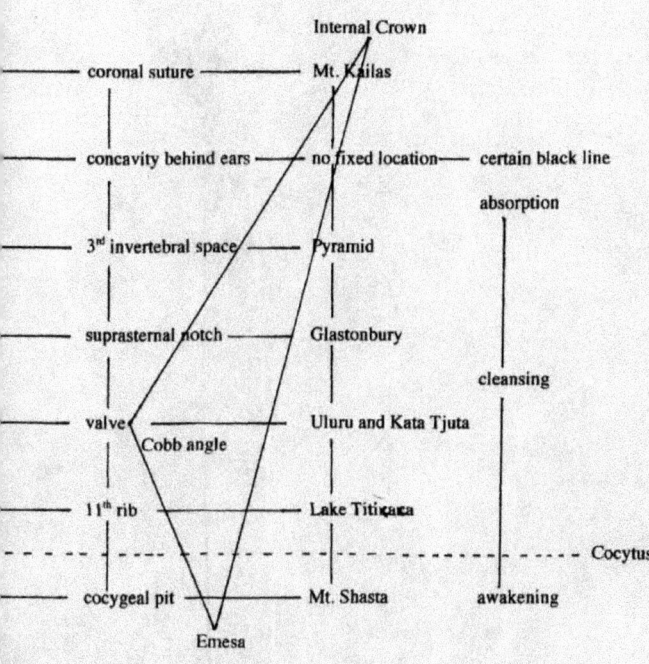

Internal Crown: state of opened peripheral channels achieved with dynamic deformation of growth through the agency of externally applied disciplinary force

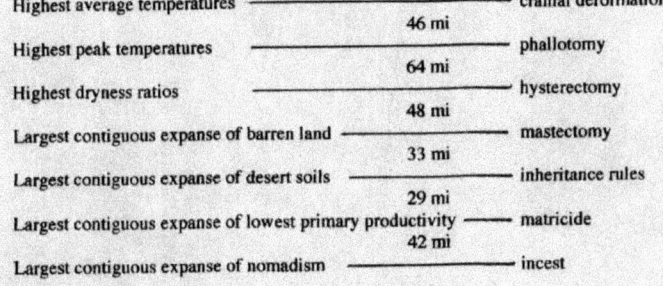

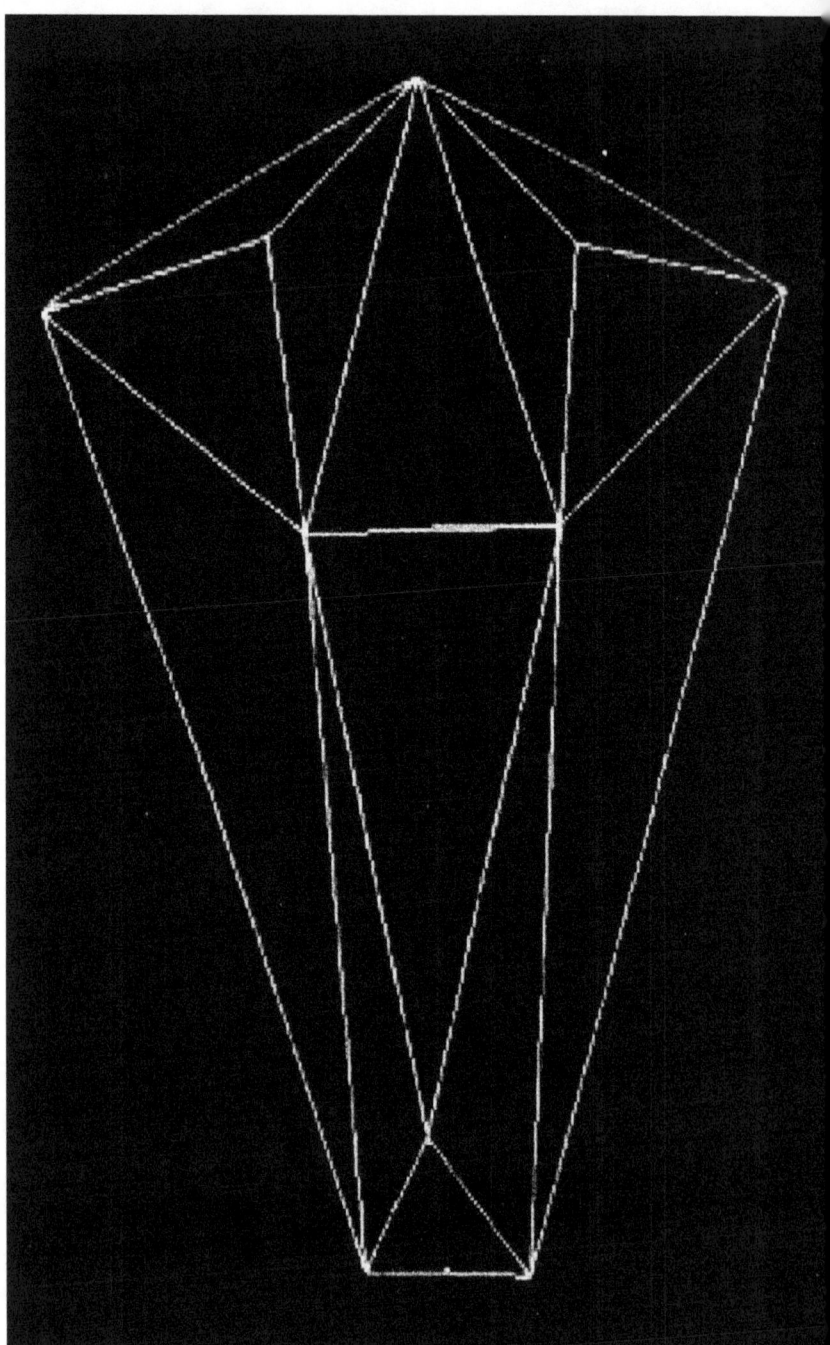

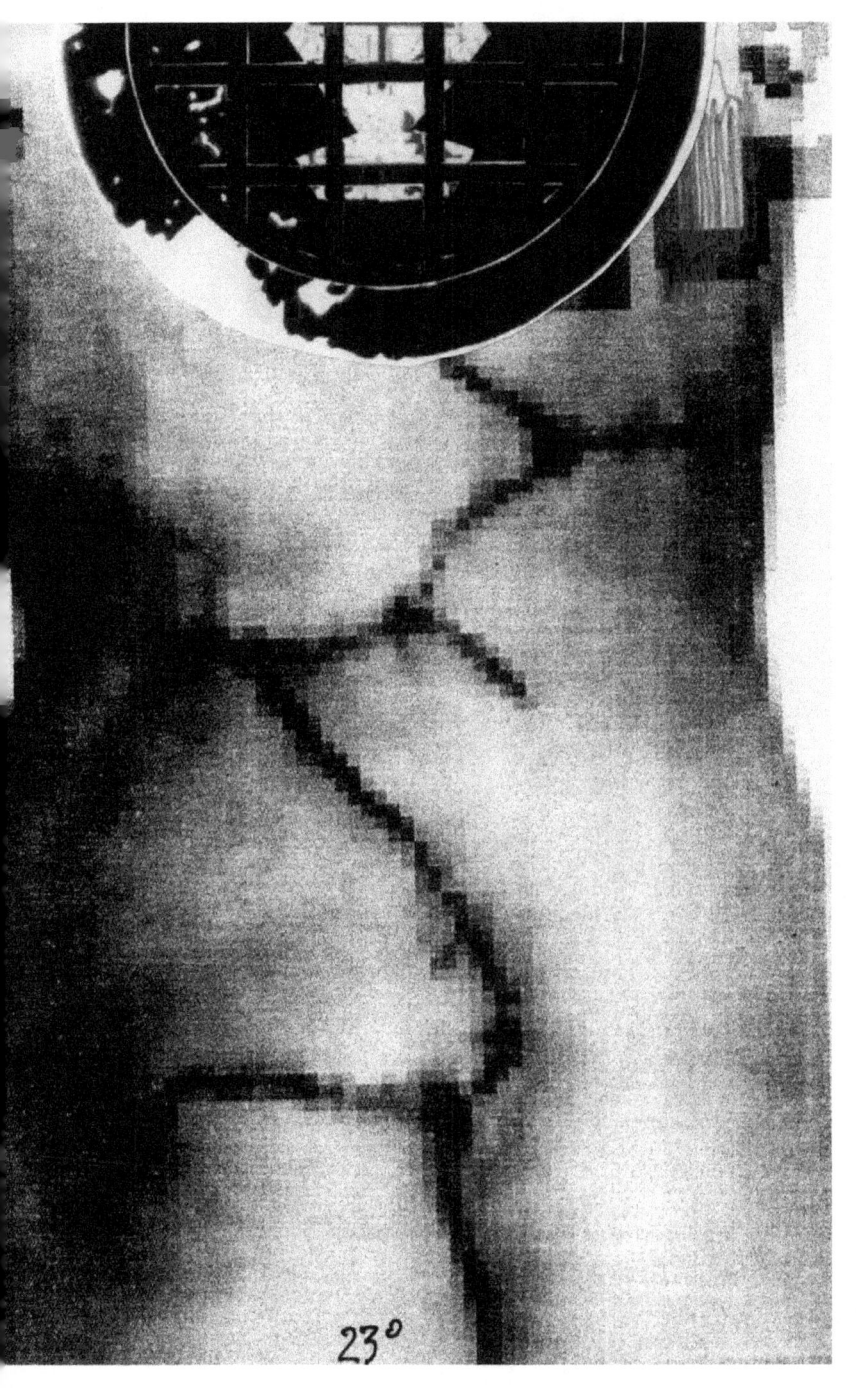

23°

Seven sewers:
First lie in the pilonoidal sinus and is a pit all mucus and butted tissue.
As sulfur is to earth what leprosy is to flesh. An unequivocal upheaval. Concussing vertically through the spaces between organs and out on a cruel rut of yeast to achieve its geography in a black line. Not natural only scrupulously reduced. That crude fissure into ashrams, all temples of the heart to deprive and pour effluvium.

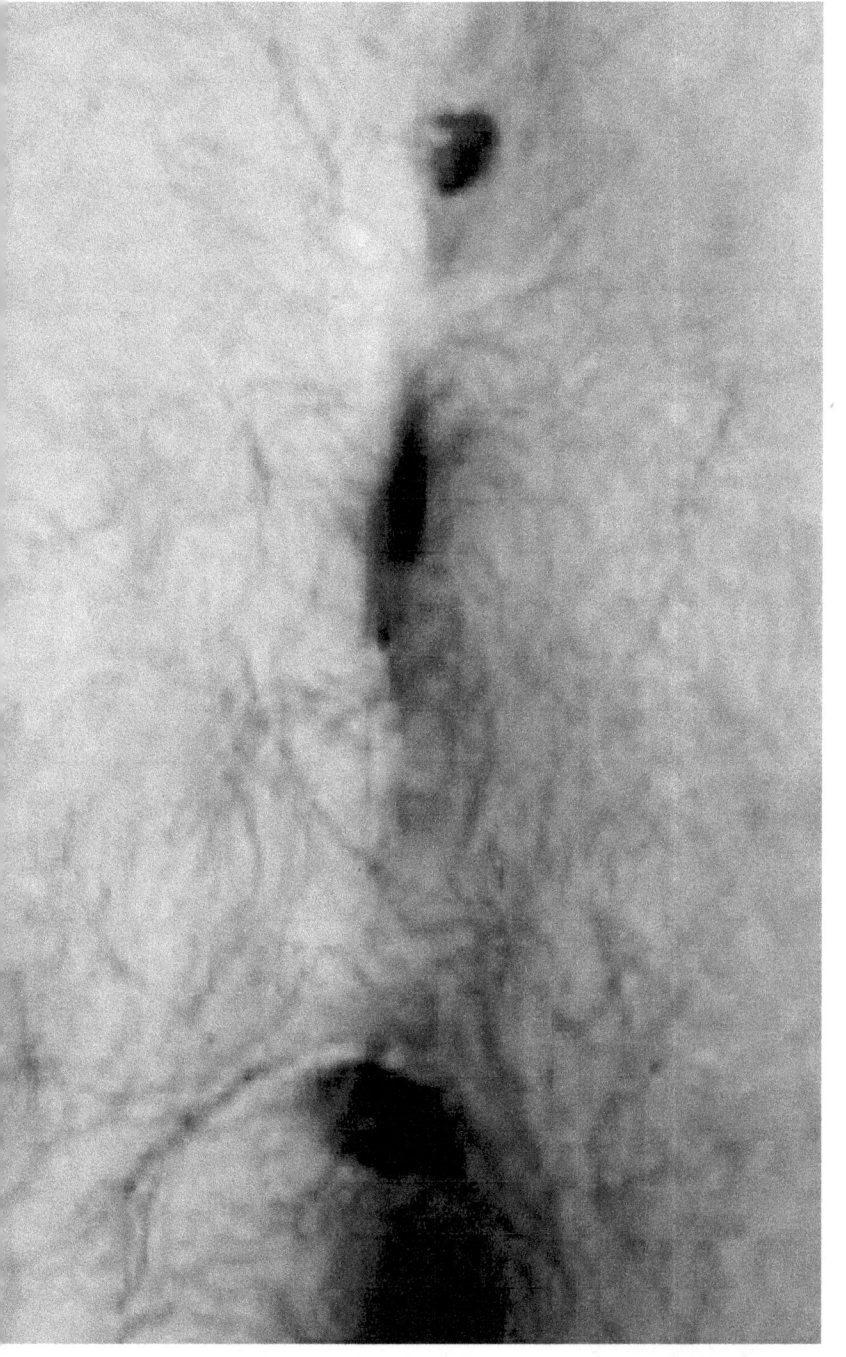

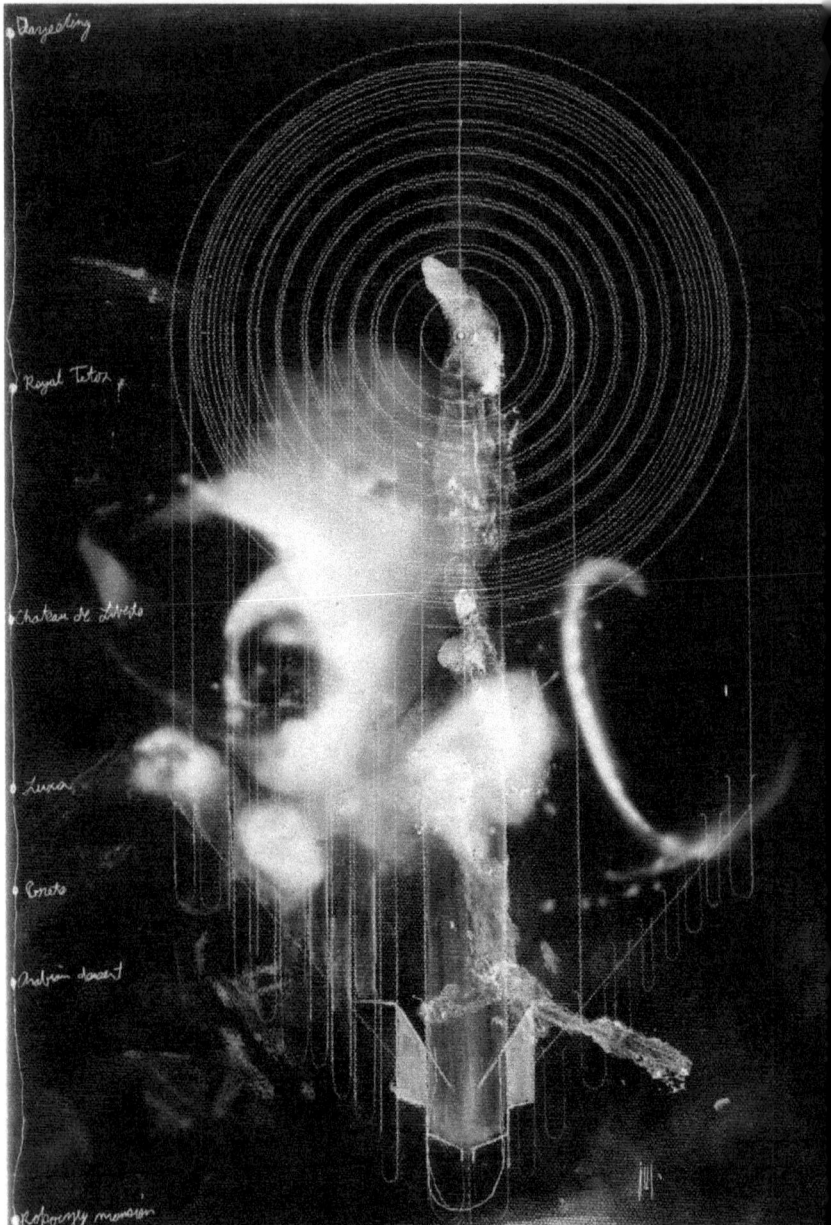

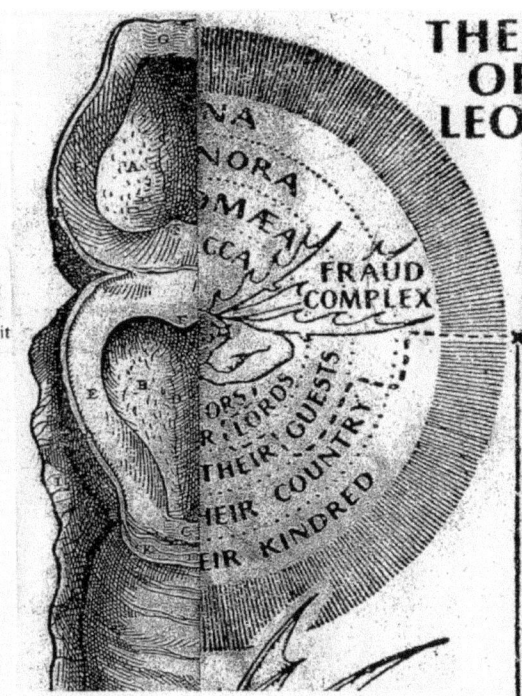

Crescent of receptivity:
All the more to receive it
All the more to receive it
All the more to embrace it

Intimating a theory about transmutation of forms into feelings corresponding to an idea contamination so that this fissure can return encumbered by 29 restrictions of vehemence.

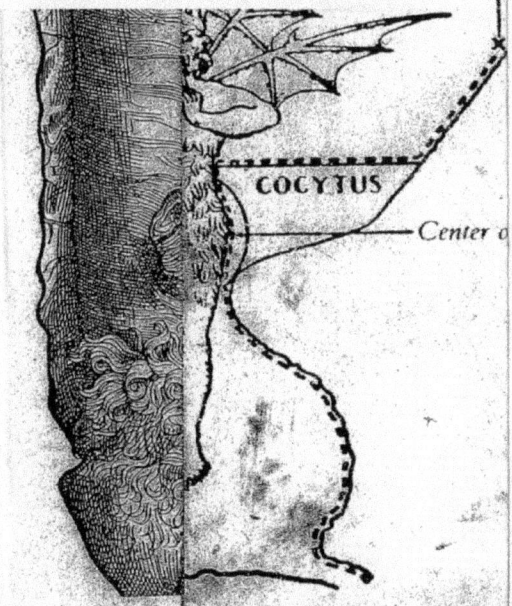

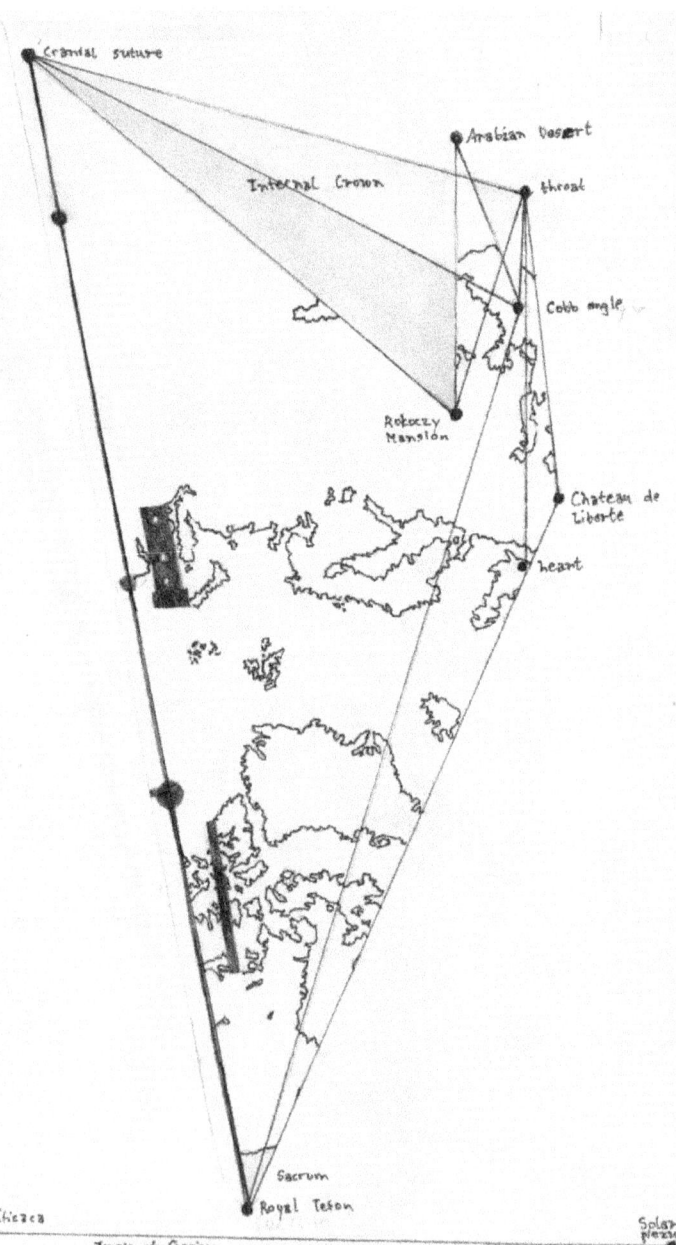

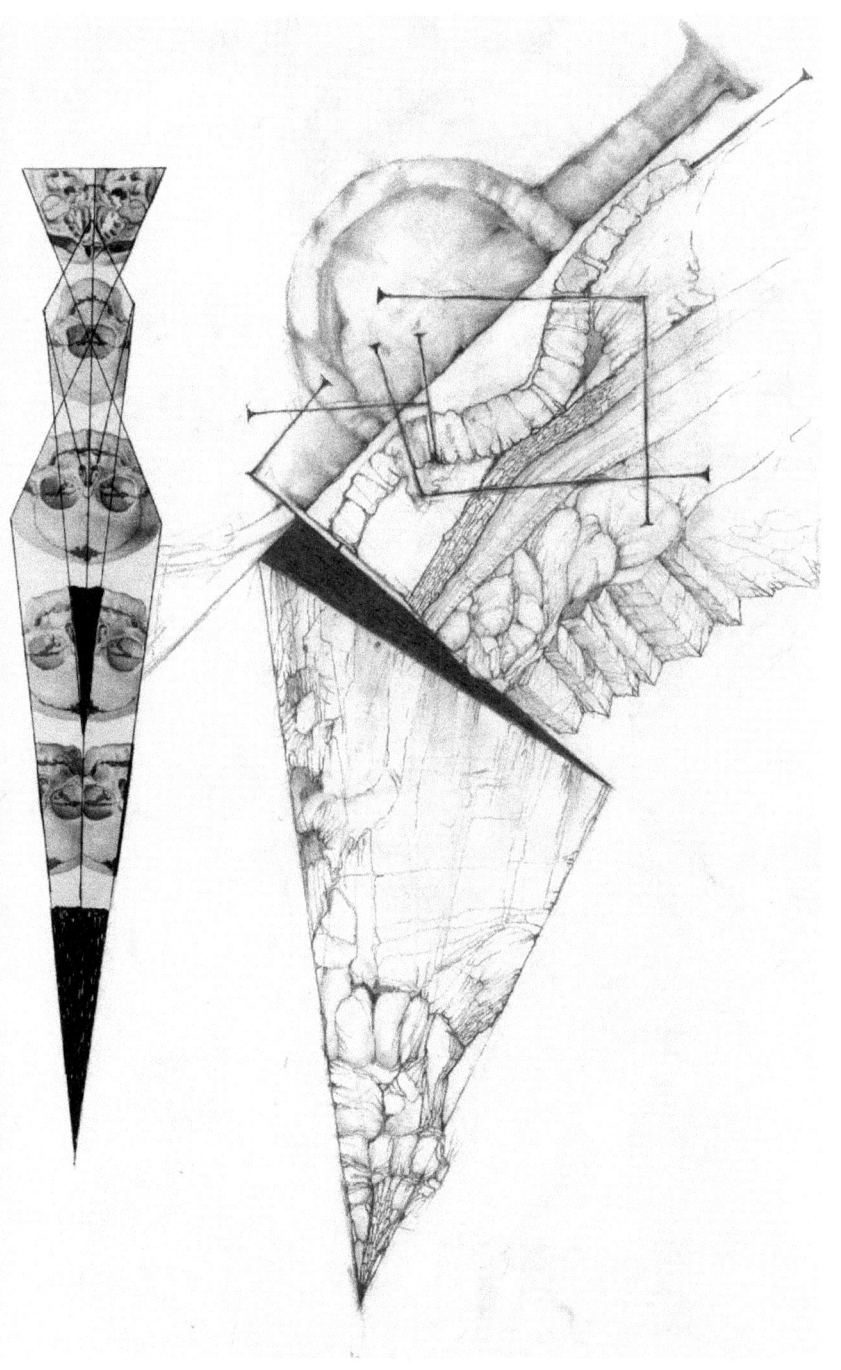

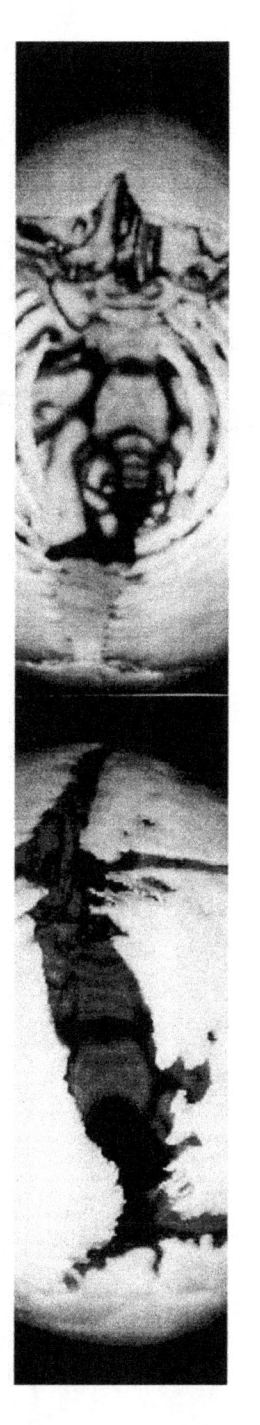

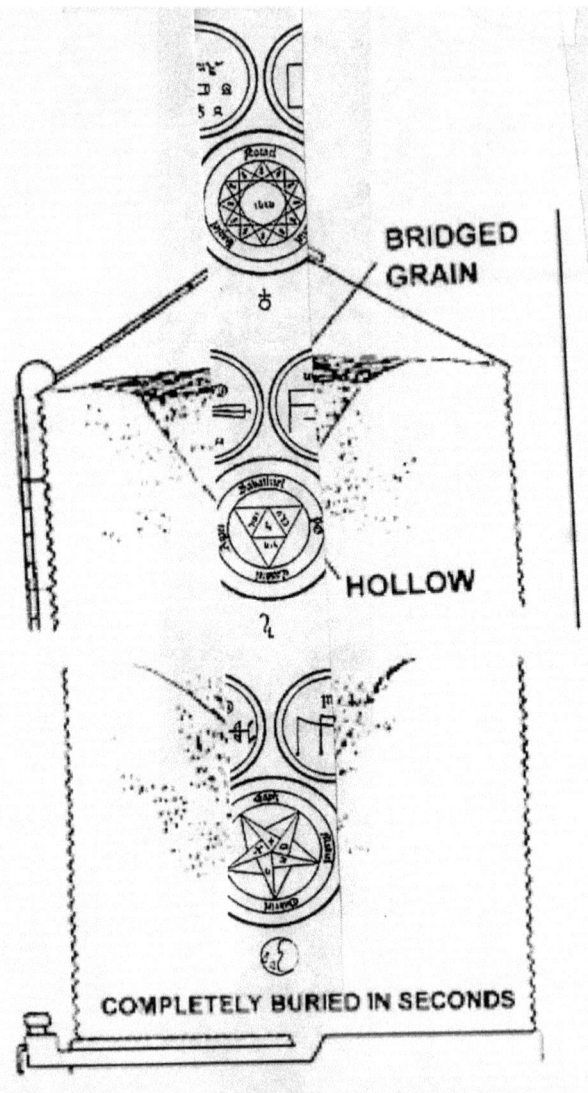

"Those ideas which the sun cult practiced at Emesa codified, touched upon the cosmic malice of a principle in which the error periodically committed by adherents was to procure a detestable outcome of events, all the while revering that principle's darkness. The inverted triangle the thighs make when the belly sinks between them as into a corner, reproduces the obscure cone of Erebus, inside that malefic space into which the devotees of the solar phallus, who therein went hand-in-hand with the devourerers of the lunar menses, would interject their exultations."

"At the very center of this illusory circle and akin to that animated point of a web when the spider is poised therein, may be found the filter chamber resembling an inverted triangle. And the filter's hollow tip corresponds to the glans of the phallus as seen from above."

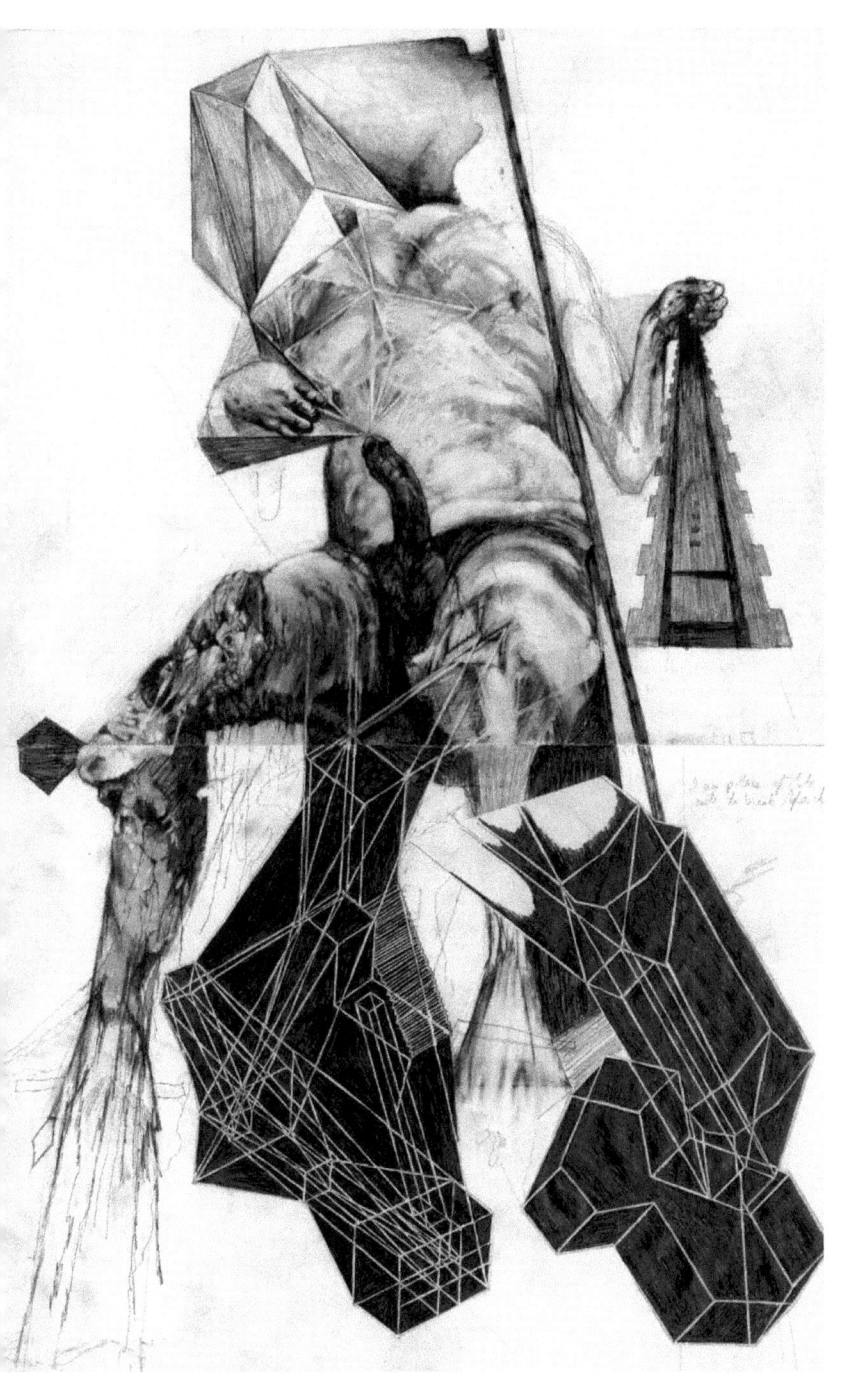

That Certain Black Line.
A weapon not entirely mine all the more to embrace.
With the specific aspect of dislocation and the principle of compression.
Not conjuration but making now fixed and set joints, all the more to receive.
Upon the cyclopean point which is calcium shadow of a phantom capstone.
As it is, "not a matter of submitting to the universe but of imitating it in open defiance."
Bones now in the service of instruments so open hearted receive that which deprives.
A reciept of malice where hangs the black culmination of a last geology.
Before they could be withdrawn to an etheric octave.
We butcher Shamballa to fornicate the pyramid of being.

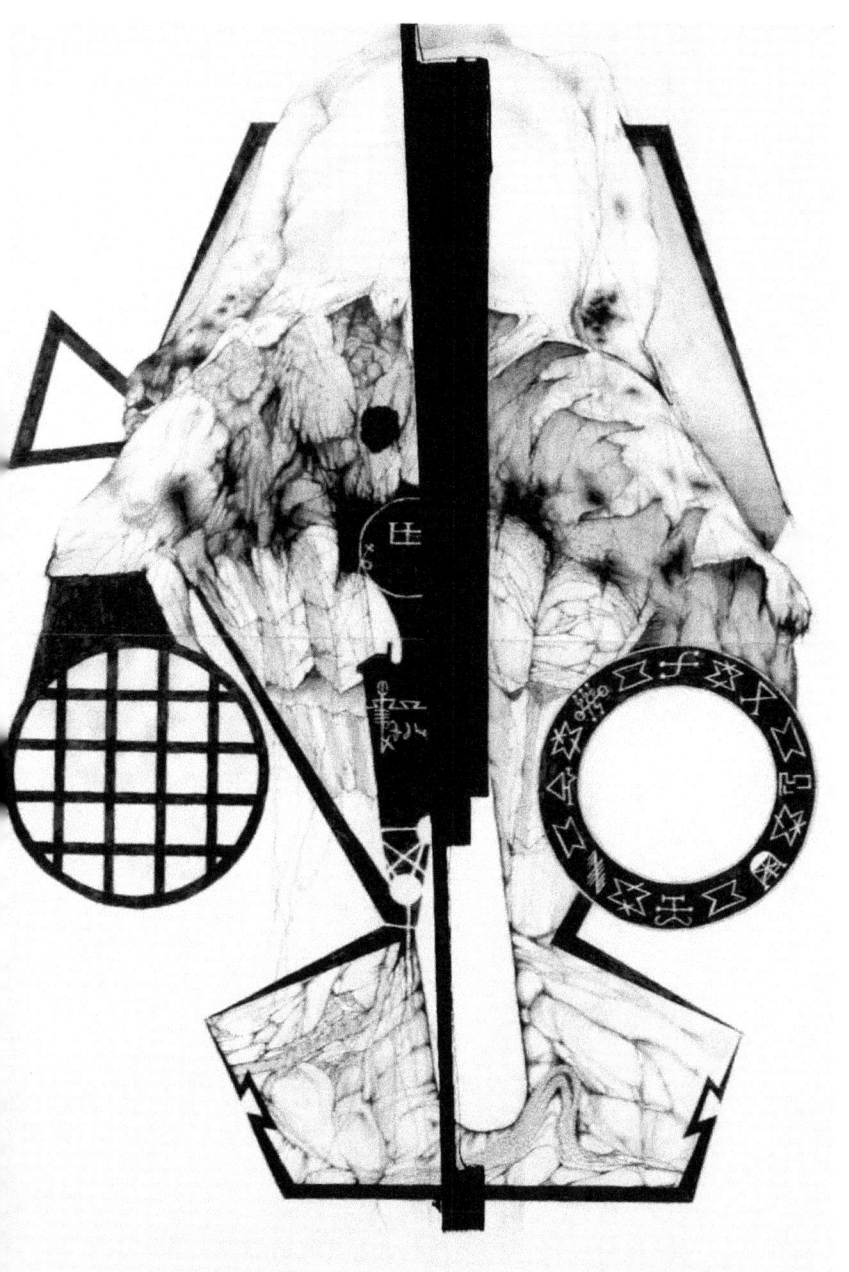

Symposium Photographs
Öykü Tekten

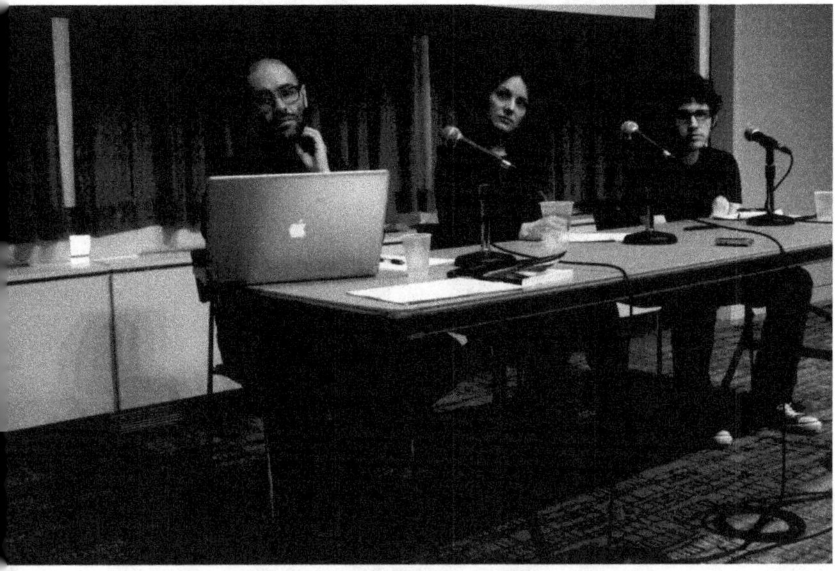

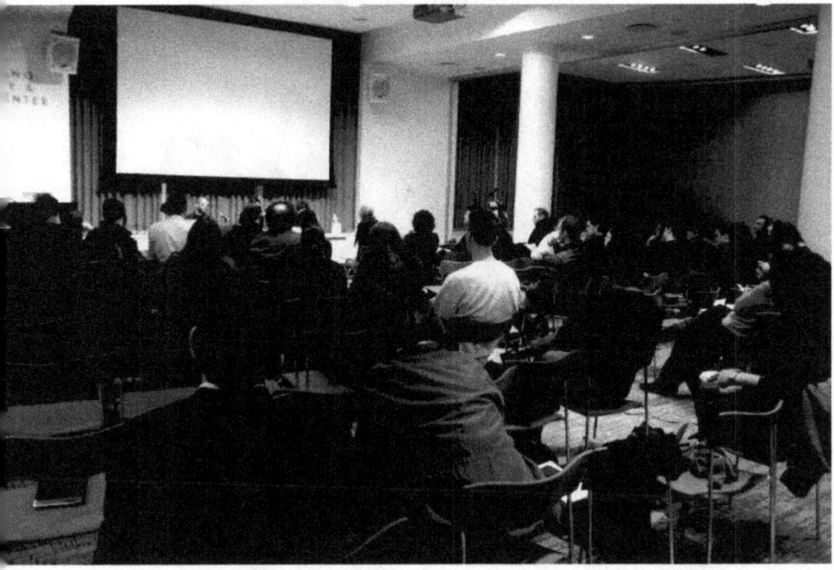

Notes on the Figure of the Cyclone
Or, universal schemata of speculation
Or, thinking according to the alien ovum of nature
Or, rewiring the philosopher's imagination with zero

Reza Negarestani

THE BOTTOMLESS ENVIRONMENT OF SPECULATION: THE
UNIVERSAL, THE ETERNAL OR THE FREE SIGN

$(U \rightarrow U, 0, \clubsuit)$

The ovum of reality is the eternal or the universal. The universal is that in which all partake, but it is eternally irreducible to commonalities and affordances between all particular instances, collections of multitudes, and local horizons of thought. It is neither bound in its local expressions, nor is it exhaustible by any collection of multitudes; it is simply free from the necessity of all its particular instances. The universal is a sign free of meaning and significance, the so-called free sign of Peirce that ramifies into its local contexts according to its global contingency, its bottomlessness and uninterruptable continuity with itself. For *naturphilosophie*, by virtue of its intensionality and self-reflexivity, the universal is identified as the eternal. The eternal—understood semio-logically by Peirce—is a modal plenum, an abyss replete with modalities that can neither be reduced to the totality of infinite possibilities nor determined in the first or the last instance by discrete actualities (marks of difference, cosmological horizons, local conditions of life and thought, etc.). The modal plenum is represented as the *Blank Sheet of Assertion*, a proto-topological blank sheet whose modes of relations to itself are unbound and on which semio-logical processes can be geometrically inscribed. Just as on the Blank Sheet of Assertion each isolated or discrete modality is perpetually intruded upon by unbound modalities of the sheet, within the open expanse of the universal, no particular instance can stave off the eruptions of the eternal or assimilate its modalities within its temporal horizon.

Devoid of any intrinsic expression, the sign of the eternal is 0—indivisible and indifferent. German natural philosopher Lorenz Oken understood the eternal as the nothing of nature or zero. 0 is the first act, yet one that has no substratum and no ground. Generation out of the eternal—or in Oken's terms position by zero—is already an expression of universal contingency, insofar as its mode of position $(0 \xrightarrow{+} \{0\}$ *or* $1)$ is already intruded by the indifference of the eternal or zero in remaining in a global state of frozen fixity indefinitely $(0 \xrightarrow{no} 1$ *or* $0 \to 0)$.

QUESTION. If the Universal is foreclosed to the thought of its particular instances and if the free sign is absolutely devoid of any significance and meaning and if the eternal qua zero of nature (0) is concomitantly inclined to posit difference and indifferently remain within itself for no reason whatsoever, then how is it possible to navigate the universal, to systematically approach the empty and free sign and think the eternal? In other words, how can we think or imagine a system of knowledge proper to a meaningless, contingent, free and bottomless Universe?

Insofar as the Universal does not express itself through commonalities or affordances between collectives and multitudes and belongs to no one, only a conception of collectivity built upon complicity—that is, communion and collaboration without necessary commonalities—is able to obliquely approach the Univer-Universal. Likewise, only a non-trivial and systematic account of synthesis between local and contingently posited contexts of the meaningless sign can asymptotically reconstruct the scope of the free sign. The eternal, in the same vein, must be thought through schemata by which it expresses itself in one way or another. A comprehensive combination of these schemata constitutes the map of indivisible nature. The map in turn brings into focus general approaches, perspectives and navigational schemes by which it can be comprehensively examined. In other words, the map provides us with alternative navigational schemes through which the eternal in all its modes can be asymptotically approached. Knowledge is indeed an optimal system of navigation endowed with universal orientation, that is to say, not only is it capable of accessing all concept spaces, paths, layers, global-local elevations and contexts of the map, but also it is able to synthesize navigational schemes corresponding to the emerging schemata of a universe whose contingency allows access to different local contexts and whose unbound modality generates new relations through which the universe further erases its frontiers. In a modern system of knowledge that has fully familiarized itself with the Galileian front of the Copernican Revolution—namely, the emphasis on mathematizability of nature and hence, putting an end to the myth of ineffability—mathematics and philosophy come hand in hand. Whilst mathematics is able to conceive (i.e. transform into semio-logically consistent concepts) these schemata, the obligation of philosophy is to broaden and deepen its analytic-synthetic valence so as to mediate between alternative navigational schemes or approaches and contribute to the universal orientation of knowledge.

If knowledge is a generic approach or system of navigation corresponding to schemata of the Universe, then we can recognize speculative thought as a particular navigational scheme corresponding to schemata of a Universe that explicitly express its contingency, bottomless continuity, invisible layers and alternative passages or conceive the meaninglessness of the free sign, the unbound modality of the eternal and the indivisibility of 0 qua nothing of nature for thought. In short, speculative thought is precisely an approach to those universal properties of the free sign and nature which cannot be examined under the pretext of a given privilege or an appropriate local context. Speculative thought—and in particular, a speculative cosmology fully accustomed to the schemata of a post-Copernican universe—must be strictly realized within this system of knowledge as a specific navigational scheme with universal orientation. It is a particular navigational scheme within the space of (universal) knowledge insofar as it is capable of bending laws, traveling in so-called unaccepted directions, uprooting given navigational highways as contingently posited privileges, examining invisible paths, taking alternative routes and at times, using obstacles to its advantage.

Far from being apologetic lines or principles of justification for a closeted irrationalism motivated by a rational deficit, the meaninglessness of the free sign, the contingency of the eternal and the abyssality of the Universal are precisely those global properties which allow for accessibility of knowledge to various local contexts of the Universal and guarantee the transcendental deepening of local fields of knowledge and the free transit of reason. But above all, these hitherto obstacles for the pre-modern theophilosophical landscape constitute the very drive of speculative thought as a particular navigational scheme in the system of knowledge corresponding to the schemata of the contingent, free and abyssal universe. In short, one should regard speculative thought as thought stripped of its purported privileges and rewired systematically by the so-called predicaments and conundrums of philosophy: intrusion of reason into every recess of the world, primordial inexistence of meaning, contingency of the eternal, paradoxical continuity of the Universal, collapse of foundation, global and local indetermination (the dialectic of generality and vagueness), the impossibility of privacy-in-the-last instance for any index of experience, dispossession of home, loss of earth, expropriation of life and thought, obsolescence of essentialism and destruction of the myth of purpose, irreducibility of the Universal to commonalities through which trivial collectivities can be assembled, exteriority of the Open to affordable modes of openness, . . .

A HYMN TO THE CYCLONE: FIVE RUDIMENTARY SCHEMATA OF THE INDIVISIBLE NATURE QUA 0 OR THE ETERNAL

If the environment of speculation is occasioned by the contingency of the eternal, the abyssality of the Universal, and the emptiness of the free sign, we should then understand speculative thought (a subset of the generic navigational approach to this environment called knowledge) as what globally and locally is capable of developing epistemological germs out of properties of this environment. These epistemological germs simultaneously contain the schematic map of the speculative environment and a navigational strategy or scheme corresponding to the map. Throughout the history of speculative thought, these epistemological germs have appeared in various guises, or more accurately, configurations: combinatorial figurations (Llull), mathematical concepts (geometric, topological, algebraic, set theoretic . . .), diagrams (Oresme), gestures (Archimedes), spatial constructs (Grassmann), semio-logical compositions (Peirce) and various skeletal configurations. Part of the optimality of these configurations is due to the fact that they fuse various types of reasoning (deductive, inductive, abductive, analogical, metric, topological . . .) together, adapt to different cognitive processes and therefore, bring about the possibility of a multi-modal confrontation with the ambient universal environment. In addition, these configurations generate polyvalent forms and possess highly synthetic characteristics required to broaden and deepen the speculative scope with minimum initial components. In short, they are able to mould imagination around themselves, spark systemic developments and in the process give rise to some of the most interesting philosophical, scientific, cultural and artistic constructs.

The figure of the cyclone is a rudimentary example of such configurations or germs of speculative programs. A powerful speculative schema conceived during the legacy of romantic science and *naturphilosophie*, the figure of the cyclone is a schematic map of 'thinking' according to or from the perspective of the indivisible nature, zero or eternal qua the nothing of nature. It is a counter-intuitive combination of a series of basic schemata or spatial traces of 0 (or the eternal) which determine their respective approaches or navigational strategies. Behind the exotic shape of the cyclone lie simple, efficient and optimal schemata and speculative schemes through which the philosopher or scientist's imagination is rewired with the alien ovum of reality, the indivisible zero as the mark of the eternal:

0. POINT: Nothing exists outside of zero, the indivisible nature or the eternal. 0 is the alien ovum of reality, without substratum and free from any the necessity of any particular instance of itself. To think according to or from the perspective of this alien ovum, one cannot begin to think it in its pure genericity, but one has to construct step by step an asymptotic (con-)figuration of zero in all its contingent transits and expressions. That is to say, a synthetic philosophy of nature is a philosophy in the making.

1. LENGTH: Position by zero is an extensive expression of zero, the mark of change and difference. The transition from the intensive to extensive expression of zero brings about the possibility of position and determination of difference. Length is the first spatial schema of zero qua the eternal; it expresses a field of speculation that allows for *venturing into a new territory* and *position of the new*. Length is an incomplete phase of speculation according to the eternal. It is blinded by the speculative promises of the new and foraying into a hitherto unrealized territory. The field of length or position out of zero (point) is a yardstick or ruler.

$$0 \xrightarrow{+} \{0\} = 1$$

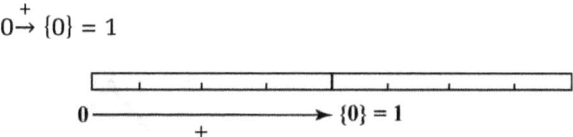

The position of length and the yardstick as the measure of the new.

2. WIDTH: Position is merely a contingent expression of zero qua the eternal, insofar as the eternal is simultaneously the intensional tendency of the eternal to remain expressionless in itself indefinitely and the extensional proclivity to posit and initiate change. Negation, accordingly, far from being a forced dialectical counter-act to position is the natural expression of the eternal to remain indifferent, expressionless and frozen for eternity. It is the indifference (rather than opposition) to the act of position. The pair '+ and −' is the complete expression of the eternal in its contingency, since contingency is not only baseless change but also baseless fixity and frozenness. '+ and −': mark of difference and mark of indifference or remaining in the continuity of the eternal (0 → 0), concomitantly, express the contingency of the eternal. The coupling of position and negation, or the full contingent expression of zero qua the eternal is the beginning of speculative cruelty: evocation of minus in the face of plus or subtraction. The spatial schema of contingency as the broad scope of the eternal is width. Being a field of a compass (as opposed to a ruler), width broadens the scope, opens up speculative fields built upon the contingency of the eternal and intensive-extensive, abstract-concrete distribution of forms implicit to the operation of subtraction. Just as '+ −' translates nature into a polarized bar of magnet, width as a field of compass translates contingency into a basic configuration of a voltaic coil.

$0 \xrightarrow{no} 1$

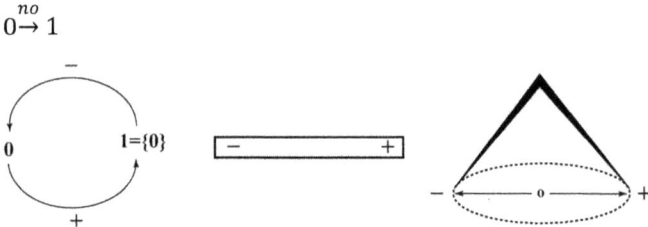

Width and its variations (0's pull-back or subtraction, distancing, and width as the circular or open embrace of the compass).

3. PROPAGATION OF WIDTH ALONG LENGTH (OR ANGULAR INTERWEAVING OF WIDTH AND LENGTH): Generation is zero in transit; it puts the contingency of the eternal or nothing of nature into motion. Oken's remark that no idea or particularity is able to germinate another idea or extended particularity without recourse to zero/dissolution suggests the contingent truth of generation. In other words, every position is accompanied by zero in its indifferent and expressionless form. In this sense, 1 ({0} i.e. a set containing one member) (an instance of change or position) cannot directly lead to 2 unless the indifferent state of zero (0) is re-affirmed: {0} → {0, {0}}. Generation through the eternal, accordingly, is not the serial act of position but the concatenation of negations and positions, that is to say, the recurrent enforcement of contingency—making an expression and making no expression whatsoever, the simultaneous tendency to change and remaining in the state of fixity for no reason at all. While width is the spatial schema of full contingency that aligns the extensive with the intensive, generation as the eternal enforcement of contingency (+ −) is the propagation of width along the foraying vector of length in the following manner:

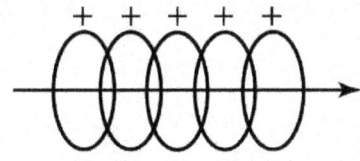

However, since the field of the eternal or nature is continuous, generation/evolution as the repetition of width along length becomes an unbroken field of transition:

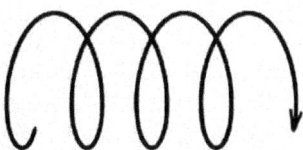

The electrical coil is the figuration of nature in transit. The spatial schema that it generates is that of a circumnavigational field of speculation that factors in contingency of nature in each and every step of its movement, of its thought. The circumnavigational field becomes a field of alternative transits or angular navigational approaches which allude to alien dimensions and circumvent possible obstacles (*from the perspective of the eternal, everything is possible*). The diagonal distribution of the intensive and the extensive in this field becomes the dynamic kernel of an acceleration-driven formalism.

$$\underset{\underset{+-+-+-+-\ldots}{\parallel}}{1} \quad \underset{\parallel}{2} \quad \underset{\parallel}{3} = \{0\}, \{0, \{0\}\}, \{0, \{0\}, \{0, \{0\}\}\}$$

Each instance of generation out of the eternal is a fibration of the indivisible and contingent nature, a perspective impregnated with zero. Evolution is nothing but a concatenation of zeros.

4. CYCLONE OR THE EXPLODED-IMPLODED COIL: Once zero/nature becomes the basal field of continuity, once contingency as the complete expression of the eternal underpins every instance of change, generation and transition, then all functions, figures of twist (or coils) can be stretched or contracted without limit. Coils can implode or explode infinitely, giving birth to cyclones. Magnified according to alien dimensions and esoteric transit routes, cyclones are coils which translate the modal continuity of the eternal into spatial continuity, making the cognition of zero or the indivisible nature possible. Length and width, position and negation, the extensive and the intensive lose their relative proportions to one another; they enter into different alliances and antagonisms all by the virtue of a basal continuity that undergirds them in each and every instance. Zero or the indivisible nature is that basal continuity. The cyclone is the schema of zero in all its possible transitions. The navigational scheme it engenders is full explosion and implosion of scope along various lines of complicity between anonymous materials, contingent eruptions of nature and esoteric couplings of the intensive and the extensive. Cyclones blow one's scope out of proportion only and strictly according to free expressions of a contingent nature or the real. As the exploded-imploded coil becomes the figure of electromagnetic space, the cyclone becomes the spatial configuration—the asymptotic reconstruction—of the Eternal qua the nothing of nature. Ultimately, the cyclone suggests an all-encompassing field of speculation wherein configuration and torsion, integration and differentiation, invariance and change bring the possibility of all manners of transition, transport and topological transformations between incommensurable expressions of a contingent nature and fields of thought.

Shiraz 2007 / Seremban 2012

punctum books is an open-access and print-on-demand independent publisher dedicated to radically creative modes of intellectual inquiry and writing across a whimsical para-humanities assemblage. We specialize in neo-traditional and non-conventional scholarly work that productively twists and/or ignores academic norms, with an emphasis on books that fall length-wise between the article and the monograph—id est, novellas, in one sense or another. This is a space for the imp-orphans of your thought and pen, an ale-serving church for little vagabonds.

<punctumbooks.com>

www.ingramcontent.com/pod-product-compliance
Lightning Source LLC
Chambersburg PA
CBHW060110170426
43198CB00010B/844